521 9/73

D0643466

THE MANAGEMENT OF
BRITAIN'S EXTERNAL RELATIONS

The Management of Britain's External Relations

Edited by

Robert Boardman
Centre for Foreign Policy Studies,
Department of Political Science,
Dalhousie University

and

A. J. R. Groom
University College London

MACMILLAN

First published 1973 by
THE MACMILLAN PRESS LTD
London and Basingstoke
Associated companies in New York Toronto
Dublin Melbourne Johannesburg and Madras

SBN 333 12259 3

Printed in Great Britain by
A. WHEATON & COMPANY
Exeter

Contents

C THE FOREIGN AND COMMONWEALTH
  OFFICE AND THE SOCIAL AND POLITICAL
  ENVIRONMENT

POSTSCRIPT

Preface

THE LAST quarter-century has seen fundamental changes in Britain's position in international society. More than ever before the British Government is involved in many international networks of consultation and decision: with other Governments, with organs of the United Nations and with other international bodies. Non-governmental organisations, from domestic interest-groups to multinational corporations, have also become significant foreign policy actors. Some form of 'islomania'* may perhaps once have informed the thinking of British Foreign Secretaries, but the epithet is hardly applicable to the Britain of the 1970s. Moreover, in many of the systems which are crucial for Britain its role is no longer a dominant one.

The Management of Britain's External Relations is an attempt to investigate some of the questions and issues raised by these developments. The volume includes the results of original research on aspects of Britain's external relations. It is also intended as a general textbook on the machinery, official and non-official, of British foreign policy decision-making which we hope will fill an obvious lacuna in the literature for courses on British Government, Comparative Government, International Relations and Foreign Policy Analysis.

We have been fortunate in being able to pool the knowledge and insights – the differing approaches and perspectives – of specialists in the study of Britain's external relations and of those who have had practical experience in these areas. In addition to academics the contributors include former officials of the Foreign and Commonwealth Office, the Ministry of Defence and

---

* Lawrence Durrell, 'Of Paradise Terrestre', in *Reflections on a Marine Venus* (London: Faber, 1960) 15.

Treasury. Their views are, of course, their own but they do help to bridge the gap between 'insiders' and 'outsiders'.

None of the chapters included in the volume has been published previously. Most of the chapters were prepared in the spring and summer of 1971 and do not take into account events occurring after that date.

Acknowledgements

THE FOLLOWING publishers, editors and authors have given their permission for a number of excerpts to be quoted in this book: the editors of *International Affairs* and Andrew Shonfield, 'The Duncan Report and its critics', 46 (1970); F. S. Northedge, Review Article, 45 (1969); Joseph Frankel, 'Comparing Foreign Policies: the case of Norway', 44 (1968); and D. C. Watt, 'Restrictions on Research: the Fifty-Year Rule and British Foreign Policy', 41 (1965); the editors of *Foreign Affairs*, for Edward Heath, 'Realism in British Foreign Policy', 48 (1969); and Michael Howard, 'Britain's Defenses: Commitments and Capabilities', 39 (1960); the editors of *Journal of Contemporary History*, for David Thomson, 'The writing of contemporary history', 2 (1967); the editors of *Contemporary Review* and General Lord Bourne, 'The Place of British Defence', 218 (1971); Northwestern University Press and James N. Rosenau, 'Pretheories and Theories of Foreign Policy', in R. B. Farrell, ed., *Approaches to Comparative and International Politics* (1966); George Allen and Unwin Ltd., for Peter G. Richards, *Parliament and Foreign Affairs* (1967); The Macmillan Press Ltd., for Nigel Forward, *The Field of Nations* (1971); and J. D. Singer, ed., *Quantitative International Politics: Insights and Evidence* (1967); and Hamish Hamilton Ltd., for A. J. P. Taylor, *The Trouble Makers* (1957).

We should also like to thank Professors Donald G. Bishop and Arnold Toynbee for permission to quote from private correspondence and Miss Gillian Hoxley for secretarial assistance far beyond the call of duty.

The research for the chapters by Christina Larner and Peter Byrd was supported by the Social Science Research Council.

1 Introduction: The Study of Britain's External Relations

ROBERT BOARDMAN
and A. J. R. GROOM

SYMPTOMATIC of Britain's changing position in international society in the 1960s was the fact that the *leitmotiv* of most discussions of the subject was no longer Sir Eyre Crowe's memorandum of 1907, in which the British role as maintenance-man of the European balance-of-power machinery was described and prescribed [1]. Nor could the pronouncements of Gladstone or Palmerston earlier, or of Churchill later, on the character of British foreign policy provide a satisfactory starting point. It fell to an American statesman, in 1962, to set the theme of debate for the decade. When British opinion had recovered from the shock of Dean Acheson's claim that Britain had lost an empire and had not yet found a role [2], there grew a conviction that it rang true. It hung in the air for the rest of the 1960s almost like an accusing finger, triggering a period of introspection at times virtually un-British in its intensity. At the beginning of the next decade, moreover, the former Secretary of State commented that his earlier opinion was 'demonstrably true today' [3].

The analyses of Britain's 'role' in the world tended to form a consensus. The crux of the argument was that fundamental changes had taken place, and were taking place, in international politics. Britain, it was felt, was responding inadequately. Its many former roles and aspirations – as the hub of Empire or Commonwealth, as joint moulder with the United States of Western destinies, or as benevolent protector of stability in continental Europe – had been ruled out of court by the economic and political upheavals of the wartime and post-1945 years. The resources and conditions were simply no longer there for the British Government to play the global role of a first-rank Power.

The most frequent prescription, and the one officially advocated by the Government, was 'Europeanisation', or, more concretely, British participation in the European Economic Community. This was not always the case of course. A minority argued that traditional policies should be pursued more vigorously, and called for a much closer identification with the United States or the Commonwealth. Still fewer thought in terms of 'little England' or of non-alignment. But more significantly than the conclusions reached was the stress on the need for basic decisions, for a heightened awareness of changing circumstances and a rigorous evaluation of options. In a word, the search was for an alternative conception of 'greatness'. The fact of choice was emphasised by Arnold Toynbee in 1968 :

> I think Britain today is in much the same position as Spain, the Netherlands, and Sweden at the turn of the seventeenth and eighteenth centuries. Spain has always looked back, so she has never recovered from having ceased to be a first-class power in the military and political sense. Sweden and the Netherlands, after a spell in the doldrums, turned their backs on their irrecoverable past and looked forward [4].

The present volume is not concerned with policies or options. Its focus is rather the process whereby, and the machinery, official and unofficial, through which such decisions will be made. We shall be examining therefore an area broader than that usually implied by the term 'foreign policy'. This emphasis has to some extent been dictated by the transformation of Britain's international position since the end of the Second World War. It makes little sense in the 1970s, even assuming that it did once, to confine the discussion solely to the activities of Ambassadors and Foreign Secretaries. It makes even less sense to begin with the postulate that the character of Britain's external relations is something wholly 'decided' in some mystical fashion by the British Government and purveyed to a waiting world. Foreign policy may most usefully be considered not in terms of the legal and constitutional framework of sovereignty and statehood, of law-making and war-making, but rather as the product of a complex interplay of international, transnational and domestic influences. On a particular issue pressures from the United States State Department might be crucial, while demands from the National Farmers' Union could be important for another and the recommendations of the Secretariat of the World Health Organisation even more significant for a third.

I BRITAIN AND THE INTERNATIONAL SYSTEM SINCE 1945 : SIX DIMENSIONS OF CHANGE

In what ways then have the changes of the past thirty years or so undermined the applicability of the traditional 'billiard ball' model of State interaction to the analysis of British foreign policy? Any summary is bound to lead to over-simplification. But there would seem to be at least six valuable perspectives from which to view Britain's changing position in the international system.

(a) The end of Empire
One of its authors has written that what the Duncan Report on Overseas Representation of 1969 was really doing was 'to spell out, belatedly, the logic of the end of Empire'. The implications of this end, Shonfield adds, had been obscured by the east-of-Suez military presence, 'and by the way in which, initially at any rate, the new mould of political relationships within the Commonwealth seemed to provide a ready substitute for the old relationships of Empire' [5]. Certainly in 1945 the continued existence of these older relationships was not generally disputed in Britain. The granting of independence, soon after the termination of hostilities, to the Indian subcontinent was for the most part considered a foretaste of a more distant future. And with the exception of Burma, the new states remained in close association with Britain through the Commonwealth link.

Conveniently for the tidy-minded historian, Mr Macmillan publicly acknowledged the 'wind of change' blowing through Africa at the beginning of the 1960s. By the close of the decade, the imperial past appeared to exist only in the realms of memory and nostalgia. Yet in other ways it was very much a political and diplomatic reality. The areas at the tail-end of the decolonisation process posed, and are posing, some difficult problems.

One has been the 'mini-State dilemma' [6] : territories with
meagre resources, small geographical size, and minute popula-
tions. A further complication arose from ethnic divisions within
some States of the former Empire, which later presented the
British Government with serious foreign policy issues such as with
Cyprus and Nigeria. In other similar cases, the nature of the
linkages with Britain assumed considerable local political significance, as in Mauritius, Fiji, or Guyana. There have been diplomatic repercussions for Britain's relationships with other States :
Spain in the case of Gibraltar, the People's Republic of China
in relation to Hongkong, or Argentina over the Falkland Islands.
Last but not least, the unilateral declaration of independence by
the Rhodesian authorities in 1965 became a major diplomatic
problem for Britain in the years following.

The transition from Empire to Commonwealth had repercussions in other directions. Strategically, for example, the Indian
Ocean territories have been seen in Western defence analyses as
crucial assets in parrying the expansion of Soviet naval capability.
Indeed the very rapidity of the process of de-colonisation was
sometimes thought to indicate the need for a re-introduction in
some form or other of the British presence. The Conservative
Party won the 1970 General Election with a manifesto which
included the promise to explore this possibility further. Writing
in *Foreign Affairs* in 1969, Mr Heath drew attention to the use of
British troops in Kuwait in 1961, in East Africa in 1964, and
during the Malaysia-Indonesia confrontation. The lesson to be
drawn, he concluded, was that 'a British military presence can be
effective if the political context is right' [7]. Britain's first priority,
the new Conservative Foreign Secretary stated in July 1970, was
to the NATO alliance, but there was an independent British role
in three other areas : east of Suez, the Persian Gulf, and the
South Atlantic.

The imperial past moreover has structured Britain's relationships with the non-aligned Governments of the Third World
and the Western-oriented administrations of the older white
Dominions. Given the context of the cold war, influence in the
former could not become a one-way affair from London to the
ex-colonial capitals. British sensitivity to the potency of memories
of imperialism, and to the cry of 'neo-colonialism' as a tool
for national integration within the new States, muted the reaction

to some of the features of the political life of some of the newly-independent Commonwealth countries which were distasteful to the Westminster palate. The attitudes of the Asian Member-States of the Commonwealth helped to shape the British Government's response to issues in the 1950s such as relations with Peking or the conflicts in Korea and Indo-China. In the second half of the 1960s, African Commonwealth opinion had constantly to be borne in mind in London on the Rhodesian question. It was strongly felt in Britain that the idea of the Commonwealth could survive only to the extent that a cleavage by race or wealth could be avoided. The imperial link moreover was as much economic and commercial as political and constitutional. In each of the Brussels negotiations on British entry to the European Communities, for example, the status of New Zealand primary produce became one of the more intractable agenda issues. Even so, the important Commonwealth ties have often been those least publicised : the work of the Secretariat, the regular meetings in New York and in other United Nations forums, or the technical assistance programmes and aid operations within the Colombo Plan framework.

These few instances illustrate the magnitude of the task of post-imperial readjustment in terms of domestic British politics and administration. In the defence field, British commitments often remained after independence, even if Governments did not always allocate sufficient resources to meet them. But the ending of a large-scale military role east of Suez meant the return to British bases of more units of the armed forces. With the services not having yet found their place in a 'new-look' Britain, this might in turn have important social and political repercussions during the 1970s. Similar difficulties of administrative reorganisation arose with the recall of personnel from the former Empire. Even if in the early 1950s a career in the Indian Civil Service was not open to a young Briton as it might have been to his father, colonial administration in Africa and elsewhere remained as a possibility to be considered seriously. Finally, the institutional machinery of foreign policy decision-making underwent important changes in the 1960s, with the Commonwealth Office assuming the responsibilities of the Colonial Office in 1966 and with the formation of a single unified Foreign and Commonwealth Office in 1968.

(b) The cold war

The link between London and Washington has been traditionally regarded, as least from the British side, as the 'special relationship' *par excellence*. Indeed so 'special' is it that one analysis concluded that it is inexplicable in terms of conventional alliance theory : factors such as history, tradition, affinity, and cultural values and beliefs were crucial rather than peripheral [8]. The transparency of such ties may well induce future historians to question the existence of the 'special relationship'. Whatever the merits of this view in operational terms, British Governments certainly claimed that it existed. The character of the tie, though, has obviously changed. From the pre-eminent maritime grandeur of the late nineteenth century, Britain emerged from the Second World War at best a *secundus inter pares* with her powerful ally : thereafter a slippery slope led inexorably to the temporary role of acting deputy or lieutenant, and from there to the rank of one middle Power among several in the Western alliance. As designated by the Prime Minister towards the end of 1970, Britain is 'a medium Power of the first rank'.

What impact has the emergence of a bipolar nuclear international system had on British foreign and defence policies? Most British politicans had few doubts in the years after 1945 that close alliance with the United States was the only option for Britain. Little thought for example was given to the questions whether a Gaullist foreign policy of independence-cum-alignment might best serve British interests, or whether a fully aligned stance was required over all areas of policy, including those outside Europe. It is perhaps not surprising that there has sometimes been a sense of resentment or hurt pride in British attitudes. This has found expression in complaints about lack of consultation on important international issues, or in behind-the-scenes irritation at the style, if not the content, of United States policies in the Middle East, South-East Asia and elsewhere, Criticism of Washington is not solely a left-wing phenomenon; it is also a favourite Conservative parlour game.

Two analytically distinct processes have operated here. Nuclear capability ruled out large-scale conventional warfare between the two super-Powers through mutual fears of escalation to and across the nuclear threshold. Tolerance of separate national nuclear deterrent forces has also been low both in Washington and Moscow for similar considerations. Britain's attempts to sustain an independent nuclear programme were gradually eroded during the late 1950s and early 1960s. Indeed the British Government may itself have contributed to the limiting of its area of choice by emphasising its nuclear vocation while eschewing conventional and sub-threshold alternatives. Secondly, the scope for independent British strategic action has been whittled down by the complex international superstructure of the NATO alliance, with its related consultative and integrated command procedures. Taking the two together then, the condition of nuclear bipolarity has in practice eliminated for Britain the independent exercise of the option of major war, traditionally the crucial attribute of sovereignty.

British official opinion has in general been a willing and active participant in these changes. The perceived threat from the Soviet presence in Eastern Europe, combined with a perennial anxiety at the possibility of United States' withdrawal into thermonuclear isolation, have been the twin spurs to British defence thinking throughout the cold war. As Mr Macmillan put it in 1966 : 'I am only upset when foolish people complain about America taking the burden which we can no longer fully carry. We can carry some of it . . . but they have taken the great burden we carried for two centuries and I rejoice at it' [9]. Older British fears were aroused and lent powerful reinforcement to such thoughts when the Soviet Union in the early 1970s expanded its naval operations in the Mediterranean and the Indian Ocean.

But Anglo-American disagreements, for example over policies towards the Arab States, indicated that cold war imperatives and more traditional British inclinations did not always coincide. The conflict between these two aspects of British foreign policy thinking was intensified in the 1950s as the Government turned a receptive ear to the views of the Indian and the other Asian Commonwealth Governments. Clashes between British interpretations of international law and practice and commercial needs on the one hand, and the Western strategic interest as defined in Washington on the other, occurred with the establishment of revolutionary regimes in China in 1949 and in Cuba in 1959. Britain's position as a trading nation has been circumscribed by the cold war regulations governing East-West transactions, even though these do recognise the special needs for export outlets of countries like Britain. 'Trading with the enemy' was a familiar Congressional cry against British firms during the 1950s.

The British Government has tried to respond to such conflicts by polishing its self-image as the exerter of a mediatory or con-ciliatory influence in world affairs. Eden and Macmillan sought in the 1950s to narrow some of the gaps between Moscow and Washington, just as in the 1960s Wilson saw it to be a major British objective to ward off the more dangerous consequences of the Sino-American confrontation. But there was no easy answer to the question how best such potential influence could be wielded. One answer was that 'Britain must maintain modern forces which entitle her to join in talks at the "top table", though without her former influence' [10]. On the other hand, Labour Party critics tended to stress the virtues of more public and more frequent dissociation from the Washington line, and to argue that the close official identification of views between the two Govern-ments was costly for Britain's Third World relationships. It was increasingly apparent however that a British voice could not carry the weight it had done in 1945. Indeed the decision-making process in the United States is now so complex that it is difficult to imagine any participant, foreign or domestic, influencing it consistently over a period of time. Conditions at the beginning of the 1970s drove the point home; for example, the American obsession with Indo-China, British withdrawal from east of Suez, and Washington's attempts through the SALT talks and in other ways to consolidate the rapproachement with the Soviet Union [11]. At other levels the Anglo-American relationship seemed to remain as firm as ever, although Russett's statistical analysis has pointed to a slight drawing apart over a longer historical period [12].

(c) Western Europe
Economic considerations played a major part in persuading British official opinion of the advantages of membership of the European Economic Community. But they were not the whole story. The case put forward for greater British involvement in continental affairs also included a blend of political, strategic and cultural arguments. Britain's imperial and Atlantic roles were gone; aloofness from her immediate neighbours was an anachronism in an age in which Western Europe was no longer

the pivot of international life; and only on a regional basis could Britain and other Western European States achieve a say in international politics comparable to those of the two super-Powers.

Equally, opposition to the European idea, in the particular form it had taken, was not always grounded in strictly economic assessments. Where it was more than an expedient negotiating tactic, resistance to the provisions of the Rome Treaty reflected on uneasy suspicion that the EEC, even with an expanded membership, would be too 'inward-looking'. There are, as Buchan has pointed out, at least six models of Western Europe for the 1970s [13]. The alternatives canvassed in Britain were symptomatic of this feeling : a revitalisation of EFTA, closer economic links with the United States and other countries in a new North Atlantic grouping, or a strengthening of existing Commonwealth trading arrangements. It is interesting to note that a policy of vigorous independence or non-alignment found little support.

The outcry in Britain at the French Government's veto on British entry into the EEC in 1963 demonstrated well the ambivalence of British attitudes to 'Europe', and perhaps vindicated the reference earlier of one writer to 'the chronic schizophrenia from which Britain suffers as an offshore island, at once part of the continent of Europe and detached from it . . .' [14]. Directed as it was almost entirely at General de Gaulle, this wave of national indignation tended to gloss over significant trends in Britain's de facto relationships with other West European States. Clearly Britain was not to be an isolated outpost, shunned by her neighbours; trade flows on. Thus it has been argued that the important structural change in economic interaction in the North Atlantic area occurred during the Second World War, from which Western Europe emerged 'more economically and politically "European" than it had ever been in the inter-war period' [15]. Since then British commercial links grew until in 1970 British exports to EEC countries exceeded for the first time exports to the Commonwealth. The 'enforced isolation' image of Britain has also been undermined by the somewhat controversial findings of Deutsch and his colleagues that 'European integration has slowed down since the mid-50s, and has stopped or reached a plateau since 1957–58' [16].

(d) The Third World

Earlier we looked at Britain's changing international position in
the context of East-West relations. An increasingly relevant
alternative perspective however is developmental and economic
rather than ideological and strategic. Britain, according to this
viewpoint, could be placed firmly in the affluent industrialised
North of world society. The implications are important. The
Commonwealth emerges as an even more heterogeneous entity,
with the underdeveloped African and Asian Members in a
different economic situation altogether from Britain, Canada,
Australia and New Zealand; and the patterns of cold war interaction become criss-crossed with others in which the Soviet Union
and the NATO allies are in not too dissimilar categories.

These developments were often interpreted in Britain and the
West in cold war terms. Non-alignment, the distinctive foreign
policy of the new States, was received coolly in the 1950s, and
not only by the over articulate Mr Dulles. Suspicions of Communist machinations lurking behind non-aligned masks grew
with the appearance of constitutional forms, especially in Africa,
at variance with those of the West. What was seen as an irritating
eagerness to jump nimbly upon any passing anti-Western band-
wagon frequently confirmed this distate for post-colonial developments. When thought genuine, Third World suspicions of
Western intentions were sometimes attributed in Britain to over-
zealous American anti-Communist policies, and in the United
States to a lingering British nostalgia for Empire. Cold war
considerations also moulded policies. The sale of certain categories of armaments to the South African Government, for
example, a major British foreign policy issue at the beginning
of the 1970s, was both justified and condemned on the criterion
of minimising potential Soviet or Chinese influence in the continent's affairs. And from the outset, British approaches to the
EEC were encouraged in Washington not least for strategic
reasons.

Other considerations than strategic of course have provided a
stimulus to Britain's aid policies. Aid figures, counting both
official aid and private investment, have nevertheless failed to
reach the one per cent of the Gross National Product set as a
target by the United Nations Conference on Trade and Development in 1968. The Pearson Report, which set the additional goal

of 0·7 per cent for Government aid by 1975 or 1980, pointed out that Britain was among the countries which had been devoting a diminishing percentage of GNP to foreign aid [17]. This brings us back firmly to the theme of the present discussion. The complexities of the relationships involved – with the Government departments and intergovernmental agencies overlapping with private bodies and non-governmental organisations, and with aid questions inextricably linked to issues of international trade and to British balance-of-payments, budgetary, and other problems – illustrate still further the intricacies and interdependencies of Britain's contemporary involvement in world society.

(e) *Economics and technology*

Of the many caricatures of Britain which have been prompted by post-1945 history, the least flattering is that of the 'sick man of Europe'. It could be argued that the British economy never fully revived after the severe jolt of the Second World War. During the war, large-scale disinvestment of overseas capital took place, and war debts to the United States were incurred which are still being repaid annually. One estimate is that the war effort cost about one quarter of Britain's national wealth, or about £7,300m [18]. Immediately afterwards, the sudden termination of Lend-Lease, although followed by the inauguration of United States aid through the Marshall Plan, made British official opinion even more sensitive to the need for an expansion of exports. The reorganisation of the foreign policy machinery in the 1960s stressed the necessity for matters of trade and economics to be more explicitly and professionally related to more traditional diplomatic concerns. The Duncan Report, indeed, went so far as to refer to the 'towering importance' of achieving a surplus in Britain's balance of payments [19].

Changes since the second half of the 1940s have been great. To the degree that GNP and economic growth rate are factors in the evaluation of 'great Power' status, Britain's international political position has been significantly affected by such developments as the rise of Japan as an economic super-Power, and the emergence of an EEC grouping which includes the West German economy. Shifts in economic and technological parameters also exerted an 'internationalising' effect on Britain. Anglo-French cooperation on the *Concorde* supersonic airliner and other capital-intensive projects involving substantial investment in research and development suggested that Britain alone was no longer in the same class as the United States or the USSR. It seems fair to say that before the end of the century, advances in aerospace, computer, telecommunications, nuclear, electronic and other technologies will have crucial ramifications for the British Government's international policies [20]. Further, the interdependence of the economic and the political, and the domestic and the international, is shown clearly in the close consultation of the British with other Governments maintained through such organs as the OECD and the IMF. It was in the 1960s that there appeared the popular image of the 'gnomes of Zurich' as the watchdogs and manipulators of the British Government's economic and financial policies.

(f) Interdependence and linkages
It is not only in the field of inter-governmental relations that British links with the rest of world society have grown in importance since 1945. Sectors of society and the economy have moved in similar directions. Companies such as Unilever and Shell have been important multinational concerns for some time, but it is only comparatively recently that the multinational corporation has made its mark as an international actor. Essentially this means American rather than British-based capital. Of the eighty-seven corporations whose 1965 sales exceeded US$1 billion, sixty were registered in the United States and only seven in the United Kingdom [21]. Their international nature moreover is reflected in the fact that Unilever for example aims to accommodate in the parent companies in Britain and the Netherlands people of every nationality [22]. But despite occasionally vocal trade union indignation – for example in the British automobile industries at the fact that decisions affecting British workers could be taken in Detroit boardrooms – *le défi américain* [23] has not assumed the ogre proportions which are apparent at times in France.

Similarly, Britain experienced some of the international labour problems of the EEC countries even while outside the formal Brussels framework. The numbers of British workers under contract in West Germany for example underwent significant expansion. These transnational linkages of industry and trade unions – and even of private social organisations concerned with anything from pigeon-racing to stamp-collecting – are phenomena the importance of which is at last being studied by political scientists [24]. And for Britain, the direction of such links is changing : relatively more to continental Europe, relatively less to the old Dominions and the United States. Hence the paradox, evident in Britain as in other Western countries, that at the same time as there is increased Governmental participation in domestic society, so more activities are escaping from the Nation-State to be organised in a transnational systemic framework largely outside the formal international governmental system.

II CHANGE AND THE ANALYSIS OF BRITISH FOREIGN POLICY

Brief though it is, this survey reveals a number of interesting trends affecting Britain's position in international society in the period since 1945. First, the altering international environment – the rise in the number of States following the end of Empire, improvements in communications, the growing importance of multilateral diplomacy – have occasioned an almost continual restructuring of the British Government's administrative machinery for handling foreign policy questions [25]. This fact alone would be sufficient to warrant more research attention being paid to the organisational context of policy-making. As diplomacy has become more concerned with economic and social questions moreover, closer attention is due not only to the Foreign and Commonwealth Office, but also to other departments and to interest groups outside Whitehall.

Secondly, the British Government has had to face many constraints, domestic and international, on its external policies. It is true that the Government experienced real and sometimes formidable barriers to the implementation of its foreign policy choices during the nineteenth-century *pax Britannica*. But, enmeshed as it is in the 1970s in a complex network of often competing demands, the reality of the constraints is both more self-evident and yet at the same time more difficult to analyse. This paradox can be seen in the Suez intervention of 1956. Similar dilemmas for the Government in the face of conflicting advice, and difficulties for the researcher in the face of its complexities, were all too apparent in the Rhodesian issue in the late 1960s. Public debates in the press, Parliament and elsewhere during that decade often tended to underestimate the circumstances which in practice set limits to the range of tenable foreign policy options for British decision-makers.

Thirdly, interdependence at governmental and at other levels, and the growing inseparability of the foreign and domestic spheres, is the other side of this coin. It raises comparable analytical problems. As James Rosenau has argued :

> . . . the national society is now so penetrated by the external world that it is no longer the only source of legitimacy or even of the employment of coercive techniques. The probability that most social processes will culminate at the national level has diminished, and instead the 'most inclusive' structures through which groups strive to attain goals are increasingly becoming a composite of subnational, national, and supranational elements [26].

In Britain in 1970 the decisions called for in connection with the situation in Northern Ireland, or the East-African Asian holders of British passports, or the negotiations between the international oil companies and the oil-producing states, highlighted the definitional problem of trying to isolate a specifically and exclusively 'foreign' area of policy.

Recent developments in foreign policy studies have indicated the advantage of pursuing alternative models of Britain's external relations to those which have conventionally, if implicitly, been adopted. Dissatisfaction with traditional metaphors has come from other sources. The historian A. J. P. Taylor, for example, has criticised a tendency of some of his professional colleagues : 'Great Britain is made to move with the ponderous certainty of John Bull. In the end we build up a picture of an apostolic succession, in which statesmen moving from one muddle to the next display "the continuity of British foreign policy"' [27]. But perhaps a more important need is to recognise the growing significance of extra-societal formative influences on British foreign policy. In an attempt to come to grips with these and other problems, Rosenau has suggested the utility of the notion of a 'penetrated political system' ; that is,

. . . one in which nonmembers of a national society participate directly and authoritatively, through actions taken jointly with the society's members, in either the allocation of its values or the mobilisation of support on behalf of its goals [28].

The definition has been taken up for one analysis of West German foreign policy [29]. Some of its implications for British foreign policy studies will be discussed in a later section.

III THE LITERATURE ON BRITAIN'S EXTERNAL RELATIONS

Surprisingly, we cannot refer to a large body of published literature on the management of Britain's external relations. Indeed, Donald Bishop, before writing *The Administration of British Foreign Relations* [30], was 'puzzled . . . at the failure of British scholars to analyse such matters, thinking it almost impertinent for an American to write on it' [31]. In the Preface to his *Parliament and Foreign Affairs* [32], Peter Richards reinforces the point :

> The number of detailed research studies now appearing on various aspects of the British Parliament is greater than ever before; but its function in relation to foreign policy has been ignored. . . . The British approach to our own institutions is excessively insular : far too little attention is paid to the role of the State in the international community [33].

Whatever the reasons for this neglect, the gaps remain formidable ones. Before the 1960s virtually nothing was available for the student interested in the machinery of British foreign policy decision-making. Library shelf space on the history of modern British foreign policy was almost as meagre. There are still no specialist journals on the subject along the lines of publications like *Australian Outlook, German Foreign Policy, the Indian Yearbook of World Affairs,* or the *Czechoslovak Foreign Policy Review.** The first study of Britain's foreign policy institutions appeared in 1942. After classifying already published material over the whole field of British foreign policy, Langford com-

* There is now a yearly publication including relevant documents: *Current British Foreign Policy* (London: Maurice Temple Smith).

mented: 'Oddly enough, it is only the formulation of British foreign policy that has been neglected; a detailed study of the subject has never appeared in print' [34].

Even so, there followed a lengthy delay before the two major studies of the 1960s, by Bishop [35] and Vital [36]. Northedge has put forward one explanation: 'there is simply not enough to say about how British foreign policy is made to fill a book . . . the making of British foreign policy, for good or ill, does not lend itself to textbook exposition, because the basic constitutional facts are so simple and the nuances communicated by personality so varied and elusive' [37]. Having attempted to fill the present volume with germane material, we may be forgiven for thinking this judgement over-pessimistic. The lack of British research initiatives may be due in part to methodological difficulties, or to a relatively unco-operative attitude in the past by some of the relevant actors and institutions. We shall come back to this point later. But on the other hand, this has not prevented some American scholars from making headway. In the study of British defence policy, for example, the major surveys have been carried out in the United States [38]; only recently have British scholars entered this field [39]. Similarly, Epstein's study of British politics during the 1956 Suez crisis has, generally speaking, not been followed up by British studies of the social and political environment of decision-making [40].

IV   RECENT DEVELOPMENTS IN FOREIGN POLICY STUDIES

Given this paucity, it seems entirely appropriate to ask whether recent theorising in the field of foreign policy decision-making can offer any insights into possible directions for research on Britain. Clearly, with such a large and growing field, we can do little more than single out a few themes – while bearing in mind the conclusion of one 1969 review that 'The study of foreign policy is underdeveloped; its theoretical content is inadequate; and analysis for the most part lacks rigour' [41].

First, the focus on 'decision-making' as a key to the understanding of foreign policy has been influential since the work of Snyder and his colleagues in the early 1950s [42]. One criticism of developments since has been that, perhaps because of diffi-

culties of gaining access to data, researchers have for the most
part shied away from empirical investigations. A major emphasis
has rather been on the refinement of models and analytical
categories [43]. There are exceptions of course. Pruitt examined
at first hand decision-making processes within the State Department [44], while other studies have been made of the processes
which culminated in the United States decision to enter the
Korean War [45] and in the Japanese Peace Settlement [46].
But there have been no comparable studies of Britain. Considerable scope exists therefore for investigations of processes both
within the FCO and in the wider perspective of official transactions with other Departments; the workings of Embassies; the
character of links with other Governments; the bargaining and
negotiating behaviour of diplomats; or the impact of pressures
from the social and political environments of policy-making. As
Nigel Forward has commented: 'Who can say what would be
revealed by a systems analysis of the Foreign Office?' [47].

Secondly, the value of comparative work has increasingly been
emphasised. The drawback of 'single-country' research is clearly
that it will not necessarily generate findings applicable to other
national contexts. The chances of building a body of comparative
empirical theory on foreign policy decision-making are accordingly diminished. It has been argued, therefore, that there is a
need for teaching and research to develop much more along the
lines of recent texts in comparative government [48]. Obstacles
to success do exist however. Simply in terms of practicability it
might be difficult, to say the least, to co-ordinate and implement
a programme of research into, say, the comparative structure and
functioning of West European foreign ministries. So, while
acknowledging the virtues of comparability, especially in the
West European context [49], the more intensive analysis of
particular foreign policies remains a valuable research option.

Thirdly, the areas sketched out in volumes such as those edited
by Rosenau on *Linkage Politics* [50] and *Domestic Sources of
Foreign Policy* [51], have tremendous ramifications for any
attempt to study more closely Britain's external relations. Some
of these research fields – for example, the foreign policy role of
political parties or pressure groups – can be absorbed within the
decision-making framework mentioned earlier. Others cannot:
and hence our general preference in the present discussion for

using the term 'external relations' rather than 'foreign policy', the traditional usage of the latter term being subsumed under the connotations of the former. Many of the changes affecting Britain's international position since 1945 have involved transnational links at non-governmental levels. These are of interest *per se*, and not only as relevant factors in the policy-making process. The operations of non-governmental organisations are a good example [52].

V   METHODOLOGY AND THE DATA PROBLEM

Before we can venture much further however, a serious barrier must be recognised. Detailed and useful information about foreign policy processes in Britain is simply not available. The situation is perhaps better in other countries, though Pruitt's State Department study [53] was restricted to a few area-desks and to an issue not officially considered of great importance. But it is a little ironic that British scholars have sometimes in the past been given a degree of access to ministries in other European countries and elsewhere that they could not hope for in Britain.

The problem is admittedly not one exclusive to research into the making of foreign policy. Special factors of national security accentuate but do not create it. A reluctance to reveal its processes to the outside observer, including the researcher, is a characteristic common to most organisations, from car assembly-plants to hospitals. Indeed, as Allen has pointed out, researchers can be refused access by Government Departments in Britain over the whole field of public policy. The reasons, he suggests, are numerous, including confidentiality, political-cum-administrative 'sensitivity', paternalism, inadequate resources, or even sheer disorganisation. It is, for example, a common complaint of economists that they are not allowed to know the assumptions on which Whitehall forecasts are based [54]. On the foreign policy side, sources such as *Hansard*, or the Command Papers and publications of HMSO and the Central Office of Information, are not augmented by any periodical such as the United States' *Department of State Bulletin* or Australia's *Current Notes on International Affairs*.

If full documentary evidence were taken as the goal of research methodology – and not even the diplomatic historian would take the argument that far – the foreign policy researcher would find himself in an impossible situation. At best he could examine, and at that inadequately, issues no more recent than thirty years old. Other sources, it is true, are available : the United States archives [56], for example, or memoirs, or informal remarks by officials. After all, the judicious leakage of information is just as much an instrument of State policy as its restriction. George Brown gave as one of his reasons for leaving the FCO that 'we were very leaky. Things were in the press and it was being used . . . to mould decisions in the Cabinet Room' [57].

Fortunately however the methodology of foreign policy studies is not a question of accumulating and absorbing documents from official archives. This is not to deny the utility of documents. The Stanford University studies of North and his colleagues on the 1914 and other international crises made systematic use of documentation with the aid of content analysis [58]. The argument is rather that it is more profitable, from the research point of view, to concentrate on the *processes* of decision-making : on *how* and *why* decisions are taken and policies implemented, instead of on specific outcomes in actual situations. Given this orientation, it becomes quite possible for foreign policy decision-making to be studied more rigorously without the researcher's infringing or being unduly impeded by the Official Secrets Acts. Research methods do differ from those of the traditional diplomatic historian. But, slowly perhaps, the International Relations scholar and the practitioner are beginning to work out a *modus vivendi*. As the contributions to the present volume indicate, the relationship is one of mutual advantage.

VI OUTLINE OF THE VOLUME

To summarise then, we have argued that Britain's international position has undergone a number of fundamental changes since 1945; that these changes suggest the need for fresh approaches to the study of Britain's external relations; that foreign policy decision-making in Britain is however a field which has been sadly neglected by researchers; that recent developments in foreign policy studies can lend insights into potentially fruitful research directions; and finally, that the very real problems of access to relevant data do not present insurmountable obstacles to such research.

It remains to introduce the contributions. Practical considerations dictate that we cannot include a full treatment of the operating environment of Britain's external relations. Discussion has for the most part been restricted to the British context, even though this means excluding questions such as the impact of NATO, Commonwealth, or United Nations demands on policy outcomes. This is unfortunate; but we had proceeded on the principle that half a loaf is better than none, and in the hope that the present volume will stimulate further research into these important areas.

Part A concentrates wholly on the Foreign and Commonwealth Office itself. The implication, that the FCO can be viewed as the heart of the decision-making process, is debatable; but it does provide an initial working picture of reality [59]. The image becomes more accurate when the chapters in Part B are taken into account. These examine more closely the relationships between the FCO and other major Departments or fields of policy : trade and aid, economic and defence. The section begins with an evaluation of the relationship between the FCO and the political machinery, and the foreign policy role of the Cabinet. Parliament itself however is included in Part C on the grounds that the legislature has not in general played any crucial role in the formulation of British foreign policy. This third section also incorporates discussions of the significance of pressure groups, non-governmental organisations and the mass media.

REFERENCES

[1] See 'Memorandum by Sir Eyre Crowe on the Present State of British Relations with France and Germany, January 1, 1907', in *British Documents on the Origins of the War, 1898–1914*, ed. G. P. Gooch and Harold Temperley London, HMSO 1928) III, 403. 'So ample, so lucid and so authoritative was it a statement of what British diplomats and statesmen held to be the aims of British diplomacy,

that it must be regarded as the starting point in any attempt to understand British foreign policy in the first half of the twentieth century' : John Connell, *The 'Office': A Study of British Foreign Policy and its Makers, 1919–51* (London : Wingate, 1958) 11.

[2]   Speech at the United States Military Academy, West Point, 5 December 1962. Younger has referred to the 'extraordinary violence of the reaction in the highest political circles' in Britain to this 'obvious truth' : Kenneth Younger, *Changing Perspectives in British Foreign Policy* (London : Oxford University Press, 1964) 137.

[3]   Interview on *The World This Weekend*, BBC Radio 4, 26 April 1970.

[4]   Personal communication, 31 July 1968.

[5]   Andrew Shonfield, 'The Duncan Report and its Critics', in *International Affairs*, 46 (1970) 247. See further *Report of the Review Committee on Overseas Representation, 1968–1969, Chairman Sir Val Duncan* (London : HMSO, 1969) Cmnd. 4107.

[6]   Patricia W. Blair, *The Mini-State Dilemma* (New York : Carnegie, 1967).

[7]   Edward Heath, 'Realism in British Foreign Policy', in *Foreign Affairs*, 48 (1969) 49. On some of the implications for Britain's traditional naval role, see J. L. Moulton, *British Maritime Strategy in the 1970s* (Royal United Service Institution, July 1969).

[8]   R. Dawson and R. Rosecrance, 'Theory and Reality in the Anglo-American Alliance', in *World Politics*, 19 (1966) 21–51.

[9]   Interview in September 1966 : cited in E. F. Penrose, 'Britain's Place in the Changing Structure of International Relations', in *New Orientations: Essays in International Relations*, ed. E. F. Penrose, Peter Lyon, and Edith Penrose (London : Cass, 1970) 73.

[10] General Lord Bourne, 'The Place of British Defence', in *Contemporary Review*, 218 (1971) 118.

[11] See further *Europe and America in the 1970s: I. Between Détente and Confrontation*, Adelphi Paper No. 70 (London : Institute for Strategic Studies, November 1970); and Hans J. Morgenthau, 'Western Europe', in *America's*

World Role in the 70s, ed. Abdul A. Said (Englewood Cliffs, N.J.: Prentice-Hall, 1970) 43–53.

[12] B. M. Russett, *Community and Contention: Britain and America in the Twentieth Century* (Cambridge, Mass.: MIT Press, 1963).

[13] *Europe's Futures, Europe's Choices: Models of Western Europe in the 1970s*, ed. Alastair Buchan (London: Chatto and Windus, 1969).

[14] Michael Howard, 'Britain's Defences: Commitments and Capabilities', in *Foreign Affairs*, 39 (1960) 81.

[15] Hayward Alker and Donald Puchala, 'Trends in Economic Partnership: The North Atlantic Area, 1928–1966', in *Quantitative International Politics: Insights and Evidence*, ed. J. David Singer (New York: Free Press, 1967) 315.

[16] Karl W. Deutsch, 'Integration and Arms Control in the European Political Environment: A Summary Report', in *American Political Science Review*, LX (1966) 355. For a conflicting conclusion – indeed, that 'in some respects, European integration may have moved into full gear only *since* 1958' – see Ronald Inglehart, 'An End to European Integration?', *ibid.*, LXI (1967) 91.

[17] See further Reg Prentice, 'More Priority for Overseas Aid', in *International Affairs*, 46 (1970) 1–10.

[18] F. S. Northedge, *British Foreign Policy: The Process of Readjustment, 1945–61* (London: Allen and Unwin, 1962) 33.

[19] *Duncan*, p. 10. See further Michael Donelan, 'The Trade of Diplomacy', in *International Affairs*, 45 (1969) 605–16. On the political and diplomatic significance of the changing role of sterling, see Susan Strange, *Sterling and British Policy: A Political Study of an International Currency in Decline* (London: Oxford University Press, 1971).

[20] One important motive for *Concorde*, begun in 1962, was British and French fears that their aerospace industries might come under the domination of the United States: John Calmann, *European Co-operation in Defence Technology: The Political Aspect* (London: Institute for Strategic Studies, April 1967) 7. On future developments, see Victor Basiuk, 'The Impact of Technology in the Next Decades', *Orbis*, XIV (1970) 17–42.

[21] George Modelski, 'The Corporation in World Society', in *Yearbook of World Affairs*, 22 (1968) 75.

[22] ibid., 77. See also Caroline M. Miles, 'The International Corporation', in *International Affairs*, 45 (1969) 259–68.

[23] Jean-Jacques Servan-Schreiber, *Le Défi Américain* (Paris: Denoël, 1967); also translated by Ronald Steel as *The American Challenge* (London: Hamish Hamilton, 1968).

[24] Robert C. Angell, 'The Growth of Transnational Participation', in *Social Processes in International Relations: A Reader*, ed. Louis Kriesberg (New York: Wiley, 1968) 226–45; and *Peace on the March: Transnational Participation* (New York, 1969).

[25] The impact of changing external factors on the organisation of diplomacy is discussed in J. Niezing, 'Diplomatie, een organisatie in beweqing: een evaluatie van literatuur', in *Acta Politica*, 4 (1969) 139–72.

[26] James N. Rosenau, 'Pre-theories and Theories of Foreign Policy', in *Approaches to Comparative and International Politics*, ed. R. Barry Farrell (Evanston: Northwestern University Press, 1966) 63. See also John W. Burton, *Systems, States, Diplomacy and Rules* (Cambridge: University Press, 1968).

[27] A. J. P. Taylor, *The Trouble Makers: Dissent over Foreign Policy, 1792–1939* (London: Hamish Hamilton, 1957) 11–12.

[28] Roesnau, 'Pre-theories and Theories of Foreign Policy', 65 (italics omitted).

[29] Wolfram F. Hanrieder, *West German Foreign Policy, 1949–63: International Pressure and Domestic Response* (Stanford: University Press, 1967). See also his article 'Compatibility and Consensus: A Proposal for the Conceptual Linkage of External and Internal Dimensions of Foreign Policy', in *American Political Science Review*, LXI (1967) 971–82.

[30] Donald G. Bishop, *The Administration of British Foreign Relations* (New York: Syracuse University Press, 1961).

[31] Personal communication, 13 December 1969.

[32] Peter G. Richards, *Parliament and Foreign Affairs* (London: Allen and Unwin, 1967).

[33] ibid., Preface.

[34] R. Victor Langford, *British Foreign Policy: Its Formulation in Recent Years* (Washington, D.C.: American Council on Public Affairs, 1942) vii.

[35] *The Administration of British Foreign Relations.*

[36] David Vital, *The Making of British Foreign Policy* (London: Allen and Unwin, 1968). See also the valuable essays in D. C. Watt, *Personalities and Policies: Studies in the Formulation of British Foreign Policy in the Twentieth Century* (London: Longmans, 1965). Other references are given in the Bibliography at the end of this volume.

[37] Review in *International Affairs*, 45 (1969) 524.

[38] For example William P. Snyder, *The Politics of British Defense Policy, 1945–1962* (Columbus: Ohio State University Press, 1964); and R. N. Rosecrance, *Defense of the Realm: British Strategy in the Nuclear Epoch* (New York: Columbia University Press, 1968).

[39] Michael Howard, *The Central Organisation of Defence* (London: Royal United Service Institution, April 1970); and A. J. R. Groom, *British Thinking about Nuclear Weapons*, forthcoming.

[40] Leon D. Epstein, *British Politics in the Suez Crisis* (London: Pall Mall, 1964). There have been some interesting studies of international attitudes in Britain: for example, Morris Davis and Sidney Verba, 'Party Affiliation and International Opinions in Britain and France, 1947–1956', in *Public Opinion Quarterly*, 24 (1960) 590–604; and M. Abrams, British Elite Attitudes and the European Common Market', ibid., 29 (1965) 236–46.

[41] Michael Brecher, Blema Steinberg, and Janice Stern, 'A Framework for Research on Foreign Policy Behaviour', in *Journal of Conflict Resolution*, XIII (1969) 75. For further references see the Bibliography.

[42] *Foreign Policy Decision-Making: An Approach to the Study of International Politics*, ed. Richard C. Snyder, H. W. Bruck, and Burton Sapin (New York: Free Press, 1962). See further, James N. Rosenau, 'The Premises and Promises of Decision-Making Analysis', in *Contemporary Political Analysis*, ed. James C. Charlesworth (New York: Free Press, 1967); James A. Robinson and Richard C. Snyder, 'Decision-Making in International Politics', in

International Behaviour, ed. H. C. Kelman (New York: Holt, Rinehart and Winston, 1965) 433–63; *The Study of Policy Formation*, ed. Raymond Bauer and Kenneth J. Gergen (New York: Free Press, 1968); David Braybrooke and Charles E. Lindblom, *A Strategy of Decision* (New York: Free Press, 1963); and Oran R. Young, 'A Note on Snyder, Bruck and Sapin', in his *Systems of Political Science* (Englewood Cliffs, N.J.: Prentice-Hall, 1968) 62–64.

[43] See for example, George Modelski, *A Theory of Foreign Policy* (New York: Praeger, 1962); Karl W. Deutsch, *The Nerves of Government* (New York: Free Press, 1963); John W. Burton, *Systems, States, Diplomacy and Rules* (Cambridge: University Press, 1968) 58–79; Roy E. Jones, *Analysing Foreign Policy: An Introduction to Some Conceptual Problems* (London: Routledge and Kegan Paul, 1970); James N. Rosenau, 'Pre-theories and Theories of Foreign Policy', in *Approaches to Comparative and International Politics*, ed. R. Barry Farrell (Evanston: Northwestern University Press, 1966) 27–92; and James N. Rosenau, 'Foreign Policy as an Issue-Area', in *Domestic Sources of Foreign Policy*, ed. James N. Rosenau (New York: Free Press, 1967) 11–50. The field is reviewed in William Wallace, *Foreign Policy and the Political Process* (London: Macmillan, 1971).

[44] Dean G. Pruitt, *Problem-Solving in the Department of State* (University of Denver: Monograph Series on World Affairs, 1964–5, No. 2). See also Charlton Ogburn, 'The Flow of Policy-Making in the Department of State', in *The Formulation and Administration of United States Foreign Policy*, ed. H. Field Haviland (Washington, D.C.: Brookings Institute, 1960).

[45] Glenn D. Paige, *The Korean Decision (June 24–30, 1950)* (New York: Free Press, 1968).

[46] Bernard C. Cohen, *The Political Process and Foreign Policy: The Making of the Japanese Peace Settlement* (Princeton University Press, 1957).

[47] Nigel Forward, *The Field of Nations: An Account of Some New Approaches to International Relations* (London: Macmillan, 1971) 3. As Joseph Frankel comments: '. . . we

know much less about the details of British foreign policy
than about those of American foreign policy. Certainly we
have no insights into the working of the Cabinet and of the
Foreign Office even remotely comparable with the information available about the White House and the Department
of State': 'Comparing Foreign Policies: The Case of
Norway', in *International Affairs*, 44 (1968) 482.

[48] For example, Jean Blondel, *An Introduction to Comparative Government* (London: Weidenfeld and Nicolson,
1969).

[49] See for example D. C. Watt, 'The Reform of the German
Foreign Service: The Herwarth and Duncan Reports
Compared', in *The World Today*, 26 (1970) 352–58.

[50] *Linkage Politics: Essays on the Convergence of National
and International Systems*, ed. James N. Rosenau (New
York: Free Press, 1969).

[51] *Domestic Sources of Foreign Policy*, ed. James N. Rosenau
(New York: Free Press, 1967).

[52] Jeffrey Harrod, 'Non-Governmental Organisations and the
Third World', in *Yearbook of World Affairs*, 24 (1970)
170–85.

[53] *Problem-Solving in the Department of State.*

[54] David Allen, 'Problems of Access to Government Data', in
Social Science Research Council Newsletter, 9 (1970) 26–
28. On sources relevant for foreign policy studies, see
Government Information and the Research Worker, ed.
Ronald Staveley and Mary Piggott (London: The Library
Association, 1965) Ch. I, IV, VII. Late in 1970 it was
announced that the Government intended to reduce secrecy
in Government Departments (*The Observer*, 1 November
1970).

[55] 'Any assiduous student can soon know more about quite
recent events than the most erudite historian will ever know
about many remoter events': David Thomson, 'The
Writing of Contemporary History', in *Journal of Contemporary History*, 2 (1967) 25–26. Indeed, the opposite might
be the case: when documents for the 1970s became available for study, the researcher might find there are too many
for comfort.

[56] 'Like it or not, all concerned . . . have to face the fact that

there will shortly be in existence in the United States a group of academics interested in, and intimately informed on, a wide area of British political and diplomatic activity on which research in Britain is virtually impossible' : D. C. Watt, 'Restrictions on Research : The Fifty-Year Rule and British Foreign Policy', in *International Affairs*, 41 (1965) 92. See also his 'United States Documentary Sources for the Study of British Foreign Policy, 1919–39', ibid., 38 (1962) 63–72.

[57] Interview reported in the *Guardian*, 22 August 1970. Leaks, whether for accidental or other reasons, underwent a marked increase in the later 1950s : see Laurence W. Martin, 'The Market for Strategic Ideas in Britain : The "Sandys Era" ', in *American Political Science Review*, LVI 1962) 31. Some of the problems are examined briefly in Hans Schauer, 'Journalisten und Diplomaten : Kollegen oder Rivalen?', in *Aussenpolitik*, 20 (1969) 763–66.

[58] R. C. North, O. R. Holsti, M. G. Zaninovich, and D. A. Zinnes, *Content Analysis: A Handbook with Applications for the Study of International Crises* (Evanston : Northwestern University Press, 1963); O. R. Holsti, R. C. North, and R. A. Brody, 'Perception and Action in the 1914 Crisis,' in *Quantitative International Politics: Insights and Evidence*, ed. J. David Singer (New York : Free Press, 1967) 123–58.

[59] Friedrich has suggested a three-level scheme for the analysis of democratic foreign policy : the technical and bureaucratic level of professional diplomacy; particular interest groups; and the emotional level of broad popular participation : Carl J. Friedrich, 'Die öffentliche Meinung Amerikas in der Krise', *Aussenpolitik*, VII (1956) 502; cited in his 'International Politics and Foreign Policy in Developed (Western) Systems', in *Approaches to Comparative and International Politics*, ed. R. Barry Farrell (Evanston : Northwestern University Press, 1966) 108–10.

A The Foreign and Commonwealth Office: Organisation, Planning and Personnel

2 The Organisation and Structure of the Foreign and Commonwealth Office*

CHRISTINA LARNER

I THE HISTORICAL BACKGROUND

THE PRESENT Foreign and Commonwealth Office (FCO) is the end product of a series of unions of government offices and organisations for the administration of Britain's overseas affairs. These mergers (which are set out in Chart I) reflect the changes in Britain's overseas commitments over the past fifty years. In the early years of this century when there was an extended empire to administer, and when the number of important foreign countries was relatively few – there were eight ambassadors in 1920; now there are over seventy – the administration of Britain's overseas services was covered by numerous specialist home and overseas organisations. These included the Foreign Office, the Colonial Office, and the India Office at home; the Diplomatic Service, the four separate Consular Services, the Colonial Service, and the Indian Civil Service abroad.

This high degree of specialisation with its concomitant diversification of organisations became unpopular among administrative reformers towards the end of the nineteenth century. It was thought that centralisation would improve the efficiency of the services, and that unification of these services for foreign, though

* The sources for this chapter are the yearly Diplomatic Service Lists, the Reports of the Civil Service Commissioners, the Foreign and Commonwealth Office and HMSO publications mentioned in the text and notes, and interviews with officials.

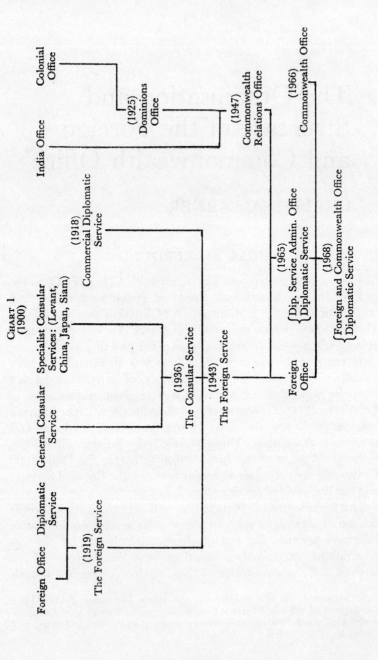

CHART 1
(1900)

not yet for colonial affairs, was desirable. This became the dominant reforming idea from the report of the MacDonnell Committee of 1914 [1] onwards. Immediately after the First World War there was a partial amalgamation of the personnel of the Diplomatic Service with that of the Foreign Office under the new title of 'the Foreign Service'. Probably the most important merger before 1968, however, was that made under the Foreign Service Act 1943 which amalgamated the Consular Service and the Commercial Diplomatic Service with the Foreign Service. This Act also had the effect of completing the unification of the Diplomatic Service with the Foreign Office by providing financial disincentives to members to spend more than five years at a time in London. The prevailing philosophy among Foreign Service reformers at this time was that a mobile generalist service, all of whose members could serve equally well in a variety of diplomatic, consular, and administrative posts, was the ideal both from the point of view of the service as a career, and from the point of view of the work to be done.

The Foreign Service between 1943 and 1965 was essentially the creation of the 1943 Eden proposals. During this period a genuine attempt was made to distribute and circulate Foreign Service officers around the new greater range of jobs, and to make this easier the balance of consular and political work was redistributed. It was urged in the *Proposals for the Reform of the Foreign Service* [2] that it was in any case desirable to increase the number of political postings. At the same time the number of consular posts was reduced which meant that new recruits did not have to spend the major part of their time in consular work.

An indication of the completeness of the post-1943 amalgamation is that the fears of those who opposed it on the grounds that there would be a loss of expertise in the office seem to have been realised. Complaints have been levelled at the office end rather than at the work of embassies, for diplomats are not sufficiently long at a London desk to lose diplomatic skills; the problem is more that they are not in London long enough to gain administrative ones. These complaints are of a lack of continuity of personnel, of administrative and financial incompetence, and of a lack of parliamentary expertise.

The other main reform of 1943, the effects of which have been felt since the war, has been to make the Service open to wider social strata. It was for the first time made accessible to all by the provision of adequate allowances for travel and for the education of children, and by the removal of the qualifications of a high level of French and German before entry.

Apart from the differences already noted between the pre-war and post-war Foreign Office, the post-war period saw a rapid expansion. This is so marked that twentieth-century Foreign Office history can be seen as falling into two parts : a pre-Second World War period in which Britain played a world power role with an embryonic organisation, and a post-World War period in which she has played a reduced role with an ever-expanding organisation. But it is fair to point out in passing that the Foreign Office has increased through amalgamation as well as through internal expansion, that the expansion is reflected in all other aspects of the central government machine, and that Britain is not in any way abnormal in this respect. Most major powers in the first half of the century did their business with small home organisations : today, major, medium, and minor powers all tend to have large organisations.

By 1962 there was felt to be a need for a review of the overseas services. By then there were two main problems which could not have beeen detected or dealt with under the conditions prevailing in 1943. The first was that the Commonwealth countries and ex-colonial territories had become more obviously 'foreign' than they had appeared in the middle of the Second World War when many of their armed forces served alongside those of Britain. The number of independent countries in the Commonwealth had increased. The work of officers of the Commonwealth Services now appeared to have more in common with that of the Foreign Service than with that of the Home Civil Service of which they were still officially members. At home, the work of the Colonial Office and Commonwealth Relations Office [3] often appeared to overlap with that of the Foreign Office, and the process of amalgamation now appeared to be incomplete. The second problem was that Britain's position in the world had been greatly altered, and in terms of military power at least was seen to be reduced.

The Committee on Representational Services Overseas which was set up in 1962 under Lord Plowden reported back in 1964.

The suggested solution to the first problem was the amalgamation of the Commonwealth Service, Foreign Service, and Trades Commissioner Service (belonging to the Board of Trade) into one Diplomatic Service. This Service was to be administered by a new office called the Diplomatic Service Administrative Office. This was to take place immediately and it was thought that it might be followed by a union at the offices at home, though there was no firm agreement on that.

Britain's reduced role in the world, however, was not fully accepted. The Service was not found to be expensive considering the task it was expected to fulfil :

> Britain retains many wide responsibilities and a high degree of world-wide influence. We believe that the British people wish to sustain that influence and share Sir Winston Churchill's view that Britain should not be content to be 'relegated to take a minor role in the world'. If our influence is not felt, not only national but international interests and objectives will suffer. It is in the general interest that Britain's voice should continue to be heard and to carry weight in the world. If this is to be achieved, despite the narrowed limits of our economic and military resources, we shall require to make the best possible use of 'diplomacy' and 'persuasion'. What we can no longer ensure by power alone, we must secure by other means [3].

It was partly this determination to fight for a world role rather than work out a policy for a new, reduced one, which ensured that the Plowden Report, despite the implementation of many of its practical suggestions for updating and reforming the Service, belonged to the past and would soon be superseded.

On the Commonwealth issue, the report came out against the immediate amalgamation of the Commonwealth Relations Office with the Foreign Office, lest such a step at this juncture could be interpreted as implying a loss of interest in the Commonwealth partnership. The Plowden Committee thought, however, that 'the logic of events' pointed to an eventual amalgamation, although in fact 'the logic of events' proved a stronger force than they had anticipated. The new combined Diplomatic Service was formally established in January 1st 1965. In 1966 the Commonwealth Relations Office (itself the result of the 1947 amalgamation of the India Office with the Dominions Office)

amalgamated with the Colonial Office to form the Commonwealth Office, which in October 1968 amalgamated in turn with
the Foreign Office. This last amalgamation appears to have been
an impulse of the Prime Minister, and it, in a sense, completed
the unification of Britain's overseas representational services : it
meant that her dealings with the whole globe were administered
by a single organisation.

The creation of the new Diplomatic Service in 1965 had led
to a reconstruction of both the Foreign Office and the Commonwealth Relations Office. They were streamlined with the help of
a new Organisation and Methods team and with advice from
the Treasury Management Services Division. A common communications system was set up, the Diplomatic Service Administration Office unified the administration of personnel, and other
departments were established as 'joint departments' where there
was obvious overlapping. By early 1968 the planners believed
that the process of forming joint departments had been taken
as far as was practical so long as there were two separate
ministries, and in March it was announced that the Prime
Minister proposed to bring about the amalgamation of the
Foreign Office and the (since 1966) Commonwealth Office. By
this time about two-thirds of the diplomatic staff of the two
offices were serving in joint departments.

In the post-amalgamation period there have been some personnel problems. These are not regarded as serious as they are
expected to be phased out in time. Members of the former
Commonwealth Service, when asked to fill in a form giving their
preference for postings, still tend to write in, 'any Commonwealth
country'. Colonial Office staff who had not reckoned on serving
abroad have been given the option of transfer to the Home Civil
Service, and a number have been accommodated in this way.
Others are still happily serving in the department of the new
FCO equivalent to the one that they were in in the Colonial
Office.

The Duncan Report, July 1969 [4]

It may be wondered why another review of the overseas service
should have been required so soon after the Plowden Committee
reported. The Eden proposals of 1943 had sufficed for over
twenty years. Many reasons could be advanced.

The Plowden Report and the 1968 amalgamation, it could be said, ended an era; an era in which it was central firstly that Britain had a world, and in some places a paternal, role to play, and secondly that the men best fitted to run Britain's overseas affairs were generalist diplomats with some commercial and administrative experience. The Plowden Committee therefore had made recommendations for a situation which was changing. They were overtaken almost as soon as they had pronounced, on the one hand by a much wider recognition of Britain's vulnerable and reduced world position and on the other hand by the anti-generalist ideals of the Fulton Report on the Home Civil Service of July, 1968. Probably, however the weakness of the Plowden Report, from the point of view of the problems of the Government late in 1967, was that it found that 'the present cost of these Services is not unreasonable' [5].

The major change in foreign policy, which included withdrawal from the 'East of Suez' military commitments, was announced in January 1968. This change was dictated by a recognition of Britain's deteriorating economic circumstances. And so even before the new merger had been completed, a committee of three was set up with an urgent brief to report back in six months (they took from September 1968 to publication in July 1969) on the implications of the foreign policy change, and to suggest ways in which the foreign services could be run more cheaply.

The Duncan Committee appears to have been set up mainly to effect economies; as a *quid pro quo* for similar economies already agreed on the home front. The FCO, which had worked extremely hard at practising economy and retraction during the build-up to the merger, felt injured by the early setting up of this committee with a clear mandate to cut back still further. Most of the other reasons were regarded as window dressing, although an important subsidiary one does seem to have been a response to Parliamentary and intra-governmental signs of more official support for export promotion.

The Committee interpreted their terms of reference to mean that all activities financed out of public funds which are concerned with the conduct of British external relations lay within the scope of their enquiry. They found that the new circumstances in which they had to make recommendations were :

(1) That Britain was now 'a major power of the second order'. This was taken to mean approximately equal to France and Germany.

(2) That British foreign policy now has two central commitments

      (i) to an increasingly integrated Western Europe on as wide a basis as possible;

      (ii) to a North Atlantic Alliance under United States leadership as the main instrument for the conduct of East–West relations.

And their main recommendations were :

(1) That political diplomacy (increasingly expected to be multilateral rather than bilateral) would be confined to countries in Western Europe and North America, described as the Area of Concentration.

(2) The rest of the world, called tactlessly the Outer Area, should be covered by reduced, flexible, 'selective' posts as opposed to the 'comprehensive' posts in the Area of Concentration. Work in the Outer Area would be largely commercial, but the system should be sufficiently flexible to allow for reinforcing a Selective Mission 'if unexpected demands are placed upon it in times of crisis'.

The fate of the Duncan Report since July 1969

The Duncan Report has now become simply a point of reference. The Labour Government said in the autumn of 1969 that the report was accepted and would be implemented. So far as the present Government are concerned, it is in the spirit of the renewed Conservative orthodoxy on the necessity for cutting back on government expenditure. FCO opinion is that the report exists, its recommendations are a point of reference for discussion, and when any moves or reforms in Diplomatic Service organisation are in accordance with the letter or spirit of the Duncan Report this will be clearly pointed out.

Its intellectual status can be followed in the press and Parliamentary discussions of July 1969 and later reactions in the academic journals. In general praise has been awarded to it for its realism, and blame for its insensitive and tactless use of language. It suffers from the fact that the Committee looked at the Diplomatic Service abroad and hardly at all at the Office, but there are naturally many implications for the Office as well as for the Diplomatic Service as a whole, and reference will be made to the report where it seems relevant in the pages that follow.

II THE STRUCTURE OF THE FCO

(a) Personnel: grades, classes; and numbers in the Diplomatic Service

The FCO is the headquarters of the Diplomatic Service, and is staffed by members of the Service who are required to serve interchangeably at home and abroad, thought in fact, for most, the greater proportion of their career will be spent abroad. In order therefore to describe the hierarchy in the FCO it is necessary to look at the system of ranks and classes in the Diplomatic Service as a whole.

The Diplomatic Service is composed of five branches. The first two branches, in their case normally known as classes or streams: the A Class (Administrative) and the E Class (Executive), are together divided into nine grades. The third branch, the Clerical Branch, is officially known as the tenth grade of the Diplomatic Service. The other two branches have their own grading structure. The Secretarial Branch consists of Grades S2 to S5, and the Security Officer Branch has its own Grades 1 to 3.

But it is the Administrative and Executive Classes of the Diplomatic Service that chiefly concern us here. Chart 2 shows that an officer's diplomatic title, unless he is in the top four grades and working in the Foreign and Commonwealth Office, is not a clear indication of his grade, his stream, or his career prospects. It only suggest the kind of work that he may be doing. The ambiguity is intentional. It disguises the difference in career expectations beween members of administrative and executive streams doing the same work, and will ease the present movement towards a unified grading structure. In the representational field it gives to the Ivory Coast at Abidjan a proper British Ambassador in full diplomatic kneebreeches and cocked hat, looking like and having the same credentials as our knight in Bonn. The exact truth about an Ambassador's rank cannot even be found

CHART 2A. RANKS IN THE FOREIGN AND COMMONWEALTH OFFICE

Title	Grade (A Class)	Grade (E Class)	Home Civil Service Equivalent
Permanent Under-Secretary	1		Permanent Secretary
Deputy Under-Secretary	2		Deputy Secretary
Assistant Under-Secretary	3		Under Secretary
Counsellor (Head of FCO Department)	4		Assistant Secretary Principal Executive Officer
First Secretary	5		Principal Chief Executive Officer
		6	Senior Executive Officer
Second Secretary	7A	7E	Assistant Principal Higher Executive Officer
Third Secretary	8		Assistant Principal
(No Title)		9	Executive Officer

CHART 2B. RANKS IN THE DIPLOMATIC SERVICE WHEN SERVING ABROAD

Title	Grade (A Class)	Grade (E Class)
Ambassador	1–4*	
Minister	2–3	
Counsellor	4	
Consul-General	4	
First Secretary	5	6
Consul	5	6
Second Secretary	7A	7E
Third Secretary	8	
Vice Consul	8	9
Junior Attaché		9

* There are also some headships of missions at Grade 5.

in *The Diplomatic Service List*. To find it recourse to *Whitaker's Almanack* is necessary.

And just as knowledge of an officer's title and type of work does not tell you his grade, neither does knowing his grade necessarily indicate his stream, unless he is in Grades 9, 8, or 6, which are confined to one stream. The two streams enter the Service at different ages and levels of educational attainment. The Administrative Class are almost invariably honours graduates with first or second class degrees; the Executive Class are recruited at the age of 18 from among sixth-form leavers, although the recruitment of graduates for this class is on the increase.

The Executive Class recruit in the Office is simply known as a Grade 9 officer. On promotion to 7E he is officially given the Diplomatic Service title of Second Secretary whether he is at home or abroad, though they are not used in the Office. There are no Executive Class titles in the FCO equivalent to those in the Home Civil Service, although the actual grades are more or less equivalent to particular Home Civil Service old-style executive titles.

At the time the Duncan Committee reported, the FCO was in advance of the Home Civil Service in its plans for a unified grading structure. The Diplomatic Service Grade 4 was already then an integrated grade, and this has now been extended to include Grade 5. That is to say there is only one salary range for Grade 5 and an executive class officer on promotion to Grade 5 ceases automatically to be in the executive stream. At Grade 7 there are still different pay scales for A and E streams.

The FCO approach the problem of a unified grading structure from the opposite end from the Home Civil Service. The FCO are planning to extend unification downwards; the Home Civil Service, in their post-Fulton period, are planning for a common entrance with accelerated promotion for a fast stream selected on the job. The FCO plan has the advantage that their Executive Class recruits, some of whom can stay at Grade 9 for as long as ten years or even more, are not necessarily given inflated expectations of their career chances; but it could have the disadvantage, which the Fulton proposals for the Home Civil Service were seeking to overcome, of failing to attract sufficiently high quality personnel to do the kind of jobs traditionally done by the executive class. The FCO however does not regard itself as having at present the same recruitment problems at this level as the Home Civil Service. It has always had a much lower proportion of executive to administrative class personnel, and partly for this reason, partly because the Service still has high prestige among entrants, they feel they have kept up the standard of recruitment for this class. Their problem is not so much how to attract good executive class material in the first place; it is rather how to accelerate the promotion and integration of the best of them once they are in.

Despite this current difference of approach possibly reflecting different needs, there is a close relationship between the grading system and pay scales in the Foreign and Home Civil Service, which rests partly on history, partly on present convenience. Until the Foreign Service Act 1943 the Foreign Office was officially part of the Home Civil Service and under direct Treasury control. Since that date it has proved convenient for salary rises in the administrative class to be negotiated together. The administrative class of the Diplomatic Service and FCO have a separate union from that of the Home Civil Service called the Diplomatic Service Association, but it is formally affiliated to the Association of First Division Civil Servants. The Diplomatic Service Association (to which between 90 per cent and 95 per cent of all those eligible for membership belong) feel themselves to be too small to negotiate a salary rise every time it is appropriate and rely on the Home Civil Service union to do it for them. The D.S.A. feel that they are at a disadvantage in being tied to the Home Civil Service because promotion comes to them at a later average age, but that owing to their relatively small size the present arrangement is worthwhile.

The executive classes have separate associations, but at the time of writing the unions are in flux. There is a move towards unification in accordance with the present policy of integrated hierarchies. Both the past and hoped-for future connections between the unions and between the Home Civil and Foreign Services have forced a fairly close correspondence between the ranks of the two services in both classes. It is for this reason that there is in the FCO hierarchy an executive Grade 6 which corresponded to the Home Civil Executive grade of Senior Executive Officer, but which had no administrative class equivalent in either Service.

NUMBERS OF STAFF IN THE FCO. The present establishment in the FCO consists of 1 Permanent Under-Secretary, 10 Deputy Under-Secretaries, 15 Assistant Under-Secretaries, 78 Counsellors (heads of departments), and a fluctuating number of First,

Second, and Third Secretaries, but not fewer than about 600. The highest levels, the Deputy and Assistant Under-Secretaries, were much reduced at the time of the 1968 merger, and have been further reduced since then, when they stood at 12 Deputy Under-Secretaries and 21 Assistant Under-Secretaries. But the present strength is still thought to be top-heavy, and the Duncan Committee recommended the elimination of one level of Under-Secretary, at least so far as differentiation of function is concerned. The FCO itself regard this as already happening in practice, though they agree the actual numbers could still be slightly reduced. But at departmental level all departments regard themselves as extremely hard pressed in terms of the amount of work routinely coming through their hands. Here the question is whether the amount of paper could or should be reduced before there is any question of reducing staff.

The Duncan Committee calculated in July 1969 that at any given time one-third of the total service was at home. There is not quite the same proportion if the Administrative and Executive classes are considered on their own, because a large number of clerical staff are recruited locally. But this would still appear an alarming proportion in staff-line terms if it were not for the fact that only one-seventh of the FCO departments are actually managing the Diplomatic Service. It may not in any case be a very useful concept to apply to the FCO, but it is one which they invite by using it themselves [6].

PERSONNEL : RECRUITMENT AND SELECTION. The FCO has moved a long way since the end of the First World War when open competition was first introduced and a senior FO man could write a note which invited his colleagues to worry about 'whether a public school education was to be regarded as essential', and 'how to exclude Jews, coloured men, and infidels who may be of British origin' [7]. (The exclusion of women had already been covered by an order-in-council amending the Sex Disqualification Act (1919).)

Today all these categories would officially be welcomed. All universities are circulated with recruitment posters, and invitations to visit the FCO, and all universities are visited by Diplomatic Service Officers, who address students and talk individually to those interested. Yet the steady stream of criticism which since the twenties has been levelled at the Diplomatic Service for its upper-class bias has not abated. That this bias still exists is undoubted, and comparative figures with the Home Civil Service for the proportion of public school boys bear this out. Comparative figures for Oxford and Cambridge dominance are stronger still. The principal effect of this continuous barrage upon the Service is not to make it mend its ways, but to increase its propaganda. Envoys may be sent to distant Newcastle and Glasgow in search of recruits, but those same envoys will admit that they can get all the talent they require by travelling no further than Oxbridge : 'there are some pretty funny chaps going there nowadays so we get a look at all types'. But the recruiting pamphlet *Graduate Careers in the Diplomatic Service* [8] gives stories by 'seven typical graduate entrants'; consisting of

(1) Grammar school in the West Country, Modern Languages, Durham.
(2) Famous northern grammar school and Oxford University.
(3) Woman language graduate.
(4) Modern linguist, public school and Cambridge.
(5) Welsh comprehensive and University College London.
(6) London grammar school and Oxford.
(7) First Class honours Classical Arabic, Oxford.

It all depends on what you mean by typical, but the table of actual entrants from the last four *Reports of the Civil Service Commission* suggests otherwise (see Chart 3). The class bias can be, and often has been, easily pinpointed and labelled, but it is very possibly a red herring. Various points occur here : (1) however many non-Oxbridge and provincial recruits were brought in, the FCO would soon make them indistinguishable from the rest, such is the efficiency of their socialisation; (2) the FCO cannot exactly be blamed for the fact that the people who apply are very like themselves. It could be said that by and large provincials, lower classes, and women, are less likely to see themselves in a representational capacity.

It is possible that it is rather late in the day to worry about the social composition of the Diplomatic Service, when the questions that are being asked are whether widespread resident representation is needed. Nevertheless it is worth pointing out in passing that two factors have operated in the past twenty-five

CHART 3
EDUCATIONAL BACKGROUND OF DIRECT ENTRANTS (MALE) 1966–69

Year	Number	Eton	Rugby Harrow Winchester	Major Public	Minor Public	Major Grammar	Other Grammar
1966	20	1	2	4	7	3	2
1967	23	1	3	3	13	3	
1968	24	2		7	6	2	6
1969	20	2	3	5	5	3	

EDUCATIONAL BACKGROUND OF DIRECT ENTRANTS (FEMALE) 1966–69

Year	Number	Public School	Major Grammar	Other Grammar	Mixed Grammar
1966	2	2			
1967	2	1	1		
1968	6	3	2		1
1969	4	4			

UNIVERSITIES OF DIRECT ENTRANTS 1966–69

Year	Number	Oxford	Cambridge	London	Scottish	Other
1966	22	9	9	1	2	1
1967	25	9	11			5
1968	30	14	6	3	3	4
1969	24	9	8		2	5

PROPORTION OF GRAMMAR SCHOOL ENTRANTS 1966–69

Year	Number	Grammar Schools	(non-major g. schools)	
1966	22	5	(2)	27%
1967	25	4	—	16%
1968	30	10	(6)	33%
1969	24	3	—	13½%

years towards greater social mixing which are unlikely to be repeated. The first is that after the war numbers were recruited from Oxford and Cambridge who had been doing special post-Service short courses and who would otherwise have gone to their local universities or not gone to university at all. The second is that successive mergers brought in the members of the Consular Service, the Sudanese Civil Service, the Commonwealth Service, and the Trade Commissions Service. From now onwards all recruitment (apart from special late entry recruitment or second-ments) will be direct from the universities through the Civil Service Commissioners, and if the entry for the last three years is anything to go by, a socially élitist pattern may become increasing apparent. It could only be modified by fairly large numbers of executive class officers being integrated at Grade 5 at an age when further promotion seems reasonable.

RECRUITMENT OF SPECIALISTS. The problem of specialists in the Service is dealt with later in this chapter in Section V, but it can be said in passing that there is no policy of favouring graduates in any particular subject. The Duncan Report recommended specialised training in the social sciences after joining the Service but recommended against any discrimination in favour of those with social science degrees. In their recruiting pamphlet the FCO ask themselves the question what use do they make of specialist qualifications. They illustrate their answer with the last man of their list of typical successful candidates. They take a first-class Classical Arabist and turn him into an FCO Arabist.

RECRUITMENT PROCEDURES. All candidates now enter by Method II (Method I, the last vestige of straight open competition by written examination – with an allowance of ten per cent of the marks for an oral examination – which prevailed from 1921, having been abolished in 1967). This consists of a short qualifying examination in general subjects from which candidates with a first-class honours degree or with second-class honours and a post-graduate degree are exempt, though this exemption is about to be abolished. This is followed by two days of written and oral tests at the Civil Service Commission offices and an interview before the Final Selection Board. A language aptitude test is also given from which those who have included a modern language in their degree are exempt.

Admission to the Diplomatic Service is therefore entirely in the hands of the Civil Service Commission. The Service does not recruit its own staff, although members and ex-members of the FCO serve on the Commission. The slight social differences between the Home Civil and Diplomatic Service may be due to self selection by candidates beforehand, or to a lack of conviction in the recruitment propaganda. The way in which young diplomats appear to the outsider to resemble middle-aged and older diplomats is probably due only partly to initial recruitment from one social class, and partly to the fact that, when abroad, they lead extensive social lives together in a manner unknown to the Home Civil Service.

(b) Division of Work

The FCO is divided into four blocs of departments. These are set out in Chart 4. The most striking aspect of the arrangement is the very large number of departments and the extent of the coverage, much of it duplicating or requiring liaison with divisions in various departments of the Home Civil Service. Two criticisms of this large number of departments are heard. One is that pressures of bureaucratic expansion have been allowed to have their head; the other is that the coverage is far too great. The answer to the first charge is that it is not entirely true. In the years between the merger of the services in 1965 and the merger of the offices in 1968 there was a considerable streamlining of departments where the two offices had overlapping responsibilities. In 1966 the Colonial Office had 14 departments, and the Commonwealth Relations Office had 32. On their union in 1966 the resulting Commonwealth Office had 32 and 8 joint departments with the Foreign Office. The Foreign Office at that time had 36 and the Diplomatic Service Administration Office which served both had 9. By October 1968 the new Foreign and Commonwealth Office had a total of 69, representing a reduction of 16 departments. Since then the number has further declined to 65 in May 1971.

The criticism that there is political reporting which is not needed and functional responsibilities which are duplicated, was made by the Duncan Committee :

CHART 4. DIVISION OF WORK

Geographical Departments (21)

Group	Departments
Europe	East European and Soviet Southern European Western European
Far East	Far Eastern South Asian South East Asian South West Pacific
America/The Middle East	American Caribbean Arabian Near Eastern North African
Africa—South of the Sahara	Central and Southern African Rhodesia Economic Rhodesia Political East Africa West Africa
Dependent Territories	Gibraltar and S. Atlantic Hong Kong Pacific and Indian Ocean West Indian

Functional Departments (29)

Group	Departments
Economic	Aviation & Telecommunications Marine & Transport Oil Commodities Export Promotion Financial Policy and Aid Trade Policy
United Nations	United Nations (Economic and Social) United Nations (Political)
Information and Cultural Relations	Cultural Relations East-West Contacts Information Administration Information Policy and Guidance Information Research
Planning, Research, Defence, and Disarmament	Research Library and Records Permanent Under-Secretary's Defence European Integration Science and Technology Western Organisations Disarmament European Communities Information Unit

Administrative Departments

Communications
Personnel: Operations
Personnel: Policy
Personnel: Training
Personnel: Services
Protocol and Conference
Security
Accommodation
Finance
Office Services and Supply.

Administration
{
Consular
Migration and Visa
Nationality and Treaty
Passport Office
Claims
India Office Library & Records
}

Advisers and Special Departments (5)
Arms Control and Disarmament Unit
Commonwealth Co-ordinators
Economists
News
Planning Staff.

The political officers in the chancery at Strelsau and the Ruritanian desk officer in the FCO may make more work for each other than the intrinsic importance of Anglo-Ruritanian political relations really justifies; and this tendency will only be increased by the likelihood that each group contains able and energetic men who will not be content to produce less than a full day's work [9].

They suggested here and elsewhere in the report that the amount of political reporting be reduced, particularly in the proposed 'Outer Area'. The suggestion has not been well received in the Office. Justification for the existence of more or less blanket coverage is made along the lines that the FCO has a threefold responsibility for information in the present situation. In the first place the Secretary of State for Foreign and Commonwealth Affairs is expected by Cabinet and Parliament to be fully briefed on any aspect of external relations and world affairs; in the second place, the rest of the Home Civil Service, the business world, and the public at large expect a similar service, and in the third place the FCO is still expected to act as postman to the world. In the present diplomatic situation withdrawal or reduction of staff in a particular country is interpreted by it as a rebuff by Her Majesty's Government.

It can be said that this is a circular argument which has been heard before, and which the Duncan Committee has attempted to break through; this extraordinarily extensive service is expected because it is provided. If it ceased to be provided, Cabinet, Parliament, Home Civil Service and public would get used to doing without it, and get their information from other sources. The FCO rejoinder is that the service is so useful simply because it is so comprehensive.

As affairs stand, most observers would regard the major work of the FCO as giving information and advice to the Foreign and Commonwealth Secretary on matters of long- and short-term foreign policy and on international crises as they occur. Since this is also the most sensitive area of its work, bearing as it does on constitutional theory, on ministerial responsibility, on Cabinet responsibility and on democratic control, it tends to be underplayed by the Office itself in its rare public pronouncements. Either the high theory is spelled out in simple language:

The Diplomatic Service provides continuous expertise on which the Ministers' decisions of policy are based. It also carries out the policy on which they have decided. In practice it is impossible to define what is or is not 'policy'. Part of the professional skill of the diplomat lies in judging which decision he may take on his own account within the overall policy of the government and which need to be put to the Ministers for their personal decision [10].

or part of their work most closely connected with policy is simply ignored :

The special contribution of the Foreign and Commonwealth Office to the national effort lies in its amassed and living knowledge of overseas countries. This knowledge is called upon constantly by Home Departments, by British industry and commerce and by the general public [11].

There is no mention in this paper of the Cabinet. The Office here sees itself, or wishes to be seen, as a kind of super information bureau.

The work of the FCO can be summarised as :

(1) The collection, processing and purveying of information about foreign countries in forms varying in importance from advice to travellers to near policy-making in advice to the Foreign and Commonwealth Secretary. Assistance in trade promotion is of increasing importance.
(2) The implementation of H.M.G.'s policy in negotiation and advice to embassies at home and abroad.
(3) The dissemination abroad of information about Britain, in keeping with the image H.M.G. wish to project and with H.M.G.'s foreign policy so far as these are compatible. The dissemination of information to embassies which may or may not be for further distribution in accordance with the above.
(4) Administration (e.g. of passports).
(5) Self-administration : the running of the Office and the Missions abroad.

For these purposes there are (May 1971) 21 geographical departments, 29 functional, 6 advisers' and special departments, and 10 administrative. These departments are now housed in sixteen different buildings, but this, while clearly unfortunate, is not quite as disastrous as the bald statement in the *Diplomatic List, 1971,* implies. The geographical departments are all contained in three buildings : Downing St. West, Downing St. East, and King Charles St., and these are in effect one building : the old Foreign Office, India Office, and Colonial Office, arranged round a quadrangle off Downing St. The functional departments are more diffused, though ten of them are also in the main FCO building, and another ten are together in Government Offices, Great George St., two minutes walk away. The ten administrative departments are nearly all together in the Curtis Green Building on the Victoria Embankment, and the rest are placed in other government offices which are not exclusive to the Foreign Office. The rehousing of the Office, by pulling down the old embarrassingly imperialistic building in Downing Street and putting up a more understated functional building which would house the entire organisation has been advocated regularly since 1943. In practice it is doubtful whether this geographical lack of unity matters all that much. The vast majority of the departments are in either the main building or the Curtis Green which are within easy walking distance of each other. Nearly all the others are fairly near by. There is probably rather more use of the telephone and less personal confrontation than there would be in one huge glass building, but this may well be time saving. The inconvenience of the multiple housing arrangements may be experienced more by those Home Departments or individuals trying to contact the Office than by the members themselves.

The twenty-one geographical departments, as the traditional central core, are all housed in the main Downing Street building. They have been inherited from the old Foreign Office structure, and some of the departments still bear the same names as they did in 1900 when there were only six geographical departments covering the whole of the (non-British) world.

The geographical departments were usually referred to up to 1945 as the 'political' departments. There was no doubt about their work : they channelled the political despatches and gave advice and information on problems which arose out of them to the Foreign Secretary and sent his instructions back to the embassies. The work is now a great deal more diffused, and it depends very much on the particular territories concerned to what extent the work is political and to what extent commercial, economic, or cultural.

The thirty functional departments are divided into five main blocks: the Economic; the United Nations; Information and Cultural Relations; Planning, Research, Defence, and Disarmament; and Administration. Unlike the geographical departments there is no long historical tradition behind them; the great majority of the problems deal with in the functional departments today were not regarded as the province of the Foreign Office and barely that of the government until 1945. Before this, when the Foreign Office had some particular problem to deal with, they simply tacked it on the geographical department in which it seemed most likely to occur. The Far Eastern had 'traffic in dangerous drugs'; the African had 'the slave trade'; and the Northern European, 'Bolshevism'. Until 1945 these seemed to be the only awkward specialised problems liable to be thrown up by the foreigner in his various aspects.

The United Nations block (two departments) was there in embryo in the League of Nations section of the Western General Department. The six Information and Cultural Relations Departments could be said to stem from the old News Department which among other things was responsible for propaganda, but the present News Department is listed under the specialist departments, and is the only department directly under the Permanent Under-Secretary. The Planning, Research, Defence and Disarmament group had no real precursors, and Administration developed from the old Treaty, Passport, and Library departments. The first four blocks in the Functional departments are largely staffed by career diplomats, the administrative group largely by E Class officers. The work in this group is very similar to that done in the Aliens and Nationality departments of the Home Office. Both deal with the application of specific rules to the personal problems of individuals. None of these departments are staffed by specialists, although E Class passport office men who do not expect to travel abroad are specialists of the old type.

The ten administrative departments are a development of the old Chief Clerk's department. The title of Chief Clerk has been one which the Office has been reluctant to drop. It was exchanged in 1933 for the title of Principal Establishment Officer, resuscitated by F. Ashton Gwatkin in 1940, replaced by the title of Chief of Administration in 1966, and has just been revived again. Since 1970 the title has once against been that of Chief Clerk.

III   THE FCO IN ACTION

There are two principal aspects of the FCO in action : there is first the day-to-day work and special functions associated with each grade and type of job in the FCO, and second the way in which these jobs relate to each other in terms of formal chains of command and consultation and in actual communication flows. In order to avoid repetition, the different jobs will be described in turn, and related to the system as a whole.

There are two striking features of the process of communication in the FCO. The first is that access of officers to other officers, whether of junior, equal, or senior status, is informal and flexible. They wander in and out of each other's rooms if near by; telephone if in different buildings; and they call each other by their first names, preferably in some diminutive form. But coupled with this informality of access and address, the actual working conversations which take place are conducted with quasi-legal formality and acute awareness of their relative positions in the hierarchy. The junior colleague outlines his proposed line and asks for guidance; the senior man says 'I suggest but I do not insist' that you do such and such, or he says that some other department must be consulted, or he gives the matter clearance, or he says that he must refer the matter upwards. He makes clear in his form of words the precise amount of can-carrying he is prepared to do on any given issue. This point, which seems crucial in the day-to-day working of the FCO, will be returned to.

(a)   *The work of the political members of the FCO*
The members of the Government who hold posts in the FCO vary in number according to the discretion of the Prime Minister, but at the present count (June 1971) there are the Secretary of State for Foreign and Commonwealth Affairs, one Chancellor

of the Duchy of Lancaster (dealing with Europe), two Ministers of State, and three Parliamentary Under-Secretaries. These are the political masters of the FCO, and all FCO work is theoretically directed towards pleasing and serving them. Normal FCO procedures will be bent to the whim of any of these men. But although they are given this basic theoretical dominance they are excluded by their formal treatment from the ordinary life of the diplomatic personnel. They do not get the first name, or even second name treatment, but are always referred to as, for example, 'Minister'. Personal friendships of course may occur or already exist, but in the normal day-to-day communications the contrast between the informality of officers among themselves and the high formality with which the political overlords are treated is marked and intentional. The politicians can easily be made to feel that although they are the masters, they are there only temporarily, and are deferred to by reason of the office of state which they hold rather than for personal qualities. An experienced diplomat can if he wish inject a great deal of contempt into the address 'Minister of State'. This capacity is, after all, one of his professional skills.

The members of the Government each have rooms and a small diplomatic and secretarial staff in the main building of the FCO. They are not, of course, full time in the Office. Almost all are also M.P.s with constituencies; M.P.s and peers alike must represent the Government in Parliament; and the Secretary of State himself is an important member of the Cabinet. The job of the Ministers, so far as the FCO is concerned, is to make policy recommendations to the Cabinet on the basis of advice and information offered by or sought from the Office. They are not obliged to take the advice, but the feeling among older members of the Service who have been in it throughout the post-war period is that actual conflicts between the Office and the Government have been rare occurrences. That is to say that the two have tended to view the facts of the international scene in the same way.

(b) *The work of the permanent officials*
The Permanent Under-Secretary to the Foreign and Commonwealth Office is Head of the Diplomatic Service, and is equivalent in pay and technical status to the Head of the Civil Service. His

CHART 5. CHAINS OF COMMAND

(a) *Straightforward*

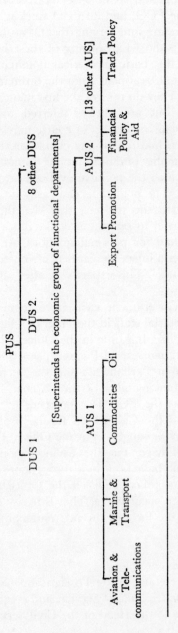

PUS

DUS 1   DUS 2.   8 other DUS

[Superintends the economic group of functional departments]

AUS 1   AUS 2   [13 other AUS]

Aviation &
Tele-
communications   Marine &
Transport   Commodities   Oil   Export Promotion   Financial
Policy &
Aid   Trade Policy

(b) *One link eliminated (most of the time)*

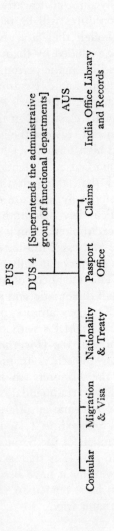

PUS

DUS 4

[Superintends the administrative
group of functional departments]

AUS

Consular   Migration
& Visa   Nationality
& Treaty   Passport
Office   Claims   India Office Library
and Records

(c) *Less straightforward*

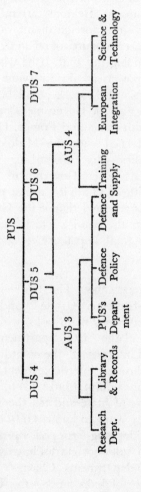

(d) *Below the level of Assistant Under-Secretary*

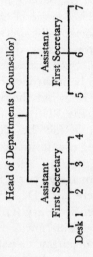

Manned by First, Second and Third Secretaries

The Number of Assistants varies: 1 or 2 are most common; some have more.

job is to ensure that the Secretary of State for Foreign and Commonwealth Affairs goes into Cabinet and Parliament properly briefed, both in terms of what he wants to know and in terms of what the Office thinks he ought to know. A whole department of the FCO is devoted to dealing with the paper work which the PUS must know about, but the greater part of his daily routine now is conversational. He must attend committees and see ambassadors and visiting foreign dignitaries in a fairly constant stream. He is the supreme pourer of oil on troubled waters in a profession devoted to doing just that. If he wishes to he can also wield great political power, as did Sir Ivone Kirkpatrick who, during the Suez crisis of 1956, kept all but two members of the Service in ignorance of the Government's policy, while working in secret alliance with Israel and France. He had all members of the Service concerned with the Middle East working towards a different policy – that of curbing Israeli aggression. Such extreme situations, when Government policy is likely to be in strong conflict with FCO advice, are at present extremely rare, but the Suez crisis revealed that if the Government and the PUS are in alliance the Service which the PUS heads can in fact be reduced to total impotence through the withholding of information.

THE WORK OF THE UNDER-SECRETARIES. The two levels of Under-Secretaries, Deputy Under-Secretary (Grade 2) and Assistant Under-Secretary (Grade 3) have four main tasks, which are (1) the co-ordination of the work of the FCO departments into groups of departments with linked interests, (2) the co-ordination of policy with other Ministries through interdepartmental and Cabinet committees and other more informal links, (3) to be the main FCO link with the Ministers of State and tell them what they need to know, and what they want to know, and (4) (and inevitably in that position) to consider long-term policy problems.

So far as (1) is concerned the Under-Secretaries have general control over connected groups of departments. Charts 5 (a) (b) and (c) show three different types of links among the Under-Secretaries. Chart 5 (a) shows a classical arrangement whereby one Deputy Under-Secretary superintends one related group of seven departments: in this particular instance the economic group among the functional departments. Two Assistant Under-

Secretaries under him divide these departments into two smaller groups. Chart 5 (b) shows a simplified version of this, with one link eliminated. Some departments, principally those administrative ones which are headed and staffed by members of the executive class, are directly superintended by a Deputy Under-Secretary without the assistance of an Assistant Under-Secretary. The explanation seems to be that the supervision of these departments is less arduous: the work is fairly routine and policy decisions are seldom involved. In some cases however, as in Chart 5 (c), the classical bureaucratic patterns are very confused. Some Assistant Under-Secretaries are responsible to more than one Deputy Under-Secretary for the different departments under them. Some Deputy Under-Secretaries have different groups of departments under them. One departmental head even has two Assistant Under-Secretaries and two Deputy Under-Secretaries interested in his department. This sort of complication occurs where departments have overlapping interests.

This system is acknowledged to be top-heavy. A recently retired Permanent Under-Secretary said that he could not imagine what all the Under-Secretaries were doing clogging up the system. Basically he saw the most important decisions as being quite capable of being handled between himself and the appropriate departmental head. He conceived of the principal role of the Under-Secretaries as being long-term policy planners. They should be a group of people who had time to reflect on things other than the immediate day-to-day problems and who would be able to give a different kind of advice to the Permanent Under-Secretary and the Secretary of State.

Such a simplified state of affairs is probably a long-lost pipe dream. With the ever-increasing interest of home departments in overseas matters, the time of Under-Secretaries is likely to be taken up more and more with co-ordinating work on inter-Departmental committees.

THE WORK OF THE HEAD OF A DEPARTMENT. The headship of a department has been described as being the most arduous job the Service has to offer. The head is invariably a Counsellor. His function is organising the day-to-day work of the department. He has to arrange a proper distribution of work in the department and know who can be trusted to do what. He takes the final decision about what information should be passed up, and which matters are sufficiently difficult to require a high policy decision. He may refer problems directly to the Permanent Under-Secretary. He is not expected to offer profound minutes about policy, but advice which he tenders has a high chance of being acted upon since he is the expert. In so far as the FCO has a voice in foreign affairs, it is likely on any particular issue to be the voice of the head of the department concerned.

THE ASSISTANT. There can be one, two, or more Assistants in a department, but two is normal. The departmental Assistant is a senior First Secretary. His job is to relieve pressure from below on the Head of Department. He has to take on as much responsibility for signing off documents as he dares. He will also be responsible for the administration of the department; for the registry staff, typists, for arrangements for leave, security; and for the training of new entrants. He may also on occasion be asked to substitute for the Head of Department.

THE WORK OF A DEPARTMENT. The work of an individual department is concerned with the day-to-day immediate matters. The work is subdivided into 'desks' manned by First, Second, and Third Secretaries, and the basic skill of the desk officer is that of drafting. The desk officers draft submissions, that is to say suggestions for action, sent upwards; telegrams to posts; letters to posts, to Government departments, to the public; letters from ministers to other ministers, and papers on subjects of immediate interest for the use of their senior colleagues and their political masters.

The procedures for the daily distribution of paper are very elaborate. There are hundreds of telegrams from posts to the FCO every day which are seen by dozens of people. Some of them may come in with a security classification or a priority marking. In the opinion of one FCO officer there were far too many telegrams and much of the information which comes in this form would be better sent by letter. But telegrams are much easier to compose than letters and get priority over letters at the FCO and so there is a constant tendency for telegrams rather than letters to be sent.

There are three types of distribution for telegrams, and the Communications Department will sometimes seek advice on the type of distribution for a particular telegram. A telegram can be generally distributed for information all over Whitehall in addition to concerned officers within the FCO. This means the circulation of about 500 copies. The second type of distribution is limited to within the FCO plus one or two copies for involved outsiders. For this about 150 copies are required. The third type is a limited distribution either for purposes of security, or simply to reduce paper, or in response to the need not to be told everything. The number of copies involved in a limited distribution can vary greatly. In addition to the telegrams there are the incoming letters and papers which are treated similarly after the telegrams have been dealt with.

The distribution process results in each department getting between 60 and 90 telegrams a day. Of these, 50 will be for information only, 20 will concern their part of the world or their functional speciality, and about 5 will require action. An ambassador says he is about to meet a key official and wants instruction. Five opposition M.P.s are taking a trip to Israel: would the FCO arrange for them to come to dinner at Tel-Aviv? Such items are the staple diet of departmental life. Letters and other papers are received in roughly similar proportions.

The principle is that paper work starts at the bottom and goes upward. Traditional Foreign Office theory has it that the despatch from Lima arrives at the desk of the newly appointed Third Secretary for Peru, Brazil, etc., in the American Department, and that he is initially responsible for suggesting what H.M.G.'s reply should be. He writes his minute, or letter, in reply to this, and passes it on to a Grade 5 officer for comment and further action. This conjures up a rather worrying picture of the novice leafing through his morning telegrams and possibly missing the flash from Lima which states that H.M. Ambassador has been kidnapped and is being held to ransom, in favour of one from Brazil which gives data on the number of brothels in Rio. In fact, actual responsibility at this level is large fictional, and not even insisted on now as FCO theory. Each day the PUS's assistant will sort through all the telegrams received by the office, offering them in some sort of order of importance. Until very recently (but pre-merger) times it was quite common for the PUS to read them all.

Some PUS's, when important matters have cropped up, have claimed they would ring straight through to the department concerned, and sometimes even directly to the desk secretary concerned, to ask what advice was being offered, and to urge some kind of minute to be sent up within the hour. This would be unusual, but the PUS is not in any case going to get surprise information gradually percolating up from below. He gets all his problems at once, and has some idea each day what items are being covered at a lower level without troubling him, and what problems may eventually filter through, quite apart from crises or high policy topics which he must cope with at once himself.

Meanwhile, the desk secretary, dealing with only minor matters, will draft a reply to a telegram and send it on to the senior Grade 5 officer – probably the Assistant in the department. He, if he is not under pressure, may call the apprentice up to take him to task on the niceties of English composition, on what Parliament will stand, on what H.M.G.'s policy is on this point – or whatever piece of education seems called for. For the novice drafter the experience is that of adapting to a particular FCO language. Regardless of who initiated the work, most FCO papers end up with a uniform stylistic stamp. They have their own set of quasi-legal formal styles to convey particular meanings; they also have their own range of dead metaphors taken largely from war and sport, which economise on effort in composition and reading among a still fairly homogeneous personnel.

If, as is more often the case, the Assistant is extremely busy, he will simply dictate an amended version to the typist. The matter is choked off at that point and troubles the system no further. But if there is any difficulty about the letter or the suggested action, if there appears to be some options open, he may refer the whole thing to the head of the department. The head of department in his turn will either finalise the matter or decide to refer it to one or more of his Under-Secretaries. At each level nice judgement is called for as to what point in the chain of command the matter can be finally despatched. Any officer can damage his career prospects either by showing himself unable to take decisions or through failure to consult. The decision whether to refer up or not will be influenced not only by the intrinsic importance or difficulty of the question, but also by the relative busyness of the particular senior officer at that time, by his general interest in the topic, and by the amount of time available before a decision must be reached.

A further complication is that in addition to the vertical referring of papers there is a horizontal one (see Chart 6). A high proportion of telegrams, letters, and papers drafted will be on subjects on which other FCO departments and very possibly other Ministries may be expected to have a view. At some stage therefore, someone, probably the desk secretary, will have to hawk his draft around other interested departments before a final draft can be reached. This final draft will be bland and

CHART 6. POSSIBLE COMMUNICATION FLOWS

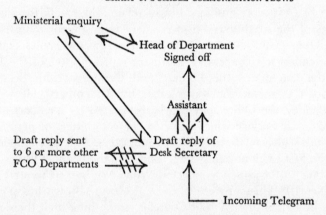

unanimous, disagreements having been ironed out or dropped on the way. This is a significant change since the days before the Second World War. At that time the Foreign Secretary would have been able to see an entire file with all the stages, suggestions of individuals, and disagreements in it. He would have been able to see arguments which had been rejected, and, if he chose, resuscitate them.

Not all departments organise their work on the hierarchical pattern described. Some, for example the East European and Soviet Department, are at present experimenting with a team system. There are a head of department and three teams, each with a team leader who is a First Secretary but less senior than an Assistant to a department would be. The advantage of the team system is that more responsibility is given earlier. The drawbacks are that there is no obvious deputy to the head, and that the team leaders are less confident about initialling papers off than an Assistant would be. The burden on the head of department tends to be greater. The general feeling in the Office at present is that the formal structure in a department is less important than the calibre of the individuals concerned.

IV   THE FCO'S OWN EXTERNAL RELATIONS

(a) *Cabinet and Parliament*

The FCO is more cushioned in its relationships with the elective parts of the machinery of government than are the ministries of the Home Civil Service [12]. So far as the mechanics of communication are concerned, the main representative of the FCO in the Cabinet is the Foreign and Commonwealth Secretary (though there are sometimes other FCO members). He will be briefed by the Office and will be supported by members of the Diplomatic Service who will be on the committees of permanent officials which relate to Cabinet committees. At least one member of the FCO will normally be seconded to the Cabinet Office, and another to the closely connected Prime Minister's Private Office at No. 10. This can result, as Lord George-Brown has pointed out, in a rival foreign policy bureau establishing itself there [13].

Formal relations with the House of Commons are confined to the preparation of statements and speeches for the members of the Government, the answering of written questions and letters from M.P.s, the preparation of the (now rare) oral answers, and the reception of M.P.s who want to make a point in person.

(b) *The relationship of the FCO with the Treasury*

The key to the relationship of the FCO with the Treasury lies in the relationship of the Diplomatic Service to the Home Civil Service as a whole. The present arrangement dates from the Foreign Service Act, 1943, which set up the Foreign Service as a separate service of the Crown. To secure his diplomatic status each member of the Service receives a Commission from the Queen. In this formal sense he is more like an officer of the armed services than a member of the Home Civil Service. However, the sense of separateness, which is jealously cherished by the Diplomatic Service, is more than purely formal. The Secretary of State for Foreign and Commonwealth Affairs can make what regulations he likes for the Service or the FCO. The Service is independent on all matters concerning recruitment, promotion, and retirement, and it is free to arrange its own grades and classes as it pleases, although, as has been indicated earlier, attempts are made to correlate with the Home Civil Service. Matters of pay, allowances, and expenses, must be arranged directly with the Treasury. But again there are differences between these negotiations and those that might take place between the Treasury and a home ministry. Some arise from the very different conditions of service. Another factor is that the Permanent Secretary of any home ministry can in the last resort be outranked by the Head of the Civil Service, the Permanent Secretary to the Civil Service Department, while the Permanent Under-Secretary of the FCO is also the Head of the Diplomatic Service, with the same status and pay as the Head of the Civil Service. Discussion takes place between equals even if the outcome is as unsatisfactory for the diplomats as it might have been for the Home Office.

(c) *The relationship with other home departments*
An ironic aspect of the history of Britain's overseas administration is that the attempt to provide a centralised organisation by successive mergers has been overtaken by the development of overseas interests in the home ministries. It is a truism that the world has become more complex, more international, smaller – in the sense of the greater ease of communication; and the consequence is that far fewer internal decision appear to be without international consequences. The FCO itself has responded over the last twenty-five years to this increase in the number of international problems, and the inflation in the functional departments is a reflection of this. The home ministries however have naturally not delegated their growing overseas interests. Instead problems are duplicated. The FCO has a section dealing with the Channel Tunnel project; so does the Ministry for the Environment.

There now appears to be a great duplication of effort and much overlapping of activities [14]. The duplication of responsibility results in two main problems; the first concerning the machinery of consultation and the second concerning which office is likely to prevail in a conflict of policy. The problem of consultation is dealt with at lower levels by telephone and letter; at higher levels by interdepartmental co-ordinating committees of Under-Secretaries and experts in the field. The question of conflicts on policy is a difficult one. It seems that the voice of the home ministry normally carries more weight because its members are more likely to be expert in the particular problem. The FCO is more likely to anticipate long-term or wide-ranging repercussions, but these may well be seen as less cogent in an inter-departmental wrangle. The Cabinet finds value in different voices being heard, and it is in Cabinet committees that such problems are very often worked out. But it would be unwise to suggest that there is no problem here. It is a sensitive area, and the problem looks likely to intensify. It is not simply a question of working out a policy within Britain between interested parties; the field of international agreements negotiated directly by officials of the Home Civil Service without the aid of the Diplomatic Service appears to be widening.

(d) *Relations with the London Diplomatic Corps and with diplomatic visitors*

The primary duty of the FCO to the diplomatic corps in London is to act as the link in the exchange of messages between the Government and the London representatives of foreign powers. The Foreign and Commonwealth Secretary may invite the ambassador of Ruritania to meet him, or the Ruritanian ambassador may request an interview if some problem crops up between Britain and Ruritania. But in addition to political consultations, the diplomat in London still has some social duties to perform similar to those he has abroad. They are fewer in number because of the very large number of British diplomats available in London. Nor is the individual diplomat expected to entertain foreign colleagues himself; he is merely expected to attend certain functions. Members of the FCO do get a personal entertainment allowance, but it is very small : First Secretaries are allotted £100 a year for this purpose.

The entertainment of distinguished foreign visitors on brief visits is usually done at formal luncheons and receptions under the auspices of the FCO, with the Foreign Secretary, one of the Ministers of State, or a senior permanent official acting as host. These occasions are duly reported in *The Times* the next day, and are purely for the encouragement of good relations.

V FCO PROBLEMS

(a) *The Diplomatic Service as a career: the after effects of the Fulton Report on the Home Civil Service and of the Report of the Duncan Committee*

The problem of providing an attractive career revolves around the fact that the Diplomatic Service, although numerically smaller than the Home Civil Service, is required to perform a much wider range of tasks. Any man within the Service who is unwilling or incompetent to perform any of these wide-ranging tasks damages his career prospects. There is a direct conflict here between the interests of efficiency (as it is now beginning to be understood, i.e. specialisation) and of the career, in which complete interchangeability of personnel is an advantage.

The FCO is at present running a fully generalist service while rapidly having its convictions on the subject eroded. From 1943 until 1968 generalism was thought to be not only compatible with but necessary for efficiency, in that individual members were enabled through their varied experience to see the wood as well as the trees. The Plowden Report on the Foreign Service endorsed the well-established generalist tradition. Indeed the setting up of the new joint Diplomatic Service which it recommended was in itself yet another step in the same direction. It was pointed out in the Plowden Report that while members of the Foreign Service were accustomed to deal with economic and commercial matters, members of the Commonwealth Service had had this done for them by the Trade Commission officers of the Board of Trade. The proposed merger of these three services would, it was hoped, give the old Commonwealth men the opportunity of commercial work.

The shock waves of the Fulton Report of July 1968, which was far more highly critical of the Home Civil Service than the Plowden Report had been of the Foreign Service, certainly reached the newly formed Diplomatic Service and the imminently emerging FCO. The Fulton Report specifically did not apply to the Foreign Office, but the Foreign Office was so obviously vulnerable to the type of criticism levelled at the Home Civil Service that its members were bound to feel defensive. The administrative class career diplomat is expected to be political diplomatist, commercial and economic diplomatist, consular official, linguist, and administrator. But only a small part of the work, even in the FCO, can be described as administration, and this means that while the Home Civil Service officer can at least claim to be a professional administrator, the Diplomatic Service officer cannot even claim that.

Members of the Service were therefore talking – early in 1969 – of 'out-Fultoning Fulton' in their new Forward Planning Unit, in their use of computers, in their semi-integrated grading structure; but the verdict of the Duncan Report on the 'Fulton' aspects of their work was awaited anxiously. In fact, as the terms of reference make clear, the Duncan Committee was not set up as a Foreign Office version of Fulton. It was to make recommendations on how to meet an urgent need for economy involving major changes in foreign relations, rather than in answer to an internal administrative need. Nevertheless the Duncan Committee did make some direct comparisons with the Fulton Report. It defended the generalist principles of the Diplomatic Service with some qualifications. In its view, despite the fact that the contrast between the professional and the generalist was not found to be wholly applicable in the context of the Diplomatic Service, 'the aim of creating "Renaissance Men" of all parts is already out of date and will become even less practicable in the future' [15]. The Report suggested as an antidote a considerable increase in regional and functional specialisation. Each officer would then become a 'semi-specialist'. New promotion blocks would be avoided by temporarily upgrading posts.

What this would mean in practice if it is fully worked out would be three or four specialist career structures within the Services. Top jobs within the Office and in the main embassies would have to be realigned so that there would, for example, be a greater number of Grade 2 or Grade 3 commercial posts whether or not circumstances other than the career needs of the Service demanded it, and even more important, the jobs would have to be specifically reserved for officers whose previous career specialisations had suited them to these posts. There has been discontent among men who were advised on entering the Service after the war to specialise in commercial work, because of the recent filling of Grade 3 commercial ministers' posts by officers who have a largely political or Foreign Office-orientated career.

But another problem of morale, that of security of tenure, was intensified by the publication of the Duncan Report. Since 1943 it has been possible to retire early officers who could not expect further promotion, but who were blocking the promotion of junior people. Before the Duncan Report was published thirty senior officers were prematurely retired under this legislation, and the report suggested a considerable extension of this practice, though under better financial conditions than hitherto.

(b) *Forward Policy Planning in the Foreign and Commonwealth Office*

One feature of the foregoing account of the working of the FCO is that a high proportion of the activity described is administrative and practical, and one degree removed from the central theme of this symposium. Of the part played by the Office in the formulation of policy itself, there are two main criticisms. The first is that referred to in Section IV (c) of this chapter on relations with other Home departments: that the FCO voice is inclined to be overlooked or discounted in a growing number of fields. The second [16] is that the practice of dealing with problems as they crop up has led to a pragmatic and inactive foreign policy. These characteristics are said to be accentuated by the normal work process in the Office, which is the reverse of delegation : advice originates at the bottom and mellows as it goes upwards. This way of working also has much to be said in its favour. But the Foreign Office had been aware since the Suez Crisis of the need for a department entirely concerned with more long-term problems.

A Planning Staff was set up in 1957. They were at first closely integrated with the department dealing with European organisations. It was thought then that the Planning Section ought not to be divorced from all current responsibilities. The Plowden Committee, however, thought that in practice current responsibilities would always have priority and that therefore the Planning Staff should be relieved of their other duties and become completely separate. The danger of their developing an 'ivory tower' mentality was to be avoided by ensuring that the staff were all career officers. They should be allowed to see current despatches on their fields of interest, and should be brought in to office meetings connected with their current problems [17].

The present Planning Staff consists of four career officers: one Counsellor, one First Secretary, and two others. They are chosen for exceptional intellectual quality, but morale in this department is not always very high. One member put it that if this was the sort of thing he had wanted to do he would have become an academic. Members do not actually plan future policy; they prepare detailed research papers on possible future problems. The area of research is nearly always decided for them at top level. It would theoretically be possible for a member of the Planning Staff to initiate a paper himself on a subject or area he thought was about to become important, but he would have to convince a great many people of this before his work would be taken seriously. In general the Planning Staff feel that they are not taken very seriously, that members of departments concerned with the immediate aspects of their problems have a stronger voice, that the existence of the department is more for show than for serious use. The counter to this is that their very existence helps to balance the general tendency towards pragmatism, and makes the rest of the Office more ready to give weight to long-term considerations.

(c) *The future of the FCO and the Diplomatic Service*
Overall, the FCO is at present a fairly contented place, a satisfied power. There are probably two main reasons for this. One is that it is not an organisation in itself; it is the central part of a larger organisation. It is therefore staffed on the whole by its more successful members. Ageing, unpromotable Counsellors and First Secretaries can be made to circle the globe endlessly without physically disturbing the main base. A second reason for contentment is that the Office is extremely busy; it is 'running a tight ship'; its resources are stretched to capacity. There is too much work for there to be time to query the value of the work. This last problem was suggested but not explored in the Duncan Report's picture, already cited,* of the energetic officer with the

* Page 50 above.

first-class mind in Ruritania creating problems for the highly able desk officer in Whitehall.

It is difficult to foresee any radical change in this situation in the near future. There is still a worldwide momentum towards maintaining the decorative, representational side of diplomacy, however unnecessary it would be to invent it. In a further and more catastrophic economic emergency the FCO and Diplomatic Service might be vulnerable, but short of that, paper will probably continue to flow at the present, or even at an increased rate. So far as FCO influence goes (as distinct from the maintenance of its status and privileges), there may be large opportunities if Britain's application to join the Common Market is successful. There will then be new jobs for linguist-administrators accustomed to living abroad; and if the Diplomatic Service fails to make a substantial contribution here, then the justification for their separate and large-scale existence may indeed come under question.

REFERENCES

[1] *Fifth Report of the Commissioners* (HMSO, 1914, Cd. 7748).
[2] HMSO Cmd. 6420.
[3] *Report of the Committee on Representational Services Overseas* (HMSO, 1964, Cmnd. 2276) pp. 2–3 ('Plowden').
[4] *Report of the Review Committee on Overseas Representation 1968–69* (HMSO, 1969, Cmnd. 4107) ('Duncan').
[5] Plowden, p. 145.
[6] *The Merger of the Foreign Office and the Commonwealth Office, 1968* (HMSO, 1968) p. 8.
[7] F.O. 366/780 : Letter of Theo Russell to J. A. C. Tilley, 14th June, 1918.
[8] *Graduate Careers in the Diplomatic Service* (HMSO, 1967).
[9] Duncan, p. 56.
[10] *Graduate Careers*, p. 20.
[11] *The Merger of the Foreign Office and the Commonwealth Office*, p. 8.
[12] See Chapters 5 and 10 below.
[13] Lord George-Brown, *In My Way* (London 1971) p. 134.

[14] Chapters 7 to 10 of this symposium suggest some of these areas.
[15] Duncan, p. 31.
[16] Levelled by D. Vital at the pre-merger Foreign Office. See *The Making of British Foreign Policy* (London 1968) passim.
[17] Plowden, p. 56.

BIBLIOGRAPHY

At the time of writing (June 1971) there are no works on the Foreign and Commonwealth Office other than official publications and articles in the press and journals. These include :

The Foreign Office Lists 1968 – 71 HMSO.
The Merger of the Foreign Office and the Commonwealth Office 1968, HMSO 1968.
Michael Banks, 'Professionalism in the Conduct of Foreign Policy', *International Affairs,* October 1968.
Graduate Careers in the Diplomatic Service, HMSO 1967.
Her Majesty's Diplomatic Service, HMSO 166, amended 1969.
Report on the Committee of Representational Services Overseas, HMSO 1964, Cmnd. 2276 (The Plowden Report).
Report of the Review Commitee on Overseas Representation 1968–69, HMSO, Cmnd. 4107 (The Duncan Report).

Articles on the Duncan Report :
M. Donelan, 'The Trade of Diplomacy', *International Affairs,* Oct. 1969.
Dudley Seers and others, *Bulletin of the Institute of Development Studies,* Oct. 1969.
D. C. Watt, Review in *The Political Quarterly,* Oct.–Dec. 1969.
A. Shonfield, 'The Duncan Report and its Critics', *International Affairs,* April 1970.

Works on the pre-merger offices :
Lord Strang, *The Foreign Office,* New Whitehall Series, London, 1954.
Donald Bishop, *The Administration of British Foreign Relations,* Syracuse, 1961.
Max Beloff, *New Dimensions in Foreign Policy,* London, 1961.

D. C. Watt, *Personalities and Policies*, London, 1965.

J. A. Cross, *Whitehall and the Commonwealth*, London, 1967.

D. Busk, *The Craft of Diplomacy*, London, 1967.

D. Vital, *The Making of British Foreign Policy*, London, 1968.

3 The British Diplomat

A. N. OPPENHEIM
and IAN SMART

IN CHAPTER 2, we have seen an account of the Foreign and
Commonwealth Office as a bureaucratic organisation. A common
assumption about bureaucracies is that they are depersonalised,
that they govern according to rules applied by every member
irrespective of his own preferences. To some degree such an
assumption must always be fallacious, for the functioning of any
organisation will partly depend on the men and women who
service it : on their morale, values and attitudes, as well as on
the career structure within which they operate and the opportunities which it offers them.

In this chapter we shall be asking questions about the British
diplomat, answers to which might suggest ways in which some
of his (or her) attitudes could affect the formulation or implementation of British foreign policy. It would have been sensible
to seek those answers on the basis of large-scale data, with the
aid of a well-established framework for comparison with other
countries and with other periods in history. Unfortunately,
neither British diplomats nor the components of British foreign
policy machinery have until now been subjected publicly to the
kind of psychological and sociological scrutiny that would enable
us to do this. Indeed, with the possible exception of one
Norwegian and one Dutch study [1], the same is true of all
diplomats and of all foreign ministries : a fact which is all
the more surprising if we consider the special interests which
sociologists have in social stratification, the position of élites
and the emergence and development of professional groups in
different societies.

The absence of sociological studies means not only that we lack data; it also leaves us without an appropriate framework or set of concepts, so that we have no accepted guide which tells us what to look for or which aspects are the most relevant. One of us has recently however been engaged in trying to develop such a conceptual framework for the comparison of national diplomatic services. As it is partly reflected in this chapter, the structure of this framework is simple enough. Having defined our field, by deciding what we mean by 'diplomacy' and 'diplomats', we shall want to consider our subject under a number of principal headings, which include recruitment and selection, training, specialisation, career structure, assessment, promotion and posting.

Because the framework we shall use is still embryonic, and because deficiencies of data have had to be made up with impressions, the analysis will have inevitable shortcomings. Moreover, the result will have no face : amongst some hundreds of different individuals, the 'average' British diplomat does not exist. Nevertheless, any study of British foreign policy must consider the people who help to formulate or implement it : the standards which are set for them or which they set for themselves, and the median points around which their individual characteristics tend to cluster.

DIPLOMACY AND DIPLOMATS

Although diplomacy is widely assumed to be a profession, diplomats lack some of the important attributes of the classical professions. They are neither entrepreneurial nor self-governing, nor do they have the degree of specialisation in their upper echelons that doctors or lawyers have. They also lack a written code of ethics, although they are generally bound to secrecy. It would be more accurate, therefore, to regard diplomacy not as a profession but as a 'service', analogous to the armed services, the police service and, of course, the civil service (of which they form a somewhat atypical part). Like these other services, diplomats tend to have a strict hierarchy, a seniority list, the assumption of interchangeability, fairly frequent postings and transfers (which mean that local ties are subordinated to a strong sense of loyalty to the central organisation), a bias towards male entry, a tradition of being non-political and some emphasis on visual ceremonies and recognition symbols such as dress, badges of rank and official flags. Their position *vis-à-vis* the State is very different from that of most professions; far from being self-governing 'guilds', which might find themselves at times in strong collective opposition to proposed government measures, the services place primary emphasis on loyalty to the State and are, in many ways, the instruments through which State power is exercised.

Diplomacy in a general sense may be, and sometimes is, practised by everyone in their daily lives; in its 'service' sense, it is practised by a limited number of men and women working on behalf of, but usually outside, their own countries. In the British case, these people are neither confined to the Diplomatic Service nor make up the whole of it; one of the facts which the Duncan Report of 1969 brought out was that a significant number of government servants from outside the Diplomatic Service – from the Treasury, the Department of Trade and Industry, the Ministry of Defence and elsewhere – are now engaged in some sort of representational activity abroad [2]. At the same time, the Diplomatic Service includes a large number of people – shorthand-typists, archivists, security guards, radio operators and others – whose work is, in a proper sense, non-diplomatic. The former group should certainly be included within any detailed study of British diplomats, but this is not the place to attempt it. What follows has therefore been confined to the diplomats of the Diplomatic Service : to approximately 2,000 members of that Service whose positions in its hierarchy entitle them to appointment, when abroad, as Third, Second or First Secretaries, as Counsellors, Ministers or Ambassadors [3]. Much that will be said may apply also to the temporary diplomats who come from outside the Diplomatic Service but, in as far as it does, that will be an accidental bonus.

Just as not all members of the British Diplomatic Service are diplomats, so no member of the Service is a diplomat all the time. It has already been pointed out in Chapter 2 that in the British case the Diplomatic Service also provides much of the staff for the Foreign and Commonwealth Office in London. In numerous other countries there is still a clear distinction between the diplomatic service and the foreign ministry; the decision-making positions within the ministry are occupied by permanent administrative civil servants, who may never go abroad, while missions in other countries are manned by members of the diplomatic service, who may only come home on leave. In Britain every member of the Diplomatic Service stands, at different times, on both sides of the line. On one side he is strictly a 'diplomat'. Returning to the other side, he becomes an official of one department of the home government. The change in the nature of his activity when he returns to London from abroad is clearly marked in a number of ways. His title will change from Ambassador, Minister, Counsellor or First, Second or Third Secretary to Under-Secretary, Head of Department, Assistant or simply 'desk officer'. His legal status will also change. Abroad, he will have shared in his Ambassador's immunity from local legal process and taxation, but he will have no such extraordinary entitlement in Britain. Finally his material circumstances and standard of living, unless he has substantial private means, will be sharply altered. Abroad, he will have received substantial allowances for accommodation, for entertainment and for simply living in a foreign country at a level appropriate to his representative function. At home, where he has no representative function, he will be paid a salary strictly comparable with that of his colleagues in other governmental departments, with the addition of only a token allowance to compensate for the burdens of his peripatetic existence. By all these means, the Diplomatic Service marks the moment at which its members cease for a time to be diplomats.

Using one diplomatic service to staff both the FCO itself and British missions abroad has a number of advantages and disadvantages, some of which have already been mentioned in Chapter 2. On the 'plus' side, the system makes it likely that those in London who are, for the time being, administering the Service and formulating policy have recent knowledge of working abroad, possibly in the very countries with which they are primarily concerned. Thus it also, hopefully, tends to minimise the 'staff vs. line' type of friction by guaranteeing a better understanding for each other's difficulties. Another advantage is that the system creates relatively frequent opportunities for home postings, thus bringing the diplomat's knowledge of domestic affairs up to date and submerging him again in the atmosphere of his own country.

First among the disadvantages of this system must rank its effect upon the policy-formulating role of the FCO. Dr Larner refers to 'complaints of a lack of continuity of personnel, of administrative and financial incompetence, and of a lack of parliamentary expertise' – complaints which are more likely to be justified in respect to more junior than to more senior members of the Service. A second disadvantage is the rapid adjustment required of the diplomat to completely different occupational, economic and social circumstances – an adjustment which may affect his family even more than himself. His status, finances, social life, family circumstances, local language and official duties will probably change profoundly whenever he and his family move from London to abroad or vice versa. More subtly perhaps, those transitions will also affect the degree of influence – real or illusory – which he can feel himself to have on policy.

Thus we see that the British system imposes particular and recurrent stresses upon the Diplomatic Service; its members must not only be fit for two quite different forms of employment, but also be able to absorb without distortion the strain of moving between them. Conversely, there are the stresses of an unknown importance which the relatively rapid rotation of personnel imposes upon the Diplomatic Service's efficiency in formulating and advising on policy.

RECRUITMENT AND SELECTION

The recruitment, selection and training of entrants to the Diplomatic Service must, as we have seen, aim at producing men and women who are both effective diplomats abroad and competent officials at home.

We have come a long way since British Secretaries of State chose their staffs personally. Today, the Foreign and Commonwealth Office has officials whose full-time concern during their period of home posting is the recruitment of new members for what have come to be called the Administrative and Executive streams, but the direct, formal responsibility for that recruitment rests principally not with them but with the Civil Service Commission. The selection procedure has already been outlined in Chapter 2. What should concern us here are not only the formal requirements of that procedure but also the less formal, yet possibly more substantial considerations affecting recruitment and selection. What qualities are successful candidates for entry into what might be called the 'diplomatic cadre' of the Diplomatic Service expected – or likely – to possess [4]? What sort of background, education and inclination make it probable that a young British citizen will attempt to join this cadre, and that he or she will succeed? Can we detect dysfunctional biases in this process of selection? How relevant to the actual work of the future diplomat are the qualities for which he is in practice selected? To what extent is the system perpetuating a set of outdated norms? Has it become the victim of its own mystique?

With few exceptions, the Diplomatic Service operates a single-entry system : everyone starts at the bottom of some 'stream'. (Lateral entry, either from an equivalent grade in the Home Civil Service or by political appointment, is very rare.) As Table 1 shows, entrants may follow different 'streams', depending on whether they seek to move upwards through the clerical grades, to enter the bottom of the Executive stream from school or university or to join the Administrative stream as graduates. (The last of these routes, which provides the most direct – and most frequently followed – path to the highest levels, is taken by some 25 new entrants each year.) One way or another, however, all have to pass through the network of examinations administered by the Civil Service Commission – and thus have to satisfy standards which are ostensibly common to the civil service as a whole. This contrasts with the practice of some other countries, where the foreign service does its own recruitment and selection independently, and where much greater freedom of lateral movement exists, at every level, between the diplomatic service and other parts of the civil service, allegedly to the advantage of both. Against this, the application to Diplomatic Service candidates of standards established for civil service recruitment as a whole might be expected to reduce the chance that specific biases would operate in the selection of entrants for the Diplomatic Service itself.

In fact, it can hardly be disputed that the results of the Diplomatic Service selection process do reveal apparent biases. The high success rate of public school candidates has been alluded to in Chapter 2. Beyond this, Table 2 to the present chapter shows

TABLE 1. ADMINISTRATIVE AND EXECUTIVE STREAMS: ENTRY, MOVEMENT AND
NUMBERS

*Numbers in boxes are those of Grades. Figures beside boxes indicate the
number of people in each Grade in January 1971*

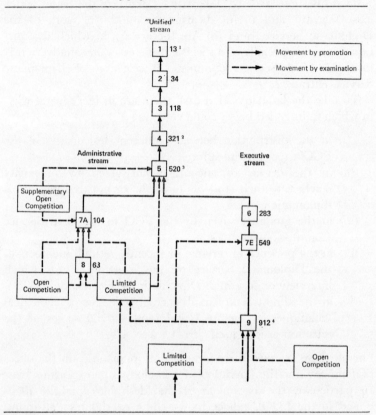

Notes:

[1] Excluding 2 non-career Ambassadors nominally in Grade 1.

[2] Including 2 remaining members of the old Executive stream Grade 4B, to
which no promotions are now made.

[3] Grade 5 was not yet "unified" in January 1971. The figures for the separate
Grades were: Grade 5A: 373; Grade 5E: 147.

[4] Grade 9, although within the Executive stream, is not within the "diplomatic
cadre" as described in this chapter.

the exceptional success rate of Oxbridge candidates (compared
both with Home Civil Service entrants and with Redbrick recruits
to the Diplomatic Service – and in spite of the rising number of
applicants from the latter source). It also reveals an even stronger

bias towards male entrants. In addition, successful candidates with a university background in law, political science or economics are remarkably few.

Two questions arise : (a) To what extent are the biases which exist relevant and useful, bearing in mind the work of the Diplomatic Service? and (b) Are there ways in which dysfunctional biases, especially of a social nature, can enter inadvertently into the Civil Service Commission's selection of Diplomatic Service entrants?

To take the latter question first, there are in fact several ways in which unintended biases could creep in :

  (i) in the distribution between different universities of the FCO's recruitment efforts;
 (ii) in the degree of encouragement given by university teachers to their students to apply, or not to apply, for a diplomatic career;
(iii) in the guidance given by the FCO to the Civil Service Commission selectors;
 (iv) in the presence of serving, or recently retired, members of the Diplomatic Service on the selection boards which interview or scrutinise Diplomatic Service candidates;
  (v) in the almost complete absence of objective psychological techniques in the final and most crucial stages of the selection process itself.

For all these reasons, there is sufficient opportunity in the selection process for the operation of conscious or unconscious bias. In particular, the assessment of the 'desirable' qualities mentioned in the FCO's advice to would-be candidates ('all-round mental ability', 'analytical skills', 'sensitivity', 'imagination', 'intellectual curiosity', 'intellectual honesty') as well as of such frequently mentioned traits as 'independence', 'self-reliance' and 'adaptivity', is almost wholly subjective, based as it is upon the personal impressions of a small group of individuals. Thus, the selection system is not automatically immune to élitism or norm-perpetuation. That is not to deny that biases may also emerge from schools and universities, in the form of self-selection by candidates. It is for example the case that, as Table 2 shows, the preference for Oxbridge candidates in selecting for the Administrative stream of the Diplomatic Service, *when related to the*

TABLE 2. DIPLOMATIC SERVICE ADMINISTRATIVE STREAM AND HOME CIVIL SERVICE ADMINISTRATIVE CLASS: SELECTION OF DIRECT ENTRANTS BY OPEN COMPETITION (METHOD II ONLY)

		Diplomatic Service							Home Civil Service						
		Oxbridge	Non-Oxbridge	Men	Women	Total	% Oxbridge	% Women	Oxbridge	Non-Oxbridge	Men	Women	Total	% Oxbridge	% Women
1967	Candidates	247	235	370	112	482	51·2	23·2	402	577	731	248	979	41·1	25·3
	Successful	20	5	23	2	25	80·0	8·0	86	44	102	28	130	66·1	21·5
1968	Candidates	213	298	369	142	511	41·7	27·8	307	672	661	318	979	31·4	32·5
	Successful	20	10	24	6	30	66·7	20·0	64	45	84	25	109	58·7	22·9
1969	Candidates	202	294	366	130	496	40·7	26·2	291	745	725	311	1036	28·1	30·0
	Successful	17	7	20	4	24	70·8	16·7	50	35	62	23	85	58·7	27·1
1970	Candidates[1]	194	337	370	161	531	36·5	30·3	422	1015	945	492	1437	29·4	34·2
	Successful[1]	18	10	26	2	28	64·3	7·1	53	43	60	36	96	55·2	37·5
Total 1967–70	Candidates	856	1164	1475	545	2020	42·4	26·9	1422	3009	3062	1369	4431	32·1	30·9
	Successful	75	32	93	14	107	70·1	13·1	253	167	308	112	420	60·2	26·7

Note:
[1] Home Civil Service figures for 1970 include all Methods of examination.

proportion of Oxbridge graduates in the original list of applications, was actually weaker during 1967–70 than it was in selecting for the Home Civil Service. Nevertheless, the evidence provided by the social and educational categorisation of Diplomatic Service entrants tends strongly to support the expectation created by the subjective quality of the selection process : that the Diplomatic Service is inclined to draw its members from a relatively narrow section of British society.

Probably no one would argue seriously that a diplomatic service should constitute a representative sample or microcosm of its own country or society – although strong political and legal pressures sometimes exist in pluralist or multi-racial societies for 'equitable' representation of the major sub-cultures. In Britain, selection is based upon a pseudo-rational model : it is assumed that the required qualifications and character attributes can be stated, and that an independent body can apply these criteria to the pool of applicants without bias, so that only those who are best and most relevantly qualified by character and ability will be chosen. Should this result in disproportionate representation of certain social, educational or geographical strata, this will merely reflect the uneven distribution, within the population at large or within the pool of applicants, of the qualities needed by the Diplomatic Service. So the argument runs. The Diplomatic Service, which is acutely sensitive to accusations of bias, élitism and self-perpetuation, would thus defend any one-sidedness in its selection of new entrants on the grounds of the relevance and appropriateness of ability and personal character, irrespective of educational or social background.

Given that bias does exist, the question of its relevance thus arises. For instance, how relevant is the male bias evident in the Diplomatic Service? After all, this bias is stronger than in the Home Civil Service and increases in the higher grades; above Grade 4, it is total (see Table 3).

Male preponderance within the diplomatic cadre may reflect a measure of prejudice, but it also has some rational justification. In the first place, the Diplomatic Service is unwilling to suppose that a woman diplomat would always accept transfer, at short notice, to any post in the world (although other diplomatic services have not found this an insuperable problem). Second, there are many diplomatic and consular posts in which it would

TABLE 3. ADMINISTRATIVE AND EXECUTIVE STREAMS: GRADE COMPOSITION
(*January* 1971)

Grade	Number in grade			Average age in grade	Appropriate diplomatic title abroad
	Men	Women	Total		
1	13	0	13[1]	58·3	Ambassador
2	34	0	34	56·5	Ambassador
3	118	0	118	53·7	Ambassador/Minister
4	315	6	321[2]	49·9	Ambassador/Counsellor
5	500	20	520[3]	43·2[3]	First Secretary
6	256	27	283	47·5	Second Secretary
7A	97	7	104	28·8	Second Secretary
7E	469	80	549	44·3	Second Secretary
8	58	5	63	24·7	Third Secretary
9[4]	711	201	912	36·8	

Notes:

[1] Excluding 2 non-career Ambassadors nominally in Grade 1.

[2] Including 2 remaining members of the old Executive stream Grade 4B.

[3] Grade 5 was not yet "unified" in January 1971. The figures for the separate Grades were:

Grade	Number in grade			Average age in grade
	Men	Women	Total	
5A	359	14	373	40·0
5E	141	6	147	51·3

[4] Grade 9, although within the Executive stream, is not within the "diplomatic cadre" as described in this chapter.

be either impossible or very difficult to employ a woman, because of the physical hardship involved or because of local attitudes to the idea of doing business with a woman. In London, whether in the FCO or in another department of government, there is no reason why women should not compete equally with men for official positions. The hard fact is however that the same is not true within a service which demands of its diplomatic members both high mobility and world-wide utility.

Many university teachers, especially outside Oxbridge, might suspect the Diplomatic Service's bias in favour of Oxbridge graduates. A number of them would also however question the absence of another bias: a bias in favour of selecting graduates trained in disciplines apparently relevant to diplomacy, including the social and political sciences and, above all, international relations. Diplomatic Service entrants have in fact included a sprinkling of those with an academic training in international relations, but the selection does not appear to reflect any preference for such candidates. The impression is created that, in addition to its Oxbridge bias, the Diplomatic Service is irremediably wedded to 'generalism' in its recruitment and moreover to a 'generalism' so traditional in its character as to have an almost Renaissance flavour – searching not for those trained in specific disciplines but rather for those with 'trained minds', capable of being moulded and re-moulded to any professional end.

Again the Diplomatic Service's answer to such questioning is that its first priority must be to recruit entrants whose individual personalities and characteristics fit them for life and work in the Diplomatic Service, and that this consideration must always override any consideration of particular academic qualification. If there is an apparent bias towards Oxbridge graduates, it says, that can only reflect the fact that Oxbridge continues to attract a high proportion of the most ambitious and generally able undergraduates in Britain, whose entrance to the Diplomatic Service is obtained by their intrinsic personal qualities rather than by their Oxbridge training. If there is an apparently inadequate emphasis upon ostensibly valuable subjects, such as international relations, that is only because individual candidates with personal qualities which fit them for the Diplomatic Service are not concentrated within such disciplines but are scattered widely across the academic field. In as far as special skills – in languages, in international relations, in economics or in other areas – are required, these can be imparted to suitable officials after their entry into the Service. If they do, in fact, exist already, that is a bonus – but it is a bonus which cannot be sought at the expense of any compromise on the personal qualities which new entrants must possess.

Other foreign services would strike a different balance between academic training and personal character. Some, for example, give systematic preference to law graduates, in the belief that, other things being equal, they will become more effective diplomats. The British Diplomatic Service has no such apparent faith in the relevance of any specific skill acquired before entry into the Service itself. Preponderance is given to character traits, rather than to skill or knowledge in specific areas. In the British case therefore questions about the relevance of different academic disciplines become subordinate to questions about the relevance of particular personal characteristics.

The difficulty here is that no observer can say with certainty what personal qualities are most relevant to the work of a diplomat, both because those qualities have never been defined or operationalised – and would probably be difficult to measure objectively if they were defined – and because there are no objective criteria for judging either the 'relevance' of qualities or the 'effectiveness' of diplomats. For similar reasons, we cannot judge whether academic training or personal qualities *should* be of greater importance in recruitment for the Diplomatic Service. Unless more objective and comparative methods of assessment are developed, the terms of the argument will remain so vague that both sides will be 'right'. We can, however, note that a primary emphasis on personal qualities – however well founded in experience and however fairly applied to the selection process – must at least make it easier for norm-perpetuation impulses to have an effect. We might also remark that even the subjective assessment of personal qualities is fraught with difficulty. Each of the 'desirable' qualities has its undesirable, but closely related, counterpart, for which it may sometimes be mistaken or into which it may sometimes develop. Quickness of intelligence lives close to the substitution of instinct for thought, oral articulateness to glib verbosity, self-confidence to arrogance, equanimity to complacency. The diplomatic virtues are finely separated from the diplomatic vices.

Despite the analytical difficulties, we must still consider whether, in general, a heavy emphasis on personal qualities – with the social bias which it does entail and the opportunity for norm-perpetuation which it may allow – is likely to be relevant or appropriate to the work of the Diplomatic Service.

There are obvious reasons why the Diplomatic Service should, in fact, lay some particular stress on personal qualities, especially when it comes to the use of its members as individual diplomats abroad. Some of the diplomatic cadre find themselves temporarily in charge of minor diplomatic posts before they are thirty. All of them act, from the first time they go abroad, as the individual voices of the British Government in discussions, negotiations or conferences with other governments. Their more senior colleagues have an obvious interest in minimising the danger that their juniors will commit serious errors, but there will be numerous occasions on which something substantial will depend upon their own judgement of a situation and their own use of personal discretion in deciding how to handle it. Particular academic skills may help them in particular circumstances; no academic experience can in general be a complete substitute for more personal qualities or for powers of individual judgement.

Given that it needs people with qualifications which are more than academic, what is perhaps surprising is that an organisation with such a powerful *esprit de corps* as the Diplomatic Service expects to get such people 'ready-made', instead of relying more upon its own ability to mould and socialise new entrants to its own image. Socialising pressures are intermittent in London, but they are constant and powerful within the more confined and tightly knit atmosphere of a mission abroad. With such forces at its disposal, saying that the Diplomatic Service must ensure that its members possess certain personal qualities is not necessarily the same as saying that it must place an almost exclusive emphasis upon those qualities in selecting its new entrants.

Quite apart from its preference for personal qualities, rather than academic qualifications, there is one reason why the Diplomatic Service may be especially prone to the perpetuation of norms – a reason which applies to all foreign services, which bears upon no other section of national governments and which emanates from international diplomacy itself. Diplomats of all countries are sometimes said to form a sort of non-national, rootless freemasonry. What is certainly true is that they influence each other's standards and attitudes, socially if not intellectually, to a very considerable extent. Diplomats from different countries and from opposed social and political systems appear to conform to a single, tacitly established, social norm with extraordinary fidelity, constituting a coherent social group and communicating in a common idiom. Whatever the reasons for this remarkable conformism, it has its professional advantages; the obvious advantage of easing working communication is coupled with the less obvious advantage of providing a common level of artificiality on which polemical exchanges can take place without impairing the future utility of personal relationships. The effect, however, is to require that all members of the group accept some degree of conformity to a set of standards which no one of the nations concerned is in a position to dictate. The point for our immediate purpose is that strong pressure for norm-perpetuation by the British Diplomatic Service may come not only from internal sources but also from the Service's perception of an internationally established diplomatic norm, defiance of which, however well justified on other grounds, might reduce the effectiveness of British diplomatic efforts within the international environment.

In all these circumstances, it would be wrong to suppose that either an emphasis on personal qualities or a tendency to norm-perpetuation is necessarily or entirely dysfunctional. The fact remains that, for whatever reason, the selection of the British diplomatic cadre does reflect a social bias. British diplomats no longer need any sort of private income, and only a very few possess one; nor will some previous family connection with the Diplomatic Service secure their entry. Nevertheless, the diplomatic cadre still seems to include a high proportion of people whose education, attitudes and social backgrounds have something in common with each other. The mixture has become a good deal less obviously and immediately homogeneous during the last twenty years, but it would still be ridiculous to suggest that the diplomatic cadre is, socially or educationally, a typical cross-section of the British nation. Indeed, it still manages to give the impression of being élitist and aloof. It also manages to give the impression of achieving a high level of norm-perpetuation, even if the means by which it is recruited appear on the surface to offer little opportunity for this to occur.

TRAINING AND SPECIALISATION

Having acquired its raw material for the 'diplomatic cadre', how does the Diplomatic Service seek to mould it? And, in planning that process, how much importance does it attach to developing a range of specialised, 'purpose-built' designs, as opposed to producing one general utility model?

New entrants to the 'diplomatic cadre' by Open Competition are given an immediate introductory course. That, at least, is the theory. In practice, some individuals who join at an inopportune moment never receive such a formal introduction. They are not however likely to find the omission a serious handicap. The course for those who enter Grade 9, at the bottom of the Executive stream, is crammed into four or five – not necessarily consecutive – days and its content is minimal. Indeed, it does little more than introduce the new entrants to the geography, office procedure and jargon of the Foreign and Commonwealth Office. The parallel course for new entrants to the Administrative stream, at Grade 8 or 7A, lasts about two weeks but is equally insubstantial. Those who take it are likely to emerge with little more than a strong – and possibly salutary – sense of the complexity of the Foreign and Commonwealth Office and the esotericism of its internal workings.

The fact is that the Diplomatic Service, faced with the task of assimilating new entrants, places its faith not in formal training but in immediate experience 'on the job'. Officially, the first year in the Administrative stream is regarded as a training year, during which recruits are given jobs in which they will acquire the rudiments of a professional equipment whilst also operating as productive components of the system. The overall objective seems to be that new entrants should acquire skills by a process of osmosis, rather than by receiving instruction. An effort is being made to introduce a $2\frac{1}{2}$-day interlude of lectures on international relations theory and major international problems into the first year of service in the Administrative stream. This, however, does little to modify the impression that the initial training of the 'diplomatic cadre' bears more relation to the flying instruction of fledgelings than to the laborious and lengthy process of tuition used by many other diplomatic services.

There is one important exception to this general statement. Some 50–65% of the year's Open Competition intake into the Administrative stream, together with a roughly equal number of Grade 9 and 7E officers from the Executive stream, are selected annually, either on entry or during the first year of service, for training in 'hard languages' : that is, in the principal languages of Asia, Africa and Eastern Europe. The requirement for such trainees is explained to new entrants, and a certain amount of gentle encouragement may be given in particular cases. Those selected are nevertheless volunteers. Some will begin their full-time hard language training immediately after entry; others will first complete their initial year of general 'on the job' training in London, although they may simultaneously undergo part-time language training in the Diplomatic Service's own Language Centre. In the majority of cases, full-time courses begin with a period at a British university—often, but not always, at the School of Oriental and African Studies in London [5]. This is followed by further academic and practical training in the country to which the language in question is native. The whole process may last anything from a few months to two years.

The significance of this hard language training is not only that it provides a pool of valuable talent but also that it constitutes the Diplomatic Service's most important element of internal specialisation. The Diplomatic Service is often thought to be preoccupied with the selection and development of 'generalists' – an impression which the Duncan Report has recently helped to confirm. The impression is nevertheless misleading. The Service is certainly intent upon *recruiting* generalists – or rather, as we have seen, upon recruiting individuals without significant reference to their particular area of academic expertise. But it is much less strongly opposed, in practice, to the development of specialised groups within its 'diplomatic cadre', at least when it comes to linguistic specialisation. A linguistic specialisation in a hard language does not mean that the individual concerned will spend all his career within the country or region of that language. In the first place, his earlier career will be punctuated by spells in London and probably in at least one post outside his linguistic region. In the second place, although skill in a hard language may bring accelerated mid-career promotion within the area of that language, it will not necessarily prevent the person concerned from becoming a generalist during the later stages of his career, when he reaches Grade 3 or above. Nevertheless, a junior member of the Administrative stream who speaks a hard language fluently may expect to spend a significant proportion of his career within his linguistic region or dealing with its affairs in London.

The effects of this form of career specialisation also tend to vary with the number of people and posts at issue, as well as with the perceived importance of the language concerned. Arabists within the 'diplomatic cadre' seem, for example, to constitute a fairly cohesive and relatively numerous group, occupying most

of the posts at all levels within the Arab world and a significant
number of those concerned with Arab and Middle Eastern affairs
in the Foreign and Commonwealth Office. Russian speakers,
although less numerous, seem to have something of the same sense
of corporate identity – possibly because of the assumption that
their linguistic skill is associated with a particular understanding
of political phenomena which are as complex as they are important. Other linguistically specialised groups appear to have
less cohesion. Together, however, these hard language specialists
constitute an important sub-division of the British 'diplomatic
cadre', the existence of which is rarely recognised and the significance of which for the conduct of British foreign policy might
merit investigation. The existence of such specialisation is, perhaps, an inevitable concomitant of the diplomatic effort of a
country which seeks to be represented throughout the world.
Indeed, the tendency towards such specialisation may be increasing. With British entry into the European Communities
an accomplished fact, it seems likely that there will be an intensification of training for new entrants in the principal languages of
Western Europe. If that occurs, the 'diplomatic cadre' may come
to be partitioned increasingly between exponents of different
languages – a development which would force some re-examination of the common assumption that the British Diplomatic
Service is one of generalists.

At present, the hard language specialists differ from their
colleagues in a number of respects. Many of them, for example,
will begin their hard language training almost immediately upon
entry, without following the otherwise normal course of completing some two years in departments of the Foreign and
Commonwealth Office before receiving their first foreign appointments. Instead, they will commonly be posted to a mission
abroad, in the area of their linguistic specialisation, as soon as
their language training is completed. In other words, they will
not normally receive the same 'on the job' training in London
which is ostensibly given to their non-specialist colleagues and,
even if they do, will be subjected to it for a shorter period. In
extreme cases, they may be forced to assume a large measure
of independent diplomatic responsibility abroad without any
preparation at all [6]. Apart from anything else, this seems to
cast some doubt upon the degree of importance which the Diplo-

matic Service really attaches to such 'on the job' training in London. The impression created is, indeed, that the analogy with the flying instruction given to young birds is a close one. The new entrant is immediately regarded as available labour, doubtless of limited utility but nevertheless capable of assuming significant responsibility without any special preparation. We may well ask, however, whether still more might not be made of the available raw material if some effort were made to explore and develop the particular talents of new entrants at an early stage.

One of the principal obstacles to the introduction of more systematic initial training for the 'diplomatic cadre' is undoubtedly the Diplomatic Service's chronic labour shortage. Without an adequate manpower margin, the Service feels itself to be incapable of providing scope for additional training. Nor can the problem be solved by reducing the number of 'working' posts for officials in order to release more people for training, since the maximum level of the Service's manpower margin is fixed by agreement with the Treasury and the Civil Service Department. The Plowden Report recommended in 1964 that the Service should have a manpower margin of 10%, which would cerainly not appear too generous to cover both inevitable and desirable contingencies in such an organisation. The maximum authorised manpower margin has never, however, risen above $7\frac{1}{2}\%$, and even this level has rarely, if ever, been reached in many grades. One result is that training programmes, both on entry and in mid-career, are fighting a constant and usually unsuccessful battle against the pressure of operational requirements. The British diplomat seems to receive training in spite, rather than because, of the system – especially during the formative years immediately after his entry into the 'diplomatic cadre'.

The lack of an adequate manpower margin impedes mid-career training, just as it does initial training. A more determined effort seems, however, to be made to overcome this obstacle in mid-career. Indeed, it is only after some years of service that a British diplomat has much chance of receiving any formal in-service training other than either language training or those brief courses in commercial, information or consular work which will precede his first appointment to a post in one of these fields.

There are current plans to introduce two new elements into mid-career training. The first is an annual course in international law, lasting one week, for some members of Grades 4 and 5. The emphasis of this course, which will be given by the Diplomatic Service's own Legal Advisers, is likely to be severely practical, but it nevertheless marks an interesting departure from the long-standing British inclination to keep law and diplomacy apart. The second new element, which runs still more strongly counter to traditions of the past, will be an annual two-week course in international relations theory, principally for members of Grade 5. If the pilot course in this series, held in September 1972, is any guide, it will consist largely of lectures and seminars by academic experts. This is therefore likely to represent the most substantial effort so far made in Britain to forge a link between the practitioners of the Diplomatic Service and the theorists of the academic world, even though the fact that it will not include more than about twenty officials a year means that many members of the 'diplomatic cadre' will never take part in it.

With these exceptions, the emphasis in mid-career training plans falls almost exclusively upon training in economics and management – the two being closely combined. The overall intention is apparently that the bulk of the 'diplomatic cadre', excluding only those who already have academic qualifications in the field, should undergo a course in management and economics between five and ten years after joining the Service. For members of the Executive stream, in Grades 9 and 7E, this would consist of a four-week course in economics and a ten-day 'junior management' course. Both these courses already exist although, especially in the case of the economics course, a significant proportion of the Executive stream still appears to by-pass them. For members of the Administrative and 'unified' stream, in Grades 7A and 5, there is a one-week 'middle management' course and a longer course in economics under the aegis of the Civil Service College, normally lasting between nine and twelve weeks. Again, however, the lack of an adequate manpower margin seriously limits the proportion of Administrative stream members who pass through this process; although the aim is that all members without some formal training in economics should take the economics course after about 6–8 years of service, only about half of them appear to do so at present.

Despite the problem of the manpower margin, the proportion of members of the 'diplomatic cadre' with some training in economics should rise slowly if current plans are put into effect. The impact of this will, however, take some time to reach the more senior levels of the 'diplomatic cadre', if only because very few people pass through this training programme after they have left Grade 5.

In principle, specialisation within a foreign service can be of two kinds: functional and geographical (or geo-linguistic). As we have seen in Chapter 2, the organisational core of the FCO itself was, until recently, strongly biased towards the latter, with functional departments added here and there on an *ad hoc* basis. Something similar seems to be happening in respect of training and career development: within the overall service emphasis on 'generalism' and interchangeability, some measure of geo-linguistic specialisation has become accepted, but functional specialisation is still resisted despite, for instance, the urging of the Duncan Committee towards commercial work and export promotion. The tendency is to add acquaintance with export promotion to the 'generalist' qualities which all members of the 'diplomatic cadre' should possess, rather than to develop a sub-category of specialists in the field. Some successful experience of commercial work is likely to be regarded as a desirable characteristic of any candidate for promotion to Grade 4 or above, but not as either a rigid pre-condition or a self-sufficient qualification. At the other end of the scale, the most junior commercial posts within the 'diplomatic cadre' are likely to go on being filled, with only rare exceptions, by members of the Executive stream (Grades 9 and 7E) rather than of the Administrative stream (Grades 8 and 7A). Of the 178 commercial jobs at these levels when the Duncan Report was written, 172 were occupied by Executive stream personnel; the proportion has changed little since.

Mid-career training is not wholly confined to subjects relevant to commercial or economic work. In addition to the practical courses in consular and information work and the proposed new courses in international law and international relations theory, a half-score of middle-grade 'diplomatic cadre' members, normally in Grade 4, are sent each year into the outside world – to universities, to other semi-academic institutions or, in a very few cases, on attachment to commercial firms. In addition, two or three Grade 4 officers join courses at the Royal College of Defence Studies or at other centres of higher defence education. There is little indication, however, that these interludes, although regarded officially as part of mid-career training activities, are related to the subsequent careers of the people concerned. Certainly, they do not seem to be treated as a foundation for later specialisation within the 'diplomatic cadre'.

The overall impression created by examining the Diplomatic Services's training programmes and their relationship to the composition of the 'diplomatic cadre' is three-fold. First, the Service appears to regard initial training in any area except hard languages as a matter indifferent; knowledge of the rudiments of diplomatic method and executive government practice is expected in the main to be the result of pragmatic experience. Second, the Service, while displaying a growing interest in mid-career training, especially in economics and management studies, is not inclined to breed specialisation by this means so much as to enrich generalism. Moreover, it is constantly forced by the lack of an adequate manpower margin to treat mid-career training as the poor relation of operational requirements. Third, while the importance of geo-linguistic specialisation has probably been underestimated and may be potentially increasing, the Service is not inclined to move significantly towards any greater degree of functional specialisation within the 'diplomatic cadre'; the highest reaches of the Service will continue to be populated by those whose special functional skills may be an incidental asset but are not a sufficient condition for their elevation.

CAREER STRUCTURE: POSTING, PROMOTION AND ASSESSMENT

The FCO operates the third largest foreign service establishment in the world, and the Diplomatic Service has one of the longest histories of uninterrupted development. Its structure and organisation have undergone a number of considerable changes (see Chapter 2); it is continuously adapting to new environmental demands, such as improved communications, a rise in the number of sovereign states, increasing numbers of international organisations and shifts in Britain's role abroad. An organisation of this size, complexity and adaptability will inevitably develop its own personnel policy for post-entry selection and for promotion to its higher echelons, a policy which in turn will partly depend on service structure: the age/grade manning schedule of its establishment. The more ranks there are, the more often a candidate can be promoted in his lifetime; the more pyramidal (as opposed to, say, rectangular) the structure of the service, the harder promotion to the upper grades becomes. Not every Third Secretary can carry an ambassador's pennant in his diplomatic pouch.

Table 3 shows the pyramidal structure of the British Diplomatic Service. It is obvious from the figures that there is a continuous risk that top-heaviness in the Service as a whole may dictate rates of promotion, a risk which – as we shall see – has at times required drastic measures.

Unlike most other departments of government, the Diplomatic Service is widely dispersed over the world. Apart from promotion, a diplomat's career is therefore also much influenced by posting and rotation. Most diplomatic services believe in moving their staff from one post to another, or back to the home base, every three to five years. It could be argued that these moves are designed in the interest of career-building, in order to give the diplomat the necessary width of experience in many functions and in many parts of the world; in the British Diplomatic Service, such moves certainly involve changes from one kind of job to another, often without much continuity or chance to specialise. However a number of other factors are also likely to determine these frequent transfers, to the point where career-building may seem to be little more than an afterthought.

Most prominent among these is the consideration of loyalty. It is assumed that after a few years a foreign service officer will begin – in his reports and recommendations – to reflect less often the interests of his government and his country, and more often those of the country in which he is stationed. A diplomat is intentionally moved from place to place so that he will not form strong local ties; after a number of years his most important reference group will be his colleagues and superiors in the service, including those in the central administration of his foreign ministry.

A second reason for the continuous rotation of personnel is the alleged development of 'localitis' – the tendency to give excessive importance to local events, and to lose the world-wide perspective. For this reason a British diplomat is likely to be moved back to London every so often, for a spell at a desk in the FCO.

Third, service morale. Some posts are classified as 'hardship' posts, for reasons which may be medical, climatic or political; in the British case they are listed as such in the Diplomatic List. Service at hardship posts is usually shorter than elsewhere, and requires relief in the interest of fairness.

Fourth, personal considerations. Diplomats would not join a foreign service if they thought they were going to stay in one foreign capital all their working life; they like to extend their experience and it is in the interest of the service that personnel administrators should give them the opportunity to do so.

There are exceptions to this general pattern. In rare cases, a British diplomat with extensive connections in a particular country may stay on for many years, if the interest of the Service would seem to require it. The exceptions, however, are few.

What would be the shape of a fairly distinguished diplomatic career?

As we have seen, there is a very high probability (over 0·85) that a direct entrant to the Administrative stream will be male and about a 0·7 probability that he will be an Oxbridge graduate. There is also a high probability that he will have entered Grade 8 through the Open Competition. He may be given the opportunity to learn a hard language on entry, in which case he will immediately spend up to two years in language training. Otherwise, those two years will probably be spent as a desk officer in one or more of the political departments in the FCO. Thereafter, in either case, he is most likely to be posted to an Embassy abroad in the rank of Third Secretary, where he will probably be engaged in general political work within the Chancery. He will be promoted to Grade 7A at the age of 26, and to Grade 5 between the ages of 30 and 31, in each case either *sur place* or on transfer. While in Grades 7A and 5, he will probably have another two tours, totalling some 6 years, in London. During the first of these, he may again be a desk officer, with the added – and desirable – possibility of being selected as an Assistant Private Secretary or Private Secretary to one of the FCO Ministers. During his second London tour, after some years in Grade 5, he may become the Assistant (that is, the assistant head) of an FCO Department. With the exception of intervals for leave, the remainder of those years will be spent abroad: as a Second Secretary (or Vice-Consul) in Grade 7A and as a First Secretary (or Consul) in

Grade 5. At least one of his foreign postings is likely to be in a commercial appointment, preceded by a short course in commercial work. Later, as a senior First Secretary, he may also serve as the Head of Chancery in a small or medium-sized Embassy, responsible for discipline and welfare as well as for the workings of the Chancery (the political reporting section) and for the smooth running of the Embassy as a whole. In most cases, he will expect to have home leave after every two years of service abroad and to spend 3–5 years in each of his foreign postings. In a post which, because of its climate or the strain imposed by its particular circumstances, is rated as a 'hardship' post, he will, however, have home leave more frequently and will not expect to serve more than three years.

From the age of 39 onwards, he will be looking for the crucial promotion to Grade 4, at which level he will hold the rank of Counsellor (or, in some small posts, even Ambassador) when abroad and Head of Department when at home. On average, however, he will wait until he is over 43 before accomplishing this step. From that point onwards, the marks of recognition will come to a 'man with a future' at an increasing pace. After four or five years of successful performance in Grade 4 he will be a strong candidate for admission, as a Companion, to the traditional British diplomatic order of chivalry, the Most Distinguished Order of St Michael and St George. With a CMG to his credit, he will look forward to higher things. As in the Home Civil Service, the process of selecting entrants to the Administrative stream is designed to identify individuals who will reach at least as high as Grade 4 before they retire. For any entrant, however, the obvious targets lie beyond this level. In Grade 3, he may be an Assistant Under-Secretary in the FCO, the Minister in a large Embassy or the Ambassador in a post of moderate importance. In Grade 2, he will be a Deputy Under-Secretary or a more senior Ambassador and will probably become a Knight Commander of the Most Distinguished Order of St Michael and St George (KCMG), with a 'Sir' before his name. Ultimately, in his later 50s, he may scale the heights to Grade 1, as one of the most senior Ambassadors in one of the most important diplomatic posts or, at the very peak, as Permanent Under Secretary of the Foreign and Commonwealth Office and Head of the Diplomatic Service, probably with the added accolade of a GCMG (Knight

Grand Cross of the Most Distinguished Order of St Michael and St George).

With this ideal career as our example, we have to ask how the man concerned has been chosen for such distinction. After all, he will have been too mobile, in every sense, for any simple system of in-service selection to follow his course. On average, he will have spent about two-thirds of his career abroad, and his promotion will have depended heavily upon his performance during those periods. We need to know, therefore, not only how his successive promotions are decided upon but also what method is used in choosing the posts in which he will serve and in scrutinising his performance, both abroad and in London.

Every direct entrant to the Administrative stream by Open Competition serves a notional probation of three years before his appointment to the Diplomatic Service is confirmed. Each direct entrant by Supplementary Open Competition completes a similar probation of two years before confirmation. During that period, as throughout the whole of his service, his performance is assessed by his superiors. Within the FCO the responsibility for this assessment lies with his Head of Department or, when he becomes a Head of Department himself, with his superintending Under-Secretary. Abroad, it lies with his Head of Chancery or, beyond that level, with the Head of Mission himself, with whom the ultimate responsibility will in any case rest. In normal circumstances, the assessment will be recorded in writing every twelve months and sent to the Personnel Departments of the FCO for scrutiny and for inclusion in the individual's confidential personal file. A written assessment will also be submitted whenever either the individual or the reporting officer is transferred to another post. If any of these reports is adverse – that is, if the individual's performance during the period examined is rated as 'unsatisfactory' – he must be told of this, and of the grounds for the adverse judgement, when the report is submitted. Less formally, a reporting officer will consider it a natural part of his duty to call to an individual's attention particular weaknesses which a periodical assessment has alleged.

The judgements which periodical reports demand are subjective. Apart from inviting reporting officers to make their general comments in prose, the report forms require in the main that the subject's performance should be rated, under several headings, on a fixed scale which ranges from 'excellent' to 'unsatisfactory'. They also call for an assessment of his ability to perform the duties of the next highest grade. None of this is surprising. What may be less obvious is that these reports also provide one of the opportunities for an assessment to be made of a married officer's wife. The Diplomatic Service is not so impertinent as to assert any right to dictate its members' choices in this matter [7]. In any foreign post, however, a diplomat's wife forms part of a representational team, constantly involved in entertaining and being entertained and probably involved in some sort of social or community work as well. Her social background is of no particular interest. What is of interest is her willingness and ability to play an active part in these aspects of representational work, since this must inevitably affect her husband's overall effectiveness as well. The extent to which wives can make their husband's diplomatic careers is probably overestimated, but they can certainly impede them, especially by a lack of interest or enthusiasm.

Beyond the probationary stage, the main importance of these periodical reports lies in the effect which they have upon proposals by the Personnel Operations Department of the FCO for postings or promotions. A report rarely reflects the isolated view of one individual. Abroad, for example, it is likely to represent the views of the Head of Mission, the Head of Chancery and, in a large post, at least one other superior officer. In London, it may only reflect the views of the Head of Department and possibly the Assistant concerned, but the FCO is small enough to enable the Personnel Operations Department to obtain any necessary cross-checks either from personal knowledge or from other senior officials with an opportunity to judge an individual's performance. Even a single report thus carries some weight. In general, however, it is the cumulative effect of several consecutive reports by several different individuals which carries real weight. The Personnel Operations Department, after all, is in an excellent position not only to compare a sequence of reports on one individual but also to compare the reports made on many individuals by one reporting officer, as well as reports on the reporting officers themselves. The complacent assessor is as easy to identify as the hyper-critical, and allowance can be made for both, especially as an individual's career provides a growing number of annual reports.

In theory, this system provides a basis for relatively sophisticated personnel assessment. The sophistication with which the assessment system is operated should not, however, be overestimated. The assessments themselves are cast in impressionistic terms and the view formed by the Personnel Operations Department is no more than an impression of a consensus of impressions. Moreover, the chronic shortage of manpower, especially at the important Grade 5 level, is such that 'career planning' in its full sense, although frequently stated as an objective, is little more than a dream. With only marginal exceptions, the evidence available from periodical assessments of individuals seems to be used in fact to serve two main purposes : to avoid disaster, in the shape of palpably inappropriate postings or premature promotions, and to identify 'flyers' whose consistently excellent performance marks them for ultimately high rank.

Finally, the whole system of promotion and to a lesser extent of posting, is still heavily constrained by considerations of relative seniority. Indeed, movement through the Administrative stream up to Grade 5 marks the inexorable operation of seniority; unless an individual's career has been marred in some quite extraordinary way, promotion to Grade 7A comes at 26 and promotion to Grade 5 at about 30·5, as the night follows the day. In theory, promotion from Grade 5 to Grade 4 is entirely by merit. In practice, this is not the whole truth. An officer who is both excellent and fortunate may achieve that promotion between 39 and 41, whereas one whose performance has been consistently mediocre may wait until 45. The great majority of new Grade 4 officers come, however, from the top 10% of the Grade 5 seniority list. It is only in Grade 4 and beyond that perceived merit comes to dominate seniority as the primary qualification for promotion. Until that point, therefore, the effect of periodical assessments on an officer's promotion prospects will be no more than marginal. The overall significance of these assessments is nevertheless great, simply because it is largely on the basis of this evidence that the Personnel Operations Department proposes the posts to which officers are appointed or transferred, and because it is largely the choice and availability of his posts which dictates the extent of the opportunities which an individual officer will have to gain the experience and to demonstrate the qualities which will eventually determine his status.

This last point deserves to be emphasised. Many organisations

offer a wide range of appointments at any level which, although
ostensibly identical in rank, vary enormously in the degree of
responsibility they carry and the amount of opportunity they
provide. The Diplomatic Service is, however, unusual (if not
unique) in possessing a range which extends not only within the
FCO but also to some 285 separate diplomatic and consular posts
abroad. During the first twenty years of a Diplomatic Service
officer's career, the most important decisions taken about him are
likely to be those which relate not to promotion, which is largely
automatic, but to posting. The man who oscillates between
subordinate positions in relatively obscure departments of the
FCO and postings to junior appointments in what the Duncan
Report characterised unforgettably as the 'Outer Area' may
nevertheless emerge in his forties as a notably successful Grade 4
officer, destined for higher things. Equally, the man who alter-
nates between 'plum' missions such as Washington, Bonn, Paris,
New York and Moscow, and the most attractive jobs in London
– as the desk officer dealing with a vital subject or country, or as
a member of the Planning Staff or as Private Secretary to one of the
junior FCO Ministers – may eventually fail to match his apparent
promise and grind to a halt in Grade 4. Such cases, however,
are unusual; the appointments given to any individual during
his passage from Grade 8 to Grade 4 will generally both reflect
his superiors' expectation and presage his own eventual attain-
ments. And the choice of those appointments will be made largely
on the collective basis of the periodical assessments of his work.

Appointments themselves, like promotions, are the product of
a complex process of review, broadly based in form but insti-
gated and heavily influenced by the Personnel Operations Department in substance. Below Grade 4, the several Selection
Boards tend to endorse the recommendations of the Personnel
Operations Department. Above this level, the process of appointment and promotion involves more people from outside the
personnel management machinery itself, and is consequently both
less predictable and less heavily dominated by the views of one
functional department. Appointments to, and promotions in,
Grade 4 are recommended to the Permanent Under-Secretary
by the No. 2 Selection Board, which because of its broad membership is in a position which allows it to modify or reject proposals
put forward by the Personnel Operations Department. An even

stronger position is held by the Senior Selection Board, which handles appointments in or to Grades 1, 2 and 3, since that Board is chaired by the Permanent Under-Secretary himself, is composed almost entirely of Under-Secretaries – often with one of the junior FCO Ministers as an additional member – and makes its recommendations directly to the Foreign Secretary. Like all the other Boards, the Senior Selection Board receives advice and a great deal of background information from the Personnel Operations Department. Its composition is so senior, however, and the individuals with whom it deals so well known to most of its members that it is much more likely than any of the lower Boards to reject the advice or to re-assess the significance of background information. Thus, although the system of appointment and promotion appears on paper to provide for impartial judgement of each candidate at all levels by his peers (or at least by representatives of immediately senior grades), there is a wide gulf between the largely formal operations of the No. 4 Selection Board – dealing with individuals who do not appear before it, whom most members of the Board have never seen and whose only 'presence' consists of the evidence provided by the periodic reports on their performance – and the substantial debates of the Senior Selection Board – indebted to the personnel managers for suggestions and information, but fully capable of forming its own judgement on people whom its members know well and with whom they have worked for years.

As with initial selection for entry into the Diplomatic Service, there are numerous questions to be asked about this process of in-service assessment and selection, some of which fall under the heading, once more, of norm-perpetuation. Impulses towards norm-perpetuation are likely to have freer play *within* the 'diplomatic cadre', when it comes to postings and promotions, than they have during the initial selection of new entrants. As always, however, it is extraordinarily difficult to be precise about the operation of such impulses. Apart from anything else, 'service' organisations, with their habitual stress on collective loyalty and corporate identity, may tend to generate a bi-directional pressure for norm-perpetuation. Those at the top may indeed be inclined to give preference to more junior members of the service who seem to reflect their own images. Indeed it is difficult for men who are still actively involved in operational work to perform that work effectively unless they have some confidence in their own characters and abilities – and it then becomes difficult for them to select potential successors on the basis of any assumption except that people with similar characteristics will be well-fitted to perform the same functions in the future. At the same time, however, there is a strong tendency in a 'service' organisation for junior members of the service not only to aspire to satisfy their superiors but also to identify men in senior positions with the organisation itself. To the extent that they do this, they may transfer a part of their organisational loyalty to those individuals, and will thus be all the more strongly inclined to model themselves upon them. Imitation of the leadership may thus become not only a prudent attempt to obtain preferment but also one side of a tacit – and largely unconscious – conspiracy to perpetuate what is seen as the ethos of the service which gives identity to all its members. As a result, it is possible that the service may become rigid and out-of-date in some of its activities.

Whether such 'conspiratorial' norm-perpetuation operates in the Diplomatic Service can only be judged impressionistically. As in all parallel circumstances, young British diplomats rail privately at the follies of their elders and resolve to behave otherwise when they attain such eminence, but this does not always prevent them from growing steadily closer to what might be described as a set of norms. Moreover, there are at least two reasons for thinking that norm-perpetuation impulses, acting in both directions, may have a particular importance in such an environment. The first reason has already been stated, at least implicitly, in the description of the selection process for postings and promotions. Up to Grade 5, the important decisions are taken largely on the basis of assessments which, if not objective in form, are balanced against each other over time to an extent which reduces the importance of purely subjective judgement; above that level, the system provides much greater opportunities for norm-perpetuation to operate directly. The second reason is also implicit in earlier comments. A high proportion of the career of any member of the 'diplomatic cadre' is spent in missions abroad, where it is reasonable to suppose that norm-perpetuation, both within the Diplomatic Service itself and in the broader context of the international diplomatic community, may operate with particular force.

It is useful to ask also whether the Diplomatic Service's process of in-service assessment and selection satisfies some criterion of relevance : that is, whether it successfully picks out people whose qualities are especially appropriate to the real functions and roles of the Service, while rarely passing over candidates who could benefit these. The question, however, begs another. What are those real functions and roles, and how rapidly are they changing? There is no entirely satisfactory answer. Some answers in general terms are available : '. . . to represent this country abroad and to conduct Her Majesty's Government's business with other governments . . . to collate and analyse reports received from Her Majesty's representatives abroad and to advise the Foreign and Commonwealth Secretary on all matters of policy' [8]. By such general standards, the Diplomatic Service's internal selection processes seem likely to produce relevant results : the overall abilities of any individual as representative, negotiator, analyst and adviser are exactly those which his more senior colleagues are well placed to judge, and it is his relative success in these areas which does, on the face of it, dominate decisions about posting or promoting him. There seems, however, to be little attempt to establish or to operate more specific standards. Two examples may demonstrate this. Firstly, the Duncan Committee asserted in 1969 that commercial work 'should absorb more of the Service's resources than any other function' and went on to suggest that, in every foreign post, the position immediately below the Head of Mission should be occupied by an officer trained for, and specialising in, commercial work. Whether or not such an emphatic assertion was justified, there is no doubt that export promotion now occupies a larger proportion of the time of most officers in Grade 4 and above than it did ten – or even five – years ago. This does not, however, appear to have given rise to any attempt to adopt skill and experience in trade promotion as a primary criterion for promotion to or beyond Grade 4. Some successful commercial experience is certainly considered to be a desirable subsidiary attribute, but it is still subordinated in importance to the traditional 'generalist' qualities. Secondly, there has been a striking growth during the last decade in the importance to the conduct of diplomacy of subjects which have some content of international economics. Multilateral negotiations concerning such matters as international monetary arrangements, transnational investments, 'off-set' payments for troop costs in Europe and, above all, Britain's entry into the European Communities have come to play an increasing part in the work of many senior diplomats. They do not need a thorough grounding in economic theory to play their alloted part in these areas, but they do need basic numeracy and at least some passing acquaintance with the workings of the international economic system. Again, however, these qualifications do not appear to have been recognised as an essential criterion for promotion to and beyond Grade 4. Indeed they have ostensibly received less attention than the much-publicised question of commercial experience, even though it is arguable that, while many senior diplomats may have only a transient involvement in commercial work, no diplomat can now perform his function of negotiation or analysis effectively unless he is equipped to weigh the wider importance of international economic factors.

Other criteria, perhaps more contentious, might also be applied to candidates for promotion. The Duncan Committee argued that it was possible within the Service to assess the utility of political reporting. It might be possible to adapt this approach in order to analyse all papers written by senior officials over a period of time, with the result serving as an additional aid to personal assessment. Particular attention might be paid to any specific forecasts of events – and to their accuracy. (The habits of the FCO seem curiously to militate against analytical post-mortems on recommendations, decisions and policies. Much could be learnt from these, and not only for the purpose of promotion.) Another useful guide might be the behaviour of individual diplomats under stress or crisis conditions; where they have been subjected to such circumstances, particular note could be taken of their ability to stay cool and to retain a wide perspective on events. A third guide might be their conduct of set-piece negotiations. Again, a subsequent dissection might show up errors or positive powers of judgement which would be highly relevant both to promotion and to future conduct and training.

There is one other aspect of in-service selection which cannot be passed over : selection for early retirement. Normally a member of the Diplomatic Service retires at 60; the theoretical power to extend his service by up to five more years is hardly ever used. In many cases, retirement will actually come earlier, because

service in many 'hardship' posts counts extra for seniority purposes and because an officer with such service to his credit will
reach what is known as 'notional 60' before he reaches actual 60.
Nevertheless, retirement will in general come between 57 and
60. Legislation exists, however, which permits the Diplomatic
Service to declare a wide range of its senior members redundant
at a much earlier age, either on the grounds that the requirements
and circumstances of the Service have changed or on the grounds
that they are not personally fitted for further promotion. The most
striking use made of these powers was the decision, announced in
March 1969, to retire some 30 members of Grades 1–3 prematurely, ostensibly as part of a general manpower-reduction
exercise but clearly also in an attempt to unblock promotion
routes for others. The powers themselves lie in the hands of the
Secretary of State, acting on the recommendation of his senior
officials. They are without parallel in the Home Civil Service and
are naturally looked upon with some trepidation by the Diplomatic Service, especially at a time when the contraction of
national responsibilities and the amalgamation of external relations services have arguably produced over-staffing at senior
levels. That trepidation is greatly increased – indeed largely
created – by the extremely ungenerous compensation offered to
those who are prematurely retired in this way. The powers are
therefore unpopular, even though, with the exception of the 30
officers already mentioned, they have not so far been used in more
than two or three cases a year.

If more generous terms were available, many British diplomats
would probably accept that powers of premature retirement are
not, in themselves, unreasonable. Indeed, they might well go
further, to the point of arguing, with the Duncan Report, that
early retirement should be suitably encouraged. Their principal
grounds for so arguing would be those already mentioned : that
the upper levels of the 'diplomatic cadre' have become over-
staffed. The reasons for this over-population are too numerous
to investigate here. The fact is, however, that as a result the pace
of promotion to and beyond Grade 4 has become the most serious
problem which the Diplomatic Service has. Whatever views outside observers may form, there seems to be very little complaint
within the Service about the methods of in-service selection for
posting and promotion or about the selections actually made. The

slowness of promotion is, on the other hand, a source of deep discontent and may well constitute not only the Diplomatic Service's most serious problem of organisation but also its most serious problem of morale.

The scale of the problem can be gauged from a comparison of promotions to and beyond Grade 4 or the equivalent in the Diplomatic Service and the Home Civil Service. The following table, quoted in part from the Duncan Report, shows the promotions made to Grades 5, 4 and 3 during 1967 of officers who had originally entered the Administrative Grades of those services by Open Competition. The position today is similar.

Promotion to	Home Civil Service			Diplomatic Service		
	Min. age	*Max. age*	*Av. age*	*Min. age*	*Max. age*	*Av. age*
Principal/ Grade 5A	26	31	28·4	30	30	30·0
Asst. Sec./ Grade 4	35	49	38·7	39	50	43·2
Under Sec./ Grade 3	43	57	46·9	47	58	50·3

The most significant fact to emerge from these figures is that, on average, Diplomatic Service officers in their thirties wait three years longer than their Home Civil Service colleagues for promotion from Principal/Grade 5 to Assistant Secretary/Grade 4 and that, again on average, they are $4\frac{1}{2}$ years older when they achieve that promotion. That gap will never be closed later in their careers. The Duncan Report argued persuasively that the best officers should be able to reach Grade 4 by their mid-thirties, Grade 3 in their early forties and Grades 2 and 1 from their late forties on. The Home Civil Service offers just that prospect; the Diplomatic Service fails to do so by a margin which seems inclined to increase. In such circumstances, dissatisfaction is not surprising.

Inherent in all this is a paradox. Recruits for the British 'diplomatic cadre' are carefully and conscientiously selected; given the assumptions on which it is based, there is no evidence that the selection process is not implemented in the most efficient way. On induction, however, the new entrant joins a service which apparently finds it impossible to give him initial training and extremely difficult to train him in mid-career, partly because of the lack of an adequate manpower margin. Yet that same service, despite in-service selection procedures which, if highly subjective, are generally accepted, has a serious problem of career structure and morale caused by over-population at the most senior levels and by the consequent slowness of promotion, especially for people in their thirties and forties. If it recruits more people in order to build up an adequate manpower margin in the mid-career grades, that will only exacerbate the structural and morale problem, immediately and in the future. There is in fact a danger that the career of the average British diplomat will lead him successively through levels which are marked, first by manpower shortage and later by over-population.

Numerous antidotes have been suggested, most of which are intended to cope both with the problem of slow promotion for people in their thirties and forties and with the linked problem of frustration due to lack of the responsibility which goes with higher rank. On several occasions, for example, it has been proposed that the Diplomatic Service should create a new grade of Junior Counsellor, covering what are now the top years of Grade 5. The attempt to find other antidotes is exemplified by the experimental introduction of a 'team' system in some FCO Departments, mentioned in Chapter 2. None of these ideas seems, however, to offer more than a palliative. They would do nothing to create a manpower margin where it is needed, or to reduce the apparent over-population in Grade 4 and above. Nor in themselves would they accomplish the redistribution of responsibility.

The resolution of the paradox seems, in truth, to demand changes involving the higher levels of the 'diplomatic cadre', at least to the extent needed to accelerate the flow of people through the levels above the Grade 5/Grade 4 demarcation line. In essence, the service structure needs to be made less narrowly pyramidal. Without this it is difficult to see that a solution of the promotion/responsibility problem can be combined with the creation of a manpower margin in Grade 5 and below, which is sufficient for training purposes. Yet the Diplomatic Service, powerfully constrained by the Treasury, is apparently unable to offer to members of Grades 1–4 the possibility of retiring prematurely on terms which they can regard as tolerable, let alone attractive. To quote the Duncan Report on the subject : '. . . a good Diplomatic Service cannot possibly be based on devices for chaining its members to their oars'. This seems to be doubly reasonable when the effect is to force people to row unwillingly on a course which, in terms of morale, career planning and efficiency, seems likely to hazard their vessel.

CONCLUSION

This patchwork account has many obvious deficiencies. We have tried to provide and discuss some of the raw evidence about the British diplomat's educational background, his recruitment, his training and the structure of his career. Even in these areas, we have said far less than we should, essentially because too few data are available. The Diplomatic Service has been studied on numerous occasions by officially-sponsored but external bodies : the Duncan Committee, the Plowden Committee and their predecessors. But, with the slight exception of some material in the Duncan Report, systematic data collection and quantitative methodology have not figured in the reports made by these bodies, from whose composition social scientists have been generally absent. Nevertheless, some evidential basis has been constructed and some issues raised, even if much of the evidence is necessarily impressionistic and suffers from over-generalisation.

We have drawn attention first of all to the dual role that is expected of British diplomats : staffing the missions abroad, and manning the FCO desks at home. We have commented on the connection between this duality and the 'generalist' emphasis which permeates so much that the Diplomatic Service does. We have shown how this generalist trend is reflected in recruitment, selection and promotion, and in the almost total absence of training (other than language training). We have contrasted this anti-specialist bias with the contention that there are in fact particular disciplines which are especially relevant to the work of a foreign service officer. We have pointed out that, even if the latter contention came to prevail, the small personnel margin available for mid-career training would make it difficult to inject new or more specific skills into the upper levels of the Diplomatic Service. Nor would the Service find it easy, as an alternative, to exploit direct exchanges with business, the Home Civil Service or the academic world, since lateral entry is virtually unknown.

We have once again documented the extent to which the Service looks to Oxbridge and to the public schools to fill its ranks. The fact that this dependence is diminishing highlights some of the other, subtler ways in which the Service finds it possible and desirable to perpetuate its own norms: the considerable elements of subjectivity in the selection and promotion processes and the vagueness of the character qualities to which more importance is given than to any academic discipline. We have indicated that there are advantages, but also risks, in perpetuating a cadre that is so inward-looking in its expectations and so adherent to the implied standards of international diplomatic circles.

We have gone on to mention the socialising pressures which affect British diplomats at home and abroad. We have also pointed out how the rotation of postings is expected to produce loyalty and a corporate spirit, as well as to build up a varied fund of experience. Some degree of functional or geographical specialisation is possible, but is regarded as relatively incidental. The service structure or manning schedule is narrowly pyramidal and, in spite of various measures taken, is likely to continue to frustrate the ambitious – the more so under conditions of diminishing global responsibilities.

Diplomats in many countries have often been perceived as a highly 'traditional' group, preserving customs and attitudes which appear archaic. There are obvious dangers in this. In the first place, accelerating societal change may not be matched by an acceleration of the process by which international diplomatic norms are evolved. In other words, diplomats, especially in countries where the pace of societal change is high, may tend to fall further behind the standards accepted by their own national societies. In the second place, diplomacy may come to appear as a refuge for nostalgia, or as an attractive haven for those who seek some shelter from the pressures within national societies. If so, then some diplomatic services may be inclined to regard themselves as bastions against the hectic flood of societal change. Such a situation might breed strong feelings of moral rectitude and simple self-satisfaction, but it would not be calculated to make a diplomatic service an effective instrument of a democratic government.

It would be wrong to imply that the British Diplomatic Service seems to fit such a description or that British diplomats seem to fall into such a category. In some ways, however, a danger may exist. There is, as there has always been, a traditional image of the British diplomat, serving as material for satirists and sometimes for social scientists. The very existence of the image may have some influence not only on British society's perception of its diplomats but also on the Diplomatic Service's perception of itself. It may thus affect recruiting, which must always reflect in some degree the expectations of potential candidates for entry. It may also affect the Diplomatic Service's internal processes, including processes of selection and training, and assessment for posting and promotion, especially as we have seen at the more senior levels. That in turn may have the effect of accentuating the public image of the Service, and thus of influencing the composition of the candidates from whom new entrants must be selected. A circular process to which the Diplomatic Service is not immune, could thus be set in motion.

The alleged inclination of the British Diplomatic Service to consider that it has some national monopoly of expertise in international affairs has often been criticised, especially of course by academic teachers of international relations. The divorce is by no means complete, and the gap between the professional diplomatists and the academic specialists is being crossed with increasing frequency. It is still, however, a gap.

The characteristic tendency of the mythically typical British diplomat to assume a great complexity in international affairs is possibly the most important part of his attitudinal make-up. It leads him to emphasise pragmatism, caution and flexibility, and often to do so in reaction to the analyses made by other groups with an interest in foreign policy. Not only his background and experience but also the balancing role he finds himself called upon to play within his own society and government incline him to regard himself as an expert whose primary task is to moderate, to qualify, to differentiate. His dominant concern for pragmatism and his strong dislike of general premises are felt to be necessary as an antidote to other factors which tend to err in the opposite direction.

It is in fact exactly the qualities of pragmatism, caution and articulateness which appear to prompt much of the praise given to the British diplomat and which he, possibly encouraged by that praise, appears to value most highly in himself. As ever, it is also the malignant reflections of these qualities – lack of principle, pusillanimity and glibness – which are commonly charged against him by his critics. Merely to list the qualities tells us little therefore about the answer to one final question : how good is the British diplomat?

To this question there is no simple answer, not only because the typical does not exist or because our data are insufficient but also because there is no role definition and no single system of standards by which 'goodness' can be measured. Using a personnel management model, for example, might lead us to ask about selection, training, career planning, promotion, mobility, service structure and morale. Judged on this basis, the British diplomat is good in some areas but much less good in others. Using a bureaucratic efficiency model, covering information processing, decision readiness, crisis management and the effectiveness of co-ordination and correlation, would probably produce a parallel answer, although it is just in these areas that the available data are most clearly inadequate. Using a 'peace oriented' model, however, would force us to ask quite different questions. How good is the British diplomat likely to be at avoiding, preventing, containing or resolving conflict? How much is he inclined to contribute to the strengthening of international organisations? What are his attitudes to sanctions, threats and power? To these questions, we do not have even impressionistic answers. Yet it is important that they should be raised.

A quite separate method would be to accept the standards set by diplomats themselves as those by which the British diplomat is to be judged. This might entail adopting the subject's personal and institutional standards, and asking how well British diplomats achieve their own stated objectives. Within narrow limits, the Duncan Committee followed that course. Alternatively, it might entail identifying and applying standards set by the international class of diplomats – the collective norms of international diplomacy already mentioned. Obviously, however, these techniques would have serious disadvantages, not the least of which is that they would effectively exclude any evaluation of the diplomatic norms themselves.

Finally, there is the *comparative approach*, as used in the social sciences. This would require intensive studies of a number of Ministries of Foreign Affairs and of their Foreign Services, including the British. The purpose of such studies would not really be to prepare a kind of 'league table' of Foreign Service qualities and abilities, but rather to determine and explain the links between such services, their Ministries, and the types of foreign policy outputs which their interactions produce, in quantitative terms. This is no doubt an ambitious proposal but one that is not beyond the bounds of present-day knowledge and techniques.

REFERENCES

[1] The possible exceptions are : Galtung, J. and M. Holmboe Ruge, 'Patterns of Diplomacy. A Study of Recruitment and Career Patterns in Norwegian Diplomacy' in *Journal of Peace Research* 2 (1965) pp. 101–35; Niezing, J., 'Diplomatie : een organisatie in beweging (II) : enig statistisch material m.b.t. de Nederlands buitlandse dienst', *Acta Politica* (Amsterdam), Vol. IV, No. 3.

[2] *Report of the Review Committee on Overseas Representation 1968–69* (Cmnd. 4107) (London, HMSO, July 1969).

[3] This definition covers Grades 1, 2, 3, 4, 5, 6, 7A, 7E and 8 of Her Majesty's Diplomatic Service. Not every individual in these Grades will bear one of the titles mentioned when abroad. In particular, those engaged in consular duties will bear the titles of Consul-General, Consul and Vice-Consul. Consular officials are not, however, accredited, in their consular capacity, to a national government, and are not concerned with representational diplomacy, in the sense of representing the policies and views of one sovereign government to another.

[4] The Administrative and Executive streams cover all grades from Grade 9 upwards. In general, however, the term 'diplomatic cadre' is used in this chapter to describe members of Grade 8 upwards.

[5] The major exception is in the case of Arabic, training in which is given throughout at the Middle East Centre for Arab Studies (MECAS), run by the Diplomatic Service in the Lebanon. Japanese training begins at Sheffield. Chinese training may be conducted throughout in Hong Kong.

[6] One of the 'real-life' stories in the Diplomatic Service's booklet of advice to graduates is of an Oxford graduate, with a degree in Classical Arabic, who was sent to learn colloquial Arabic as a student for six months on entry and thereafter, without further training or experience, put in charge of a diplomatic post in the Persian Gulf.

[7] The only exception is when a member of the 'diplomatic cadre' proposes to marry someone who is not a British subject, in which case he must first obtain formal permission. Within the obvious limits of security, this permission is readily given, although it will often be the case that he will not thereafter be posted to the country of his wife's origin.

[8] *Her Majesty's Diplomatic Service* (HMSO 1970) pp. 2, 5.

BIBLIOGRAPHY

Busk, Donald – *The Craft of Diplomacy: Mechanics and Development of National Representation Overseas* (London: Pall Mall 1967).

Report of the Review Committee on Overseas Representation 1968–69 (The Duncan Report) HMSO, Cmnd. 4107.

Vital, David – *The Making of British Foreign Policy* (London, 1968).

Chapman, Richard A. – *The Higher Civil Service in Britain* (Constable, 1970).

See also references to Chapter 2.

4 Policy Formulation and Planning*

MICHAEL KENT O'LEARY

THE NATURE OF PLANNING

'To PLAN', according to one definition offered by *The Concise Oxford Dictionary*, means 'to scheme'. 'To scheme', says the same source, means to make plans in a 'secret or underhand way'. From an etymological standpoint therefore it would appear that the function of planning is quite consistent with the practice of diplomacy, at least with the prevailing image of that clandestine profession. It is more than a little surprising therefore to find that foreign ministries on the whole have paid little formal, explicit attention to planning activities in their normal allocation of responsibilities. Few foreign ministries in the world today contain planning sections. And in those services which do have them one finds that the operations are rather recently organised, that they are generally quite small relative to the total personnel of the ministry in which they are embedded, and that their operations are often poorly integrated with the other tasks which the ministry performs.

Much of this anomaly of course is explained by the fact that the overwhelming tradition of diplomacy charges each individual practitioner to be his own planner. Every ancient and contem-

* I am deeply indebted to the courtesy of officials of the Foreign and Commonwealth Office who shared their thoughts with me in confidential interviews. I also wish to record my appreciation for assistance received as a Research Fellow of the North Atlantic Treaty Organisation and, on a different occasion, as a Visiting Scholar at the Institute for Peace and Conflict Research, Copenhagen, under the sponsorship of the Dansk Udenrigspolitisk Institut.

porary discussion of the subject would not even classify decision-making as diplomacy if it did not involve evaluating risks and benefits inherent in every alternative action considered, not excluding the responses of other nation-states which are deemed likely to be provoked by the actions of one's own state. The dominant notion that the professional diplomat should be a well-rounded 'generalist' is one aspect of this notion that each diplomat should be his own planner.

It is also true of course that only recently has society divided its labours in such specialised fashion as to produce professionals whose acknowledged expertise is planning. Accordingly, contemporary relevance requires that we examine diplomacy not in relation to the more or less intuitive attempts to anticipate the results of any course of action – which diplomats have always made – but to comment on the juxtaposition of modern diplomacy with modern planning, with its panoply of specialised procedures and techniques by which its practitioners establish their claim to make a distinct and important contribution to our highly complex society.

Professional planning activities in different fields of government, in business, and in other private sectors of society demonstrate a wide variety of procedures more or less appropriate to the substantive areas with which they are concerned. But at a very general level we may suggest that professional planning always includes a minimal core of similar activities which can be identified across the wide range of substantive fields in which they are carried out.

In this essay we shall consider the fundamental nature of formal planning in three categories : formulating goals, selecting means, and monitoring policy. Let us briefly define each of these activities in turn, before evaluating their relationship to modern diplomacy.

Formulating goals
This is at once the most fundamental and most elusive element of the planning process. Without some notion of what state of affairs a group wishes to bring about, the concept of planning is meaningless. At the same time however the specification of goals may be one of the most difficult enterprises to which a group can devote itself. We can summarise this difficulty by advancing

two conflicting propositions. On the one hand, the more that the goals of a group are set in the most general terms, the easier it is to secure consensus within the group. On the other hand, the more that goals are stated in their most general form, the more difficult it is to fashion policies appropriate to attaining goals. The degree of specificity in elaborating goals is, therefore, a matter of art and judgement relating not merely to notions about some general criteria of efficiency in carrying out policy, but also relating in important ways to the harmony and very integrity of the group itself.

Selecting means

The problem of selecting appropriate means to secure a desired sets of goals is in many ways a reflection of the problem of the level of generality in establishing goals. And, indeed, the planner's need to specify alternative sets of means is a further complication in the problem of establishing goals. For the planner's concern will be to be as precise as possible in defining goals in order that he may be as precise as possible in setting forth the proper means. A very general statement of goals allows for a multitude of different means to achieve the desired end, but at the same time provides the planner with what will seem to him an insufficient basis for selecting the appropriate means. Given the interests of the planner we can see that the planning process tends to impose upon the group doing the planning a movement towards specificity in both the goals set forth and the means selected to achieve them.

Monitoring policy

Once an acceptable solution has been achieved for the first two steps in planning, the task then becomes one of evaluating the extent to which on-going policy is, in fact, consistent with the established plans. This task itself can be subdivided into two subcategories. The planner must ask whether or not the consequences of policy are such as to advance the group towards its desired goals at an acceptable rate. And he must also evaluate the policy decision taken, to see how closely they correspond with that part of the planning process which consisted of selecting appropriate means.

Both these asks are important. Indeed, one of the chief contributions of the formal planning process is that it alerts a decision-making group to attend to both. In one sense it may be correct to say that fully satisfactory evaluation of any on-going policy is impossible without the inter-connected attention to ends and means which it is the role of the formal planner constantly to bear in mind.

One aspect of a complete plan is the sequence of events which must take place in order for the desired goal to be achieved. Without this aspect of a plan in mind, simply noting whether a desired goal is becoming more accessible as a result of policy may prove extremely misleading. Many complex social goals, no matter how constructive, can frequently be achieved only through engaging in some preliminary destructive activities. Without the comprehensive framework which a plan provides, certain short-range activities may appear highly undesirable, no matter how productive they may be in the long run. As Lenin once observed, it may be necessary to break some eggs in order to make an omelette. Accordingly, it may be necessary to be prepared to measure the number of eggs broken before it makes sense to begin trying to count the number of omelettes cooked.

In the same way, a plan must alert the group that the long-run consequences must constantly be kept in mind. Groups all too frequently fall into the pattern of complacently accepting policies which do correspond to some acceptable pattern of procedures, of means utilised, and resources allocated, when such policies may in fact be leading the group in directions which it strongly wishes to avoid.

In summary form then, the consequence of the planning activity for any group which engages in the process is a reduction in ambiguity. The planner will, in so far as he conforms to his normal role, argue for more specificity in formulating goals for the group, more precision in setting forth the alternative means which should be chosen to advance towards the goals, and more sophistication in evaluating on-going policy in terms of correspondence to appropriate means, and in terms of advancement towards longer-range goals.

PLANNING AND DIPLOMACY

The purpose of the rather extended foregoing general introduction is to establish the basis for a fundamental proposition which will be elaborated in the remainder of this essay : The needs and procedures of the formal planner exhibit a marked incompatibility with the needs and procedures of the professional diplomat. Let us consider some of the dimensions of this incompatibility by re-examining the three basic tasks of planning in relation to the general tasks and working style of the diplomat.

Formulating goals

Perhaps one of the chief characteristics of diplomacy and foreign policy of most nations today is the generality and vagueness of the goals they pursue in their foreign policy. It is true enough that diplomatic spokesmen the world over can easily invoke an impressive list of symbols to justify the policies they followed. However, a careful examination of almost all the symbols employed by officials of any nation in the world, not excepting the United Kingdom, shows that the goals articulated are among the most vague and general of all government pronouncements. They refer to idealised states of affairs which are consistent with the dominant values of the nation, they are cast so as to offend as few as possible of the government's citizens, and they are further designed simultaneously to maximise the friendly responses of international allies and the 'benign neglect' of unfriendly forces overseas. The very complexity of the modern societies, such as Britain, which diplomacy is charged with representing and protecting, coupled with the growing complexity of the international system within which diplomacy takes place, all create seemingly irresistible temptations to avoid as much as possible establishing concrete goals for foreign policy. It may in fact be possible to offer a simple proposition on this subject : In establishing foreign policy goals, both professional diplomats and politicians (that is, those most closely associated with the policy-making process) will commit themselves to precise goals only in those cases where they can be almost completely assured that there is no chance of their society's punishing them for failure to achieve the goals which they have publicly committed themselves to achieve. By way of illustration, it is noteworthy that official foreign policy spokesmen are willing to be most precise and clear-cut in discussing foreign policy goals relating to such traditional concerns as the defence of home territory against military attack. For countries such as Britain, leaders can safely associate themselves with this claim for two inter-related reasons : the probability of an attack is so low as to approach zero; and, in the unlikely event of such an attack occurring, citizens are likely to be otherwise occupied than to criticise those leaders whose promises were not kept.

On questions such as national defence, leaders have another reason for their willingness to make precise promises. This is that the fulfilment of the goal is seen as an undifferentiated benefit which can be equally shared by virtually the total population. In the jargon of economics, territorial integrity is a 'public good'. A public good has two chief characteristics : if it is made available to one citizen it is automatically made available to all; and its use by one citizen does not reduce its accessibility by others [1].

There are other areas of discussion in which governments are willing to be relatively precise because they can formulate goals which are perceived by citizens providing similar collective goods. These include the manifestations of symbolic representation which are said to be productive of enhanced prestige for the whole nation, and negotiations looking towards peaceful settlement of international disputes, which likewise provide perceived feelings of security for the entire citizenry.

On other questions governments are inclined to be much more ambiguous in their public pronouncements. Situations where the outcome is much more uncertain and situations where the benefits from a particular policy are much more likely to be to the exclusive benefit of limited sectors of society are the chief occasion for invoking the most general statements of goals. Especially important in this respect is the discussion of economic policy. Thus governments tend to state their objectives in terms of seeking unspecified levels of 'greater prosperity' for the nation, without specifying the levels or detailing which segments of the society are most likely to benefit from the prosperity such increased wealth as is attained.

From most discussion of foreign policy it would be almost impossible to obtain the sorts of specified goals with which the planner can deal professionally. In most cases governments will refuse to commit themselves to foreign policy goals of a sufficiently precise nature to permit the planner to deal with them. In the few cases where governments are willing to specify precisely what their goals are, the outcome is so certain that further planning is usually unnecessary.

Selecting means

One problem of selecting appropriate means for professional planning is clearly implied by the foregoing discussion. Without clear-cut goals, the selection of means cannot be accomplished in any reliable fashion. When the goals are vague enough it becomes nearly impossible to rule out any proposed policy as being incompatible with the end which is sought. This is, of course, one reason for the attractiveness of vaguely-stated goals. But at the same time this vagueness prevents the useful systematic selection of appropriate means, which is one of the chief skills the professional planner brings to the policy-making process.

The diplomatic enterprise presents still another problem in the planner's attempt to select appropriate means to carry policy towards a desired state of affairs. This is the fact that the burden of history has moulded most diplomatic activity into a highly structured series of procedures. Whom to consult, the channels by which to issue communications, sources of information – these and many more constituents of complex decision-making are precribed for the diplomat either by formal orders or (more importantly, perhaps) by precedent and the current practices of his bureaucratic peers.

This tendency for the professional diplomat to be guided by precedent in the means he chooses by which to carry forth his policy is scarcely a new phenomenon, being one of the most persistent characteristics of the diplomatic craft. It does, however, have especially important consequences in today's world. For today, as never before, the diplomat must expend extraordinary effort to see that the new trends, developments and inventions set loose in the modern world are so controlled that they generate their impact upon individuals only through the mediation of the traditional organisation of the nation state. And most importantly they must see to it that those transactions across national boundaries are controlled by and made to support, the established system of nation states.

In this effort to channel new developments into traditional social patterns, one must give high credit to the professional diplomats, political leaders and their collaborators, who have managed so successfully in this effort to channel new developments into traditional social patterns. They have had to counter profound forces working against the rationale of traditional nation-state behaviour. As the political scientist John Herz once pointed out, the territorial state no longer comes close to serving its original purposes as a meaningful social unit by which citizens can fulfil their traditional functions of economic organisation, self-defence, and ideological self-definition [2]. These objective changes have produced quite reasonable deductions of the demise of the nation state as inappropriate, including prophecies of such utopias as the 'global village' foretold by Marshall McLuhan [3]. Nevertheless the old system still survives. Some may speak with horror and wonder of the potentials of the work of modern man which transcend even the most well-established national boundaries – from the potential of a world-wide responsive community of mankind, to a world-wide exploitation of resources which would benefit all citizens of the globe, to the apocalyptic vision of a world-wide battlefield of universal destruction which could arise from the unleashing of military technology. But for the average citizen, in Britain no less than other nations, his view of the world, his access to values of wealth and well-being, and his feelings of physical security are still, like the life of T. S. Eliot's character, doled out with 'coffee spoons', by the venerable nation state. As we shall argue below, the Foreign Ministry can no longer count on a monopoly of control in the management of foreign relations. But what is most important here is that the chief competitors for this managerial function come from other power centres in the nation state which increasingly claim a share in shaping state policies according to their own interests. From the point of view of systematic planning, the nearly incomprehensible increase in potential means for human interaction has made only the slightest of dents upon the traditional procedures by which peoples deal with one another through the medium of their national governments.

Monitoring policy
The third of the planner's fundamental tasks, monitoring the progress of policy, points up further incompatibilities with conventional diplomatic practice. For all practical purposes, it is nearly impossible to make reliable assessments of the success of most foreign policy endeavours in the world today. One need only look at the question of how well the United Kingdom has adapted itself to changing international power relations to document this

difficulty of reliably assessing policy. It is possible to find scholars possessing every sign of objectivity and erudition who take diametrically opposed positions on this question. Some say that policy in the post-war world is an example of the classic ability of the British to appreciate and act effectively in changing international circumstances; others to the contrary, present a full indictment of errors and omissions in recent international policy.

It is a question of no small interest, but of too great complexity for discussion here, as to how officials both benefit and suffer from this unavailability of evidence and indicators which all observers will accept as valid and reliable. But the lack of such indicators is quite clear. And equally clear is the fact that their lack gravely impedes any attempt at serious policy-planning. Given the practice of producing vague symbolic goals as the purpose of policy, the so-called monitoring phase of planning is reduced to nothing more than discussions of whether or not a current set of symbols is consistent with another prior set of symbols. This degenerate form of monitoring policy can be clearly seen in the United States where, for example, it is taken to be a matter of some concern whether or not a collection of words uttered by an incumbent President concerning Latin America is consistent with another collection of words on the same subject uttered over 100 years ago by President James Monroe. The British style of diplomacy has perhaps shown less inclination towards the enunciation of doctrines, and in consequence such verbal game-playing is less common. But this characteristic, however desirable in some respects, does not do anything to render policy more easily monitored and evaluated.

One might suppose that these difficulties of monitoring policy have become more difficult with the passage of time. And they are consequently likely to become more, rather than less, severe. In earlier days foreign policy operated upon much more concrete sets of values, such as the acquisition and protection of territory; furthermore, there were much more firm guidelines as to what constituted acceptable and unacceptable regimes in other states. These conditions made it much easier to assess the desirable and undesirable consequences, of foreign political actions.

The world today is 'bigger', in the sense that there exist more independent national actors, and it is also more dangerous. But the former problem can be handled by the increase in information-processing capabilities. And the latter situation is, unhappily, not one which points to any well-defined course of action. A problem which is both more pertinent to national policies and also which has so far evaded solution by available means is what might be termed the increasing multi-dimensionality of foreign policy. The manifold nuances of military, economic, ideological and other relations among states provide so many opportunities for gains and losses that consensual standards of gains and losses are impossible to come by.

In one of his many brilliant insights into the nature of collective decision-making, Thomas Schelling has called attention to the importance of what he calls 'focal-points' – those elements in the world which two contending parties can agree upon as standards for determining gains and losses [4]. Without such consensual currency of decision-making it becomes extremely difficult to achieve agreements, strike bargains, or determine the nature of one's gains and losses in a conflict – in short to evaluate the consequences of one's policies. The acquisition and loss of territory once provided such decisional currency in the realm of foreign policy, as did the maintenance or toppling of legitimate monarchies. But one would be hard pressed to suggest the basis of such currency of decision-making relevant to foreign policy.

We have so far suggested that the context and practice of modern diplomacy in an established state such as Britain leads to fundamental incompatibilities between the foreign policy-maker and the planner's three principal tasks of goal formulation, selection of means, and the monitoring of on-going activities. We should not leave this subject without considering one much broader reason for the incompatibility between formal planning and diplomacy. This reason transcends the detailed procedures in which the planner engages in the pursuance of his job, and relates instead to the general service which the planner attempts to provide for society, or some segment of it. This broad purpose may be simply stated as the reduction of ambiguity.

Any identifiable social group must be most essentially concerned with the relationship between its own integrity and the environment – always complex and uncertain, frequently hostile – which surrounds the group. Every political group from the most narrowly-concerned interest association to the multi-faced nation state must, whatever the nature of its ultimate substantive objectives, see to it that a proper adaptive relationship to its environment is maintained. Stated briefly, this adaptive balance includes protecting the clarity of boundaries between the group and its environment, the maintenance of the group's structural forms, and wherever possible, an increased opportunity for the group's membership to extract desired values from the environment [5].

When we conceive of foreign policy according to this formulation, we must look at some age-old processes in quite a new light. For according to this notion the usual topics of foreign policy – diplomatic bargaining, military strategy and operations, economic policy, and the like – are not the end product of a social process as they are usually considered to be. Instead they are an intermediate step of a process which can be fully understood only by assessing what impact they have upon all or part of the nation originating the foreign policy in the first place.

In foreign policy as in other areas of social behaviour, a threatening and ambiguous environment stands as a formidable barrier to the accomplishment of both the immediate adaptative goals of collective survival, as well as any substantive purposes which the group is seeking. Accordingly a large measure of any group's relations with its surroundings must be evaluated in terms of how these relationships function in reducing the ambiguity in the environment. Depending upon the circumstances such ambiguity-reduction may occur in widely varying forms of co-operation and conflict with elements in the environment, and may equally range from attempting to enforce decisions upon the environment to simple measures of gathering objective information about the state of the surrounding world.

This vital social need, all the more important when the group exists in a complex social system, is one of the chief *raisons d'être* of the professional planner. He brings to his task an expert repertoire by which he can help his group to comprehend its environment and deal with its complexities. And, most significantly for our present purposes, this general social function of the planner also points out the fundamental distinction between him and the diplomat. For the professional diplomat, unlike nearly every member of a national society, not only is more tolerant of the international ambiguity in which his nation is embedded, but in fact depends upon that very ambiguity of environment as the principal justification of his profession.

The specialised diplomatic function is valued only in so far as both leader and ordinary citizen have resigned themselves to the presistent intractability of the international environment in which they must live. We can point to a duality of thought shared by all those who, whether leader or follower, only episodically turn to problems of foreign policy, in contrast to diplomats, who earn their livelihood from it. On the one hand non-professionals are quick to propose 'solutions' to foreign policy problems; on the other hand, these same groups tacitly acknowledge the futility of 'solutions' by relying upon diplomats to see them through the dangers of foreign policy by the pragmatic, short-run, marginal gains and losses so long characteristic of diplomatic relations. There is scarcely any political group which fails to find fault with the way in which professional diplomats conduct the affairs of the nation. The manifest content of such criticisms reflect of course the political preferences of the group expressing them. But such criticisms, whether from left or right, whether from economic interest or highly ideological preference, all contain a common theme : a distaste for the continued ambiguity, uncertainty, and lack of clear-cut results which characterise the professionals' conduct of international relations.

Without this generally acknowledged, if disliked, ambiguity as a feature of the international environment, the professional diplomat would find it difficult to justify his job. Accordingly, it is hardly surprising to suggest a fundamental irreconcilability of purpose between the diplomat and the professional planner, who would prefer to do as much as possible to reduce ambiguity in the international social context of the nation.

It may bear emphasising that there is not the slightest suggestion that the diplomat is motivated by unworthy impulses in this regard or that the diplomat is acting differently from any members of a well-defined group in or out of government. All available evidence about collective behaviour supports the idea that individuals selectively perceive and evaluate the 'real world' in accordance with the norms and interests of these groups which are most salient to them. In evaluating policy neither a high level of ambiguity nor its absence can be, in the abstract, held up as preferable – especially so since in some cases ambiguity may be reduced only at the expense of some highly prized values.

The notion is merely that diplomats, like members of many

groups in society, are able to appreciate how some forms of international dealings are more advantageous to them than others. And further, we should not be surprised if they tend to prefer those sorts of dealings which are more rather than less advantageous. If this self-interest makes them suspicious of certain modern practices which many people deem liberal and progressive – such as the conduct of international affairs by means of public, quasi-parliamentary institutions – it also makes them less eager than others to engage in crusades designed to eliminate intolerable elements of the world. If a tolerance for ambiguity sometimes leads to a maddening lack of decisiveness and lack of enthusiasm about working for clear-cut solutions to problems, we might observe that few people look with favour upon all state policies designed as decisive, or 'final' solutions to the ills of the world.

If, as has been argued, the decision-making style of the diplomat is so fundamentally out of harmony with the implications of formal planning, what, then, is the rationale for a formal planning operation as presently existing in the Foreign and Commonwealth Office? What sorts of functions may it perform for what must be such an unwilling client?

We should note, first of all, a suspicion that some of the motive for establishing a formal planning section may not be entirely unrelated to considerations of public relations. Formal planning has come to be one of the bench-marks of modernity and efficiency in both business and government. One would hardly be surprised to find a ministry devoted to performing one of the most ancient of government arts to be concerned about its general relevance in the modern age. Nor would it be surprising for such a ministry to equip itself with at least the forms of modern decision-making techniques.

But aside from this observation (both cynical and unproved) we can note at least two functions by which foreign office personnel might serve not only their own ministry, but also the government and society at large. The first of these is, to some extent, already being performed by the planning section of the FCO. It is the suggestion that a planning section can serve as the chief centre for promoting interchanges between ministry officials and those in the academic community who specialise in international affairs. It must be acknowledged that effecting a liaison between policy makers and intellectuals is not unlike promoting a marriage between a reluctant virgin and a suitor of doubtful potency. But it nevertheless seems that whatever the difficulties, the potential benefits are worth the price. Others have discussed the limited, but not inconsequential, benefits which might accrue to the policy-making process from greater acquaintance with members of the relevant intellectual community – social scientists as well as the historians and area specialists who are more commonly consulted. It should also be made explicit that the more theory-minded scholars should be able to derive equal advantages from increased interchanges. The extent to which intellectuals can and should become involved with policy-making activities and still maintain the desirable stance of independence poses problems which are difficult, although not necessarily insurmountable. Perhaps a first step in this regard is to consider new forms of exchanges between officials and scholars. It may be, for example, that if scholars of one nation could consult with policy-makers of another nation, this would alleviate some of the anxieties about the loss of critical independence.

PLANNING THE FCO's FUTURE

A final observation on possible diplomatic planning is the need for the foreign service to take a hard look at its own future. It might be understandable that the recommendations of the Plowden Report, which in essence urged a continuation of the diplomatic service at about the same levels, would lead to re-assurance about the future of the career service [6]. However, the more recent Duncan Report must certainly cast aside such optimistic feelings [7]. This is especially so with respect to its harsh call for reduction in the future size of the diplomatic service. Despite the chilling recommendations of that document, one suspects that even the Duncan Report may not have dealt with the full nature of the problem facing the future of Britain's diplomatic service. For that report advocated drastic cuts in the foreign service largely with respect to a fair and efficient administrative technique for dealing with redundancy. In terms of the quality, as opposed to quantity, of the diplomatic service the Duncan Report only slightly modified the recommendations of the Plowden Committee.

While the Plowden group call for 'more of the same', Duncan differs by calling in essence for 'less of the same'. It assumes that the future career diplomatic service will be most needed in those areas of the world where Britain's relations will be the closest and most important – the so-called 'Area of Concentration' which is defined by the Duncan Committee as North America plus the major industrialised countries of Western Europe [8]. It is possible to agree with this major premise of the report – that this will be the primary interest of Britain into the 1970's and beyond – without accepting the conclusion that the present skills of career diplomats will be highly valued in Britain's relations with these nations. For it is important to note that the 'Area of Concentration' is defined as that group of countries which must co-ordinate with one another in the conduct of *domestic* policies. The implication of this criterion is that the relations among these countries will be guided by a need to communicate and negotiate with respect to financial and commercial matters, labour questions, social services, and other aspects of internal governmental policy. This brings into question the Duncan Committee's conclusion that standard diplomatic representation in the 'Area of Concentration' will continue to be important.

The history of the six Common Market countries certainly casts doubt upon this conclusion. Intensification of relations has occurred in the functional, technical, spheres among the Six to the exclusion, and over the objections, of the professional diplomats of the nations involved. One study of international transactions has shown that as little as five years after the signing of the Treaty of Rome, proportionate economic transactions among European nations were much higher than world averages, but that proportionate levels of formal diplomatic exchanges among the same nations were much lower than world averages [9].

What this means is that within the 'Area of Concentration' – where more than 40% of Britain's professional diplomats are presently stationed – conditions may be changing so as to imply either a radically altered role for the foreign ministry, a radically reduced role, or possibly both. It would therefore seem the better part of bureaucratic wisdom not only to consider, as the Duncan Committee suggests, ways of justly and efficiently dealing with the forthcoming problem of redundancy of personnel, but to go beyond Duncan and consider more carefully the problem of incorporating a wide range of substantive domestic policy concerns within the practices of diplomacy. Planning for the future on such questions means introducing specialised areas of expertise into the foreign service, rendering support for the international activities of various home ministries, drawing upon home services for necessary knowledge and skills, and providing for effective overseas representation of the interests of ministries concerned with domestic policy. It does not seem unreasonable to suggest that the most salient aspects of Britain's international environment are so changing that planning in these fields is not merely a question of introducing marginal improvements into the operation of the foreign ministry, but rather a matter of the continuation of the ministry as a vital part of the British government.

REFERENCES

[1] See the stimulating discussion of this concept as it applies to politics generally in Mancur Olsen, Jr., *The Logic of Collective Action* (Cambridge, Mass.: Harvard University Press, 1965).

[2] John H. Herz, *International Politics in the Atomic Age* (New York: Columbia University Press, 1951).

[3] Marshall McLuhan, *Understanding Media* (New York: McGraw-Hill, 1964); and Marshall McLuhan and Quentin Fiore, *War and Peace in the Global Village* (New York: McGraw-Hill, 1968).

[4] Thomas Schelling, *The Strategy of Conflict* (New York: Oxford University Press, 1960).

[5] On the concept of adaptation as a basis for understanding foreign policy, see James Rosenau, *The Adaptation of National Societies: A Theory of Political System Behaviour and Transformation* (New York: McCaleb-Seiler Publishing Company, 1970).

[6] *Report of the Committee on Representational Service Overseas, 1962–63* (HMSO 1964. Cmnd. 2276). The Plowden Committee is most explicitly antagonistic to formal planning in the service of diplomacy. For a discussion of this and other biases in the Plowden Report, see Michael Banks, 'Profes-

sionalism in the Conduct of Foreign Policy', *International Affairs*, 44 (October 1968), 720–734.

[7] *Report of the Review Committee on Overseas Representation 1968–1969* (HMSO 1969. Cmnd. 4107).
[8] ibid., p. 12.
[9] Steven J. Brams, 'A Note on the Cosmopolitanism of World Regions', *Journal of Peace Research*, No. 1 (1968), pp. 87–95.

B The Foreign and Commonwealth Office and the Central Machinery: Politics, Economics and Defence

5 The Cabinet and Foreign Policy

DONALD G. BISHOP

THE CABINET plays a significant role in the management of external affairs in any country which uses the parliamentary system of government. In Great Britain this is particularly true.

What is the role of the Cabinet? How does it do its work? A common image of the British Cabinet is that of a group of senior politicians waiting in anticipation of problems arising, so that they can meet, exercise their individual judgements, and arrive at a common decision which thus becomes the Government's policy, for which they all will be held collectively responsible. In 1941 Churchill and Roosevelt met at Argentia and wrote the Atlantic Charter; British approval was thought to necessitate Cabinet action. Attlee, then Deputy Prime Minister, seemed to verify this image of the Cabinet when he wrote, 'I got a telephone call at two o'clock in the morning. . . . I called a Cabinet at 3 o'clock . . . and by four we were able to send our reply' [1]. But problems do not always arise this way, and such tidy decisions are not always possible. It is the purpose of this chapter to examine certain aspects of the Cabinet's part in the management of Britain's external affairs.

CONSULTATION WITHIN THE CABINET

One of the Cabinet's chief functions is to serve as a co-ordinating body, to draw together the ideas of the members and, whenever possible, secure agreement. This necessity for co-ordination is particularly important in the field of external relations; the Foreign Office has no monopoly over the control of British relations with other governments; there is hardly a ministry in the Cabinet which is not directly concerned with these relations.

The formal starting-point is the Foreign Office, which either formulates a policy or designates another administrative agency to do so. In the former case, the goal is to obtain a 'Foreign Office policy'. As we have seen in other chapters, the officials in the Foreign Office are constantly wrestling with each other to develop 'positions' or policies which will in their view best protect British interests in the international situations under consideration. Much intra-ministry co-ordination is necessary before they can do this. One former Foreign Secretary has written that 'the Foreign Office is equipped to give the best information, the best of briefing on any international issue. . . . But what bothered me . . . was . . . that it was they who were deciding the areas I should be briefed about, and I quickly became aware that, unless I was very determined, I would inevitably become the purveyor of views already formed in the Office' [2]. The political officers of the Foreign Office also participate in this process. These men, headed by the Secretary of State for Foreign and Commonwealth Affairs (the Foreign Secretary) are temporarily in charge of the ministry, politically and legally responsible to the Government and to the people's representatives in Parliament for the policies advocated by the Foreign Office. Since these political officers are not normally familiar with the substance of Foreign Office problems – there are notable exceptions such as Anthony Eden after the first few years of his incumbency as Foreign Secretary – they must necessarily rely on their professional advisers for proposals, for the evaluation of alternatives, and for the making of decisions. When the officials have reached general agreement on the substance of the proposal and when the political officers have considered its political effect, then there is a Foreign Office policy, ready to be launched forth to see if other interested ministries will also agree, so that a single co-ordinated Government policy can then be announced.

There has long been a special need for co-ordination between the Foreign Office, the India Office, and the Colonial Office, which was not lessened when the India and Colonial Offices were brought together to form the Commonwealth Relations Office.

Only since 1968 however have the Foreign and Commonwealth offices been unified into a single Foreign and Commonwealth Office; previously they dealt with the same problems but from different viewpoints.

The British Treasury has been a traditional co-ordinating agency, with review control over ministerial expenditures and activities. 'A Foreign Secretary and a Chancellor of the Exchequer, the Prime Minister's two principal colleagues, are apt to be thrown together, particularly if the Prime Minister is holding the reins very loosely' [3].

There is an obvious relationship between foreign and defence policy. Eden has written that 'Defence and foreign policy had to be considered together and they formed the chief topic of conversation between Sir Winston Churchill and myself in sixteen years' [4]. In the face of a reduction in British military strength during the inter-war years, every important foreign policy decision was affected. 'No British Foreign Secretary could hope to succeed when other governments had begun to question our influence in the world' [5]. In 1956, a critical year for Britain, the Prime Minister met in July with some close colleagues to discuss defence policy; among the items considered were : the forces for limited war and internal security, military facilities in the Middle East and Far East, non-military measures in the Middle East, non-military measures in South-east Asia, and Antarctica. It would be difficult to say whether these discussions dealt mainly with defence or foreign affairs.

The co-ordination of military and foreign policy is often difficult. Inter-service rivalries are one reason. Defence departments have had, on occasion, to be persuaded to co-operate with each other and with such as the Foreign, Colonial, and India offices. Attlee has referred to the story that in the mid-1930s, 'The Chiefs of Staff weren't on speaking terms, which was rather important if you were trying to plan a unified defence system' [6] – or foreign policy. There was a long-standing controversy in this same period between the Air Ministry and the Foreign Office, with each relying on its own sources of information about German air strength. 'This disagreement was the cause of much argument in the Cabinet and before ministerial committees' [7]. In 1915 Lord Kitchener, at the War Office, said that it was 'repugnant to him to have to reveal military secrets to twenty-three gentlemen with whom he was barely acquainted' [8]). No such attitude seems possible in recent years, although repeatedly Foreign Secretaries and Defence Ministers have complained of not being adequately informed about the other's activities and intentions.

Likewise, the work of the Foreign Office and the Board of Trade have long overlapped. Britain must trade if the people are to eat; this requires friendly political relations. The necessity for co-ordination between these two bodies was clear in 1935–36 when the questions of imposing and, later, removing economic sanctions against Italy were being discussed. In 1956 the precarious state of Britain's balance of payments also influenced Cabinet decisions as when, on November 6, the Treasury found it could not support the pound at the current exchange rate unless it could secure a loan from the International Monetary Fund. The Cabinet was told that the loan could be made available only if the United Nations cease-fire proposals were accepted by midnight. 'There seems little doubt that this bleak intelligence . . . almost instantaneously convinced everyone' [9].

The necessity for co-ordination has greatly increased in the past quarter century because of British membership in such international organisations as the United Nations and NATO. Since such bodies are available as instruments of British diplomacy and as forums for presenting British views, it is imperative that the British Government have clear and consistent policies whenever possible. This is not easy, in view of the nearly-universal membership of the United Nations and the wide variety of topics with which various UN bodies deal.

The main responsibility for relations between the United Kingdom Government and the United Nations lies with the Foreign and Commonwealth Office, but several other ministries are actively interested, especially in the case of the specialised agencies. Policy is always cleared horizontally before being sent up the chain of command. First a department view is obtained; this is discussed with other departments of the Foreign Office. When the latter's position is established, this must be modified, when necessary, after consultation with other ministries. The Treasury must be consulted on all financial and budgetary matters. The result is a Government view for which the Cabinet is collectively responsible, and instructions can then be forwarded to the United Kingdom Permanent Mission at the United Nations.*

In 1946 a Steering Committee on International Organisations was created to co-ordinate British policies presented in the various UN bodies, but this committee has recently been used mainly as a clearing-house for information rather than as a policy-co-ordinating body.

Whenever possible, the consultation is done informally rather than in Cabinet meetings. Prior to their integration, for example, there was close consultation between the Foreign Office and the Commonwealth Relations Office on the Rhodesian question, between the Foreign Office and the Colonial Office on matters involving dependent territories in the United Nations, and between all three offices on the trusteeship of Nauru because that territory was jointly administered by Australia and New Zealand. The Foreign Office has been charged with policy-formulation on the military aspects of atomic energy, conventional and atomic disarmament (yet the Minister of State for Disarmament has handled the question of how the United Kingdom should vote in New York or Geneva), and outer space problems. The Minister of Defence plays an important role in matters relating to the military aspects of both atomic energy and disarmament; on many questions this ministry holds an effective veto on policy-decisions.

The Board of Trade (now part of the Department of Trade and Industry) has played a vital role in supervision over British policy in the United Nations, especially through its Commercial

* The Government position may, in turn, require later modification in view of positions held by Commonwealth, West European, and other members in the United Nations. Speaking of the Anglo-French ultimatum to Egypt and Israel in 1956, Eden has written:

The question of consultation before action with the Commonwealth countries and the United States was one that troubled us greatly. Of course we would have preferred to do this. . . . On the other hand . . . such consultation was not possible within a matter of hours; it must take days at least. Nor was there any chance that all concerned would take precisely the same view of what action must follow the consultation. As a result there would be attempts to modify our proposals, to reach some compromise between several divergent points of view and, before we knew where we were, we would be back at an eight-power conference once more. This was the last thing in the world we wanted. (Anthony Eden, *Full Circle*, 588.)

Relations and Exports department. For many years it handled British contacts with the UN regional commissions until this power passed to the Ministry of Overseas Development. The Board of Trade was principally responsible for preparing Britain's policy for the United Nations Conference on Trade and Development (UNCTAD) in Geneva; the President of the Board of Trade was the leader of the United Kingdom delegation, along with representatives of the Foreign Office, Commonwealth Relations Office, Colonial Office, Ministry of Agriculture, and the Treasury. The Department also handles liaison work with the Intergovernmental Maritime Consultative Organisation (IMCO), the only UN specialised agency to have its headquarters in Britain, though a formal relation is maintained between IMCO and the Foreign Office and the Treasury.

A new Ministry of Overseas Development was created in 1964 to emphasise and co-ordinate policies in the field of overseas aid, especially related to the International Bank for Reconstruction and Development, the International Monetary Fund, the Special Fund, the Expanded Programme for Technical Assistance, and UNESCO. This ministry was given prime responsibility for the regional commissions of the Economic and Social Council, and for the Food and Agriculture Organisation. The Ministry of Health has responsibility for the World Health Organisation, the Ministry of Labour for the International Labour Organisation, and the Ministry of Aviation for the International Civil Aviation Organisation, but many of these problems overlap into the areas of the Ministry of Overseas Development, and the Foreign Office. Since most aid provided by the United Kingdom goes to dependent territories and Commonwealth countries, the Ministry of Overseas Development was assigned special relationships with the Colonial Office and the Commonwealth Relations Office. The Ministry no longer exists : it is now the Overseas Development Administration – a department of the Foreign and Commonwealth Office.

Thus, decisions on matters involving British membership in the United Nations require an immense amount of inter-ministerial co-ordination; most require the use of Cabinet machinery and not that of the Foreign Office alone. In the case of the Foreign Office and the Commonwealth Relations Office, this was facilitated by the fact that they shared the same building. Personal friendships also ease this problem, as has the use of inter-ministry committees.

In several ways the British Cabinet system is admirably suited to this task of co-ordinating policy, and of acting as a court of appeal when this cannot be done at a lower level. The larger the number of ministries to be consulted, the more difficult is the task and the longer the delay in securing approval. A Foreign Secretary who takes too many questions to the Cabinet may be criticised for being indecisive; one who goes to the other extreme may be equally criticised if his policies become politically embarrassing.

For inter-ministerial consultation to be useful, members must be familiar with current developments. Traditionally, members informed themselves by reading copies of the incoming and out-going despatches; every day they received red leather boxes filled with these materials which provided both the Sovereign and the Foreign Secretary's colleagues with the opportunity to raise questions or make objections before the despatches were sent. In an age of electronic communications this is no longer possible; today not even the Queen sees the telegrams before they are sent. When a crisis is building up, copies of the telegrams are made available to all the important officials, who thus have advance warning of what may be coming.

Does a minister have time to read what is sent to him each day?* Each has his own duties, and Foreign Office business may not be of first significance to him. Since time is short and pressures great, a minister may not actually have time to raise objections with the Foreign Secretary or the Prime Minister, even if he wishes to do so. One Foreign Secretary was absent – on business – from the country for a total of 125 days in a year, half of them while Parliament was in session. Not only could other ministers not question the Foreign Secretary during this period, but he was present to answer the oral questions of Parliamentary members on only five of the twenty-four Foreign Office days [10].

---

* In 1951, Sir Stafford Cripps submitted a long paper containing an immense amount of details, prepared for British representatives at the Japanese peace conference. He admitted that he had not had time to read it himself and realised that others could not. He 'asked us to take the paper on trust'. (Patrick Gordon Walker, *The Cabinet*, 120.)

CABINET MEETINGS

Ministers also have difficulty in raising questions or making objections in formal Cabinet meetings. Before World War I there had been about forty meetings a year; before World War II one meeting a week was usually sufficient; recently meetings have been scheduled for Tuesdays and Thursdays, especially during sessions of Parliament, and eighty to one hundred meetings a year are now not unusual. During critical periods, there is usually more Cabinet activity. During the Suez crisis in 1956 :

> . . . the morning was the only time we ever had for the urgent affairs of the nation. Into this period had to be crammed Cabinet sessions, special meetings to deal with the military, financial, economic, or diplomatic aspects of the crisis, messages to and from Commonwealth Prime Ministers, consultation with individual colleagues, and a chance to think [11].

This is not always true. In 1935 during the Ethiopian crisis, the Foreign Secretary found that Parliament was in recess, the Prime Minister had gone to the country, and the Cabinet could be convened only with difficulty even though a meeting was essential. A year later, during the Spanish Civil War, 'the Cabinet did not meet from the end of July until the beginning of September and British policy was in fact decided in the Foreign Office' [12]. The Prime Minister had promised to keep in 'constant touch' with his Foreign Secretary but this actually consisted of one letter and one telephone call, neither having anything to do with foreign affairs.

Prime Minister Macmillan found himself alone at the time of the Chinese Communist bombardment of Quemoy and Matsu in 1958. 'My colleagues have gone away. . . . The Foreign Secretary (on whose judgement I have great reliance) is on a well-deserved holiday. Sir Norman Brook is also away. . . . I composed and sent off last night without consultation with my colleagues (there were none to consult) a long reply to Foster [Dulles] and the President' [13].

Even when Cabinet meetings are held on a regular schedule, ministers may not find them useful for co-ordination. The Prime Minister arranges the agenda for the meetings and may choose to leave certain items off.* He may also exercise control when discussion occurs, since he has the advantage of advance know-ledge of the problem. Most Cabinet members are in a weak position, knowing that there have been prior discussions and agreements. In the mid-19th century there was apparently little sense of hierarchy in the Cabinet, and members spoke freely, but this is no longer characteristic. If the Cabinet work is to be finished on schedule, members must refrain from raising too many questions or talking too much.† Lloyd George said that 'a man who makes a five minutes' speech in a Cabinet is voted a bore straight away' [14]. Gordon Walker tells of one minister who was expected to make a 'long' speech; several members ran a sweepstake on the length, each putting in a sixpence; the speech lasted fourteen minutes [15]. It is said that Attlee's 'great objec-tive was to stop talk. There is evidence that two ministers simply talked themselves out of the Cabinet' [16].

On the other hand, discussion is sometimes essential. Mac-millan relates that a vital Cabinet meeting in July 1958 wrestled with the possible commitment of British troops to the defence of Jordan. There was no general consensus; two telephone calls to Secretary of State Dulles in Washington failed to provide assurances which would break the deadlock. 'I made each Minister in turn express his view without any lead from me. I was determined that if this adventure was attempted and proved a disaster there could be no question of any Cabinet Minister, including the Service Ministers not in the Cabinet, not having been properly informed' [17]. The lessons of the 1956 Suez crisis were being taken very seriously.

Some Prime Ministers 'collect the voices', permitting one or two members to speak and then offering a summary which becomes the 'sense of the meeting' unless there is objection to the summary. There is a difference of opinion on whether votes are taken in Cabinet meetings. One report is that the taking of votes is exceptional [18]; another is that 'You don't take a vote. No.

---

* Two subjects 'always' head the agenda some time each week: Parlia-mentary business for the following week, when Parliament is in session, and Foreign and Commonwealth affairs, the latter followed by discussion.

† While Foreign Secretary Eden reported: 'Cabinet in a.m. . . . Outburst from Duff (Cooper) that Cabinet were always interfering in foreign affairs, result compromise, my policy thwarted. Much better to leave matters to me – not interfere so much.' (Eden, *Facing the Dictators*, 357.)

Never' except perhaps on such matters as the time for a meeting but 'not on anything major' [19]. A recent Foreign Secretary recalls two occasions when votes were taken in the Attlee Cabinet – one a trivial matter – but says that Harold Wilson was more likely to count heads and tally votes [20]. Harold Macmillan has stated that, at the end of the long and difficult Cabinet meeting in July 1958, just referred to, 'I went around the room. All were "for". So I said, "So be it." and the Cabinet dispersed' [21]. Much seems to depend upon the Prime Minister and the circumstances.

Most Cabinets have too much to do, especially in periods of crisis. Balfour said in 1925 that Cabinet business was three or four times as great as when he first took Cabinet office in 1886. The increase has surely continued. It would not be possible for present Cabinets to deal with their work except for certain improvements in Cabinet procedures: (1) since 1919 questions are to be submitted to the concerned ministries before they are submitted to the Cabinet, thus encouraging ministers to obtain advance agreement whenever possible. (2) The Cabinet office is responsible for the distribution of memoranda – every proposal is to be accompanied by a memorandum which is to be circulated 'two clear days' before the matter is discussed by the Cabinet, except in an emergency when matters may have to be discussed with no advance warning. (3) Formal agenda for meetings also mean that ministers can be better prepared when the Cabinet meets. (4) The Cabinet now makes much use of committees.

CABINET COMMITTEES

Such Cabinet committees fulfil two very useful functions. (1) On less important matters, they make decisions and save the Cabinet from being bothered; here the committee is parallel to and equal with the Cabinet itself. Junior members of the Cabinet are very useful here, and they can also learn the working of the Cabinet system. (2) On important matters, the committee can discuss the problems, enabling the ministers to present their views, perhaps reaching a compromise but at least setting forth the points on which a Cabinet decision is required. Normally a Cabinet committee co-ordinates a group of ministries concerned with a common aspect of government, and operates under the leadership of one Cabinet minister. Churchill tried briefly to achieve the same purposes by a series of 'overlords', and, more recently, Heath has made similar groupings of departments each headed by a senior minister.

Not much is known about the operation of the Cabinet committees because of the secrecy which is a part of the collective responsibility principle.* The system developed during the First World War. In the inter-war period there were normally about twenty such committees in existence at a time; more recently as many as thirty. The existence of the Defence Committee means that the Cabinet does not have to discuss defence matters unless they involve questions of principle. A Foreign Policy Committee seems to be fairly continuous; its nine or ten members met more than fifty times in 1937–38 but in 1938 it was largely replaced by an inner Cabinet of the 'Big Four' (the Prime Minister, Chancellor of the Exchequer, Foreign Secretary, and Home Secretary.) Committees on India, Burma, Malaya, and Rhodesia have been appointed to look after problems with those countries. In 1951 Eden believed that the issue of the nationalisation of the Anglo-Iranian Oil Co. was so complicated that it could not be effectively handled by the whole Cabinet, and a committee was created for this purpose. A similar committee was established in 1956 to deal with the Suez problem, consisting of the Foreign Secretary and half a dozen colleagues, with other ministers and the Chiefs of Staff in attendance when required.

The volume of committee work for certain ministers must be very heavy, and their committee work must normally be heaviest just when their departmental work-load is greatest. Although some Cabinet members who do not have heavy departmental duties may usefully be chairman of some of these committees, the chief burden of work must fall on such ministers as the Foreign Secretary. Since most of the controversial problems before the Cabinet involve financial questions, the Chancellor of the Exchequer or the Financial Secretary of the Treasury must also participate in the work of most of the committees. One result is to concentrate much power and responsibility in the hands of a few senior

* On 4 June 1940 Attlee gave the House of Commons a detailed account of the structure of Cabinet committees (361 House of Commons Debates 769–70) and Churchill provided further information on 22 January 1941 (368 House of Commons Debates 261–64).

Cabinet members, with resultant lessened influence by other members. The full Cabinet may have the last word on decisions but it is clear that participation is not equal.

One value of Cabinet committees is to enable several problems to be studied and several decisions reached simultaneously. Co-ordination between ministries is increased by the overlapping membership of the committees. In 1967 Prime Minister Wilson ruled that a matter could be taken from a committee to the full Cabinet only with the agreement of the committee's chairman, further reducing the pressure of business in the Cabinet. It seems that much of the work which comes before the full Cabinet will be better prepared than ever before, because of the committee system.

RELATIONS BETWEEN THE PRIME MINISTER AND THE FOREIGN SECRETARY

The nature of the relations between the Prime Minister and his Foreign Secretary are vital to the Cabinet's share in the control of foreign relations.

Complete confidence between the two men is not only desirable but indispensable. Foreign affairs must be uppermost in the attention of the Prime Minister at most times,* as the wishes of the Prime Minister must be constantly in the mind of the Foreign Secretary. Winston Churchill once said that you could put him and his Foreign Secretary in separate rooms, 'put any questions of foreign policy to us and nine times out of ten we would give the same answer' [22]. In turn, this Foreign Secretary, speaking of the need to have understanding from the Prime Minister, wrote : 'In all the years that Sir Winston Churchill and I worked together, it was this comprehension . . . that was most remark-able . . . the result of our lifetimes' experience of world affairs' [23].

---

* The possibility of a Prime Minister with no interest in foreign affairs must be faced, however unlikely such a situation is in the 20th century. Stanley Baldwin was such a Prime Minister, paying little attention to foreign affairs and rarely initiating proposals. He once said to his Foreign Secretary, 'I hope you will try not to trouble me too much with foreign affairs just now'. (Eden, *Facing the Dictators*, 460.) 'He wasn't interested at all, not the least bit interested, in foreign policy, just let everything drift'. (Francis-Williams, 19.) There is no other comparable recent example.

One way to obtain such complete harmony and understanding is to put the two offices in the hands of a single man. Lord Salisbury adopted this combination in his first ministry, 1885, did not do so in his second short ministry, but returned to the practice for five years in his third ministry starting in 1895. Lord Curzon supposedly would have tried to do this in 1923 if King George V had asked him to become Prime Minister. The following year Ramsay MacDonald assumed the duties of both offices, admitting to the House of Commons on 12 February 1924 that 'Foreign affairs . . . had become so unsatisfactory that I believed it would be a great advantage if, whoever was Prime Minister was also Foreign Secretary, in order to give weight of office to any sort of policy that one might devise' [24]. But he did not do this in 1929 when he again became Prime Minister although he continued to retain control of certain foreign relations in his own hands. In 1953 Prime Minister Churchill temporarily took charge of the Foreign Office when the Foreign Secretary became ill. Churchill was then seventy-eight years old and not well, leading one of his associates to write : '. . . with a new crisis in foreign affairs every day, and no PM or FS, the position was becoming intolerable' [25].

Such a combination of the two offices is neither normal nor recommended. The duties of each office are so great and the decisions of each so vital to the national welfare that such combination is beyond the strength of one man. When Salisbury was approaching the end of his third ministry, he was described as having sat as 'a crumpled heap . . . evidently wearied out' while he became 'brisk and attentive, a changed man' [26] after giving up the Foreign Office. Both of these offices have become more onerous since that time, and neither is a suitable place for an exhausted incumbent. It was widely admitted that MacDonald succeeded in handling foreign affairs well in 1924 but at the cost of control over domestic problems. One official said that it was almost impossible to get hold of him even for a quarter of an hour.

If then these two offices are to be held separately, the question is the nature of their occupants' relationships. One problem is that of dominance. Men who have risen to this level in government have personalities and ideas which tend to clash. The Prime Minister is in the better position to dominate, because of his place as first minister and because of his political position. One former Prime Minister has said, 'Every Foreign Secretary must accept a great measure of interest, or even interference, from the Prime Minister of the day' [27] and another that 'you can't expect the Prime Minister not to interfere with Foreign Office business' [28]. It is not surprising therefore that some Prime Ministers have tried to exercise firm control over their Foreign Secretaries.

Shortly after he became Prime Minister in 1916, Lloyd George established a Secretariat for his new War Cabinet. The former has been called a means whereby the Prime Minister could 'conduct foreign policy without the inconveniences of Foreign Office intervention' [29]. He also created a private Secretariat with headquarters in the garden of 10 Downing Street, which soon became a rival to the Foreign Office. The latter was increasingly ignored, with bitter resentment between the Prime Minister and Foreign Secretary. When Curzon replaced Balfour as Foreign Secretary the situation became even worse. Lloyd George may not have been interested in dominating the Foreign Secretary so much as in ignoring, even humiliating, him but the result was that foreign policy decisions were dominated by the former and not by the latter. George Brown has written that in 1967 'we had No. 10 Downing Street trying to maintain a private Foreign Office' [30].

It is not surprising that Churchill should have played a dynamic role in foreign relations when he became Prime Minister in 1940. He had previously held a variety of Cabinet posts, giving him an unprecedented position from which to wield his power, while Eden was 'heir apparent' in several ways. Yet Churchill never tried to dominate his Foreign Secretary as Lloyd George had done; he involved himself in all important decisions, yet he did not ignore, overrule, or antagonise the Foreign Secretary. Churchill made no attempt to create a separate organisation which he could control. The Prime Minister kept a close watch on the Foreign Office and made detailed – even picayune – suggestions and criticisms about its work, but he kept the Foreign Secretary informed – 'the ·Foreign Secretary knows the whole story' – consulted with him, and respected the Cabinet's position even in the midst of severe crisis. 'The Prime Minister, unless it suited him to think otherwise, took the view that the Cabinet was entitled to a full and frank debate on all the details of foreign policy. With occasional interventions . . . Churchill left the conduct of these tangled questions . . . in Eden's hands' [31]. Since the combination of both offices in the hands of a single person is not considered wise, perhaps the best alternative is for a Prime Minister to have a Foreign Secretary whom he trusts implicitly, so that the Prime Minister can provide general policy-direction and leave detailed administration to the Foreign Secretary.

There is always the risk however that a Prime Minister may dominate his Foreign Secretary so much that the position of the latter becomes intolerable. This was the case with Neville Chamberlain. It was not surprising, in view of the attitude on foreign affairs held by his predecessor, Stanley Baldwin, that Chamberlain should say to his Foreign Secretary: 'I know you won't mind if I take more interest in foreign policy than S.B.' [32]. But Eden could hardly have been prepared for the almost complete change of course which resulted.

Chamberlain said that 'he meant to be his own foreign minister and also to take an active hand in co-ordinating ministerial policy generally, in contrast with S.B.' [33]. This need not have been a fault except that, as time passed, Eden came to understand that his role was to accept and defend the policy but not to make it. As Eden said to the House of Commons in his resignation speech, he believed it 'essential that the Prime Minister and the Foreign Secretary should have a similar outlook and wish to pursue similar methods. The more intense the interest with each one of them takes in the conduct of international affairs, the more imperative does this unity become' [34].

But these two men did not have the 'similar outlook'. Even before he became Prime Minister, while he was still Chancellor of the Exchequer and thus presumably bound to support all Cabinet policy, Chamberlain made an important speech on Britain's relations with the League of Nations. He later apologised to the Foreign Secretary that he had been so busy he had not had time to notify him of his speech, but in his diary for 17 June 1937 Chamberlain wrote, 'I did not consult Anthony Eden, because he would have been bound to beg me not to say what I proposed' [35].

In 1937, as Prime Minister, Chamberlain began and pushed conversations with the Italian government although the Foreign

Secretary was opposed to them in the form which Chamberlain used. The two men were now not pursuing 'similar methods'.* At one point the Prime Minister wrote a personal letter to Mussolini. The Foreign Secretary has written that he made no difficulty about the incident at the time, thinking that 'there was no deliberate intent to by-pass me but that it was merely a slip by a Prime Minister new to international affairs' only to discover later that Chamberlain had written, 'I did not show my letter to the Foreign Secretary for I had the feeling that he would object to it' [36]. Shortly after this, the Prime Minister invited Count Ciano to a conversation which both knew the Foreign Secretary opposed. The Prime Minister, Ciano has written, 'expected from me . . . those details and definite answers which were useful to him as ammunition against Eden' [37].

The break between Chamberlain and Eden came in early 1938 when the former replied to President Roosevelt's suggestion for an international conference without any consultation with the Foreign Secretary. 'It was difficult to escape the conclusion that the Prime Minister had deliberately withheld the information from me, sensing that I would disagree' [38]. After two hours of 'wrangling', Chamberlain 'admitted that there was a deep difference between us. . . . I determined that if the Cabinet committee would not support Roosevelt's scheme, I must resign. . . . Nothing could have exposed more sharply our differences of approach' [39]; on 20 February 1938 Eden offered his resignation. The Cabinet learned of President Roosevelt's message only when the incident was past, nor 'were we told that there had been any divergence of opinion between the Prime Minister and the Foreign Secretary. . . . The press was better informed than the Cabinet Minister' [40]. The British Cabinet system does not demand, nor even expect, that these two officials will agree on approaches and methods all the time, but it also cannot countenance a situation where one of these men runs a foreign policy 'against' the other.

---

* Like Lloyd George, Chamberlain was unwilling to rely solely on the Foreign Office for diplomatic conversations and despatches, repeatedly using Sir Horace Wilson, Economic Adviser to the Government, with continuing opposition from the Foreign Office. Chamberlain had much better relations with Eden's successor, Lord Halifax. In one case when the Prime Minister announced a possible disarmament conference in 1939, the Foreign Secretary protested that he had not been consulted, and the Prime Minister apologised.

More recently, Harold Macmillan was 'virtually his own Foreign Secretary, with Selwyn Lloyd as his deputy, until Lord Home moved into the Foreign Office in 1960, with greater independence' [41]. Thinking of himself as the heir to Churchill, Macmillan followed some of the same paths. His attempts at 'summit diplomacy' have been called 'showmanlike' and 'spectacular' – he arrived in Moscow in 1959 wearing a white fur hat twelve inches tall and with a large entourage of advisers, but the results of his talks with Khrushchev and Mikoyan were less impressive. In some ways the 1960 summit meeting in Paris marked the peak of Macmillan's foreign activity, though the conference failed because of matters over which he had little or no control. It was said that he became very aloof from his colleagues, that very few of his friends saw the inside of his home (Birch Grove), and that his only close friends were his associates at 10 Downing Street [42].

There were strained relations in the 1960's between Prime Minister Harold Wilson and his Foreign Secretary, George Brown. There was a series of problems on which the Foreign Secretary found himself increasingly unhappy with both the decisions and the decision-making process. The situation culminated in Brown's resignation in March 1968 when the Prime Minister decided to proclaim a Bank Holiday in view of the gold crisis. Brown did not object to the proclamation, even thought it 'reasonable enough'. The resignation resulted from the Prime Minister's violation of a 'fundamental principle'. It seemed to me, Brown has written :

> that the Prime Minister was not only introducing a 'presidential' system into the running of the Government . . . but was so operating it that decisions were being taken over the heads and without the knowledge of Ministers and far too often outsiders in his entourage seemed to be almost the only effective 'Cabinet'. . . . The point was that the Cabinet was not consulted. Although I was Deputy Prime Minister, Foreign Secretary, and a member of the Economic Committee of the Cabinet, I for one knew nothing

about the proposed proclamation. Other Cabinet members learned by chance that Wilson, Jenkins and Shore had already gone to the Palace to arrange matters. 'We had no idea what was happening. . . . It was a decision taken by Mr Wilson in the "presidential" manner, without consulting us, without even informing us' [43].

There is very little restriction on what a Prime Minister can do when he wishes, but a wise Prime Minister will not wish to ride roughshod over his Foreign Secretary, but rather to give him guidance, keep a finger on the pulse, and know how he is doing. The Prime Minister should work through him and not try to do his work; if he lacks confidence in the Foreign Secretary he should not retain him. When Bagehot said that the function of the Sovereign was to be informed and consulted, to encourage and to warn, perhaps he was also providing the best formula for a Prime Minister when dealing with his Foreign Secretary.

DOES THE CABINET MAKE THE FOREIGN POLICY?

Another question is, who makes the foreign policy? The theory behind the Cabinet system is that all the members, as advisers to the Sovereign, come together, discuss the problems, and make joint decisions as to what is to be done. It is clear however that this is an inadequate description. On 30 July 1914, as World War 1 was breaking out, Foreign Secretary Grey sent a telegram refusing to bind his government to neutrality on the terms suggested by von Bethmann-Hollweg. This decisive action was taken with the sanction of Prime Minister Asquith but without Cabinet notification or decision until later that same day. The ultimatum to Germany in 1914, directly related to three million British casualties, was also sent without Cabinet approval although it was a consequence of decisions previously taken by the Cabinet. In April 1938 Chamberlain and Halifax agreed on the British response to Hitler's seizure of Austria, and to naval talks with the French. In September 1938 Chamberlain arranged the meeting with Hitler and signed the Munich Declaration. More recently it has been charged that Attlee decided to make a British atom bomb and Eden to invade Suez without consulting the Cabinet. All these cases were submitted to the Cabinet only after the decisions were made and action taken. How then can it be said that foreign policy is made by the Cabinet?

The whole Cabinet does not make all these decisions in advance of action but often it only concurs in decisions already made elsewhere. The Prime Minister and Foreign Secretary agree, and if they know that several other members of the Cabinet are likely to approve, they can normally assume that the real decision is made and that a fully-attended meeting would make no essential difference. This is particularly true in an emergency.

Many Prime Ministers have an 'Inner Cabinet', a small group of close associates in whose advice they have full confidence. Such a group can be very flexible, varying from time to time and topic to topic. Thus, in 1938 Chamberlain replaced the Foreign Policy Committee of the Cabinet with an Inner Cabinet consisting of the Prime Minister, the Foreign Secretary, Sir John Simon, and Sir Samuel Hoare. At the time of Munich, this group was said to be in almost continuous session. During the Suez crisis of 1956, it is said that the Inner Cabinet consisted of the Prime Minister, Selwyn Lloyd (Foreign Secretary), R. A. Butler (Lord Privy Seal), Harold Macmillan (Chancellor of the Exchequer), and Lord Salisbury (Lord President of the Council).

One former Foreign Secretary has distinguished between an Inner Cabinet and a 'partial Cabinet', the latter being part of the organised Cabinet system, a standing or *ad hoc* committee in which the Prime Minister does not necessarily have the same influence as with an Inner Cabinet which is more personal. When a partial Cabinet has prepared policies, and made decisions, 'the Cabinet is in due course informed and consulted' [44], which may or may not be true with an Inner Cabinet. Thus the case of Attlee and the atom bomb was not a 'startling departure'; since Gordon Walker was Commonwealth Secretary, and since the Woomera range in Australia was involved, 'I myself knew about the decision to make the atom bomb. . . . There was no question of the Prime Minister alone making decisions. A number of senior Ministers shared in every decision.' Indeed, we are told that, when the matter later came before the whole Cabinet, Attlee did not even call attention to it; the minutes of the committee had been circulated to ministers who could have raised the matter. 'The outcome would have been no different' than it was [45].

The Suez decision was more controversial. It was said by some that the decision to use force was not made by the Cabinet but by a 'handful of men' [46], that some Cabinet members were sceptical about the use of force, and that the Minister of Defence was so opposed that he was shifted to another post so that the Prime Minister could have full support from that important ministry. One version is that only Eden, Lloyd, and Antony Head (the new Minister of Defence) were fully informed of what was planned. Another account says that an inner group of Butler, Macmillan, Salisbury, Lloyd, and Head knew the plans. Both authors agree that the full Cabinet learned of the plans only on 30 October, the day after the Israeli attack began and the day that the French ministers came to London to decide on the ultimatum to Israel and Egypt. Some of the Cabinet members were 'taken aback. They had not realised that war was barely sixteen hours away' [47]. In any case, any who opposed the use of force had only the choice of acquiescence or resignation, and a resignation would have threatened the Government and injured the Party.* Some believed 'that it was impossible for them at such short notice to discharge their constitutional responsibilities [48].

> . . . it was too late to do anything about it. To resign when British troops, ships and aircraft were already committed to the battle was not a thing that any patriotic man could do. And those who disliked what had been done had only four hours or so before the ultimatum became public in which to dissociate themselves, if they so wished, from what was being done in their name [49].

Prime Minister Eden's version is very different. On 27 July, the day after the nationalisation of the canal, a Cabinet committee was created and charged with supervision of the problem. During the following weeks, the Prime Minister talked with several of his colleagues.

> There was no friction of any kind between us . . . no marked divergencies were revealed. I have been a member of many Governments . . . I have not know one more united on an issue of the first importance. There were, of course, shades of

---

* There were two resignations: Anthony Nutting, Minister of State at the Foreign Office, and Sir Edward Boyle, Financial Secretary to the Treasury. Neither was a major Government figure.

opinion, but these not obtrude. . . . This calm passage during a period of many months was probably due to our having talked over the situation fully in its earliest phases. We had grown to know each other's minds. . . [50].

On 25 October the Cabinet discussed the possibility of conflict between Israel and Egypt, and the British reaction to it – including the intervention by British and French forces to separate the combatants. On 30 October, says Eden, now that this situation had arisen, the Cabinet 'confirmed its readiness to act as had been decided' [51], including the terms of the ultimatum and the Prime Minister's statement to the House of Commons that afternoon. Unless Eden's account is proved to be incorrect, it seems apparent that the full Cabinet had been informed of the potential situation, and had agreed on a British policy to be followed. Later, as Prime Minister, Macmillan spoke of this decision which Eden had taken 'with the full, complete and unanimous support of this Government', maintaining that he had the 'consistent and loyal support of all his colleagues in the Cabinet' [52].

Even if Eden had made the decision himself, on the advice of a few colleagues, this would have been consistent with the actions of other Prime Ministers, as noted. The heat of the controversy over Suez centred around the wisdom of the action taken rather than the propriety of Eden's methods.

We come then to the conclusion that the Cabinet itself is not essentially a policy-making body. The policy decisions are made in several places : by the Prime Minister, the Prime Minister and the Foreign Secretary, the Foreign Secretary alone, an Inner Cabinet, a Cabinet Committee, or by the full Cabinet. The task of the Cabinet on most occasions is to coordinate views, to approve decisions already made, and to authorise action to be taken – and not to think through alternatives to a policy.

I remember . . . many occasions when a policy . . . was discussed and accepted by the full Cabinet; not one where the discussion . . . could be regarded as adequate, and only one when the Cabinet rejected a strong recommendation of a responsible minister. . . . No Cabinet large or small can originate policy [53].

In 1958 Macmillan wrote that R. A. B. Butler was 'really shocked at the irresponsibility by which Cabinet was asked to make great changes of policy at a few days' notice, without study or preparation' [54].

Some have seen the eclipse of the Cabinet! 'The post-war epoch has seen the final transformation of Cabinet Government into Prime Ministerial Government' [55]. And yet the Prime Minister, despite his modern influence, is not independent of the Cabinet. Even so strong a Prime Minister as Lloyd George was overruled by his Cabinet on several occasions. It is doubtful that Eden could long have survived the Suez crisis or that Macmillan could long have held control when he was under party attack, even if there had not been health problems. Referring to the 1957–58 disarmament negotiations Macmillan writes that he continued to exchange possible drafts with the Cabinet until a text was finally agreed to. In so doing, the Cabinet rejected the Prime Minister's own proposal. We are told that Prime Minister Wilson and his Foreign Secretary were once overruled by the Cabinet 'on a matter of great importance' [56] though we are not told more about this incident.

In both the constitutional and the political senses, the Cabinet is essential. It remains, as it has long been, the seat of ultimate political authority. Originally the Cabinet was intended not to make the policies but rather to see that the policies were properly made, by whomever made. This may still be the essence of its usefulness: to see that all necessary views are taken into consideration, and that decisions result not from quick personal judgements but from careful evaluation of the problems. If so, the Cabinet continues to play a most important role in policy-making, domestic or external.

REFERENCES

[1] E. F. W. Francis-Williams, *Twilight of Empire, Memoirs of Prime Minister Clement Attlee* (New York, 1962), 54.
[2] George Brown (Lord George-Brown), *In My Way* (London, 1971), 129.
[3] Anthony Eden (Earl of Avon), *Facing the Dictators* (Boston, 1962), 501 : (London, Cassell, 1962).
[4] Anthony Eden (Earl of Avon), *Full Circle* (Boston, 1960), 411 : London, Cassell, 1960), 369.

[5] Sir Samuel Hoare (Lord Templewood), *Nine Troubled Years* (London, 1954), 110.

[6] Francis-Williams, 11.

[7] Eden, *Facing the Dictators*, 203 (UK ed. p. 182).

[8] John P. Mackintosh, *The British Cabinet* (Toronto, 1962), 338, quoting J. A. Spender and C. Asquith, *Life of Herbert H. Asquith,* II, 123.

[9] Randolph Churchill, *The Rise and Fall of Sir Anthony Eden* (London, 1959), 287–89.

[10] 627 House of Commons Debates, July 28, 1960, col. 1996.

[11] Eden, *Full Circle*, 615.

[12] Eden, *Facing the Dictators*, 454.

[13] Harold Macmillan, *Riding the Storm* (London, 1971), 547–48.

[14] Quoted in W. Ivor Jennings, *Cabinet Government* (Cambridge, 1961), 249.

[15] Patrick C. Gordon Walker, *The Cabinet* (London, 1970), 107.

[16] Mackintosh, 432.

[17] Macmillan, 517.

[18] Jennings, 262.

[19] Francis-Williams, 82.

[20] Gordon Walker, 26, 28, 110, 135.

[21] Macmillan, 519.

[22] Eden, *Full Circle*, 274.

[23] ibid., 776.

[24] 169 House of Commons Debates, Feb. 12, 1924, col. 767.

[25] Harold Macmillan, *Tides of Fortune* (New York, 1969), 521 : (London, Macmillan, 1969).

[26] Maurice V. B. Brett, *Journals and Letters of Reginald, Viscount Esher* (London, 1934–38), I, 270.

[27] Macmillan, *Tides of Fortune*, 529.

[28] Blanche Dugdale, *Arthur James Balfour* (New York, 1937), II, 215.

[29] Gordon A. Craig and Felix Gilbert (eds.), *The Diplomats* (Princetown, 1953), 18–19.

[30] Brown, 147. Indeed Brown has called attention (p. 134) to the fact that one of the Private Secretaries to the Prime Minister is an official of the Foreign Office, potentially

160   *The Management of Britain's External Relations*

troublesome in relations between the Prime Minister and
the Foreign Secretary.

[31] Macmillan, *Tides of Fortune*, 499.
[32] Eden, *Facing the Dictators*, 501.
[33] Quoted in Mackintosh, 417.
[34] 332 House of Commons Debates, Feb. 21, 1938, col. 49.
[35] Keith G. Feiling, *The Life of Neville Chamberlain* (London, 1946), 296.
[36] Eden, *Facing the Dictators*, 510.
[37] ibid., 706.
[38] ibid., 632.
[39] ibid., 635, 644.
[40] Duff Cooper, *Old Men Forget* (New York, 1954), 210–11.
[41] Anthony Sampson, *Macmillan* (New York, 1967), 133.
[42] ibid., 163.
[43] Brown, 169–70. For his description of this problem see also pp. 171–74, 175–78, and 180–84.
[44] Gordon Walker, 88.
[45] ibid., 89–90.
[46] On this see Paul Johnson, *The Suez War*, 70–72; Gaitskell's statement, 602 House of Commons Debates, March 16, 1959, cols 56–57; and Churchill, 277.
[47] Churchill, 277.
[48] ibid.
[49] ibid., 278.
[50] Eden, *Full Circle*, 580–81.
[51] ibid., 585.
[52] 570 House of Commons Debates, May 15, 1957, col. 425, and 602 House of Commons Debates, March 16, 1959, col. 153.
[53] Lord Eustace Percy, quoted in Mackintosh, 416.
[54] Macmillan, *Riding the Storm*, 368–69.
[55] R. H. S. Crossman's Introduction to Walter Bagehot, *The English Constitution* (London, 1963), 51.
[56] Gordon Walker, 92.

6 The Treasury and External Relations

FRANK FIGGURES

THE TREASURY is a Department of State. It has responsibilities for executing decided policy; it is concerned in the formulation of policy objectives and decisions thereon. It is centred on the Chancellor of the Exchequer and in a real sense the role of the Treasury at any time, and not least in the last thirty years, is best described in terms of the fourteen men who have held that office. That is not attempted in this chapter.

Economic policy is a matter of argument and dispute. As it is implemented it is a matter of dispute in the country, within the Government, within the department. After the event it remains a matter of controversy. To take an example from the immediate post-war period, the developments culminating in the European Payments Union, which were largely undertaken in order to make possible the progressive liberation of intra-European trade from the quantitative restrictions, were opposed on the grounds that they would encourage British exporters to concentrate on the easy European market and neglect the difficult North American area. More recently the policies of intervention in the forward exchange market are still disputed. None of these arguments are mentioned in this chapter, which may therefore give the unintended impression that all has been for the best.

This chapter is concerned with the Treasury's role in external relations, and therefore primarily with external economic policy. But economic policy is a seamless robe, and the relations between its parts are not satisfactorily separated, even for purposes of exposition.

Finally, even with all these limitations there is not room for more than a cursory treatment of the limited theme. Accordingly this chapter first describes the purpose, importance and extent of international economic and financial co-operation, and the restraining effect of the UK's economic situation and perform-ance on other external policies. The Treasury's organisation for dealing with these matters is then explained, as is the way in which the department works with the other departments with responsibilities in this area.

DEVELOPMENT OF INTERNATIONAL ECONOMIC AND FINANCIAL CO-OPERATION

In economics and in diplomacy, most memories are short. We have now become so accustomed to extensive international financial co-operation that we take it for granted. Yet the present system has worked fully only in the last decade and a half, and hardly existed at all before the second world war. To measure the benefits these arrangements have brought the western world, we must contrast the present situation with that before the last war.

In the 1920s it was appreciated in principle that international financial co-operation was necessary. There was frequent contact between a limited number of central bank governors; the Bank for International Settlements (BIS) was established in 1930 in connection with German reparations but quickly became – as Montague Norman intended it should – a forum for regular meetings, and there was also lending between central banks though on a small scale. But the policy makers thought in terms of a system of international payments based on gold; the process of adjustment of the domestic economy which would allow economic fluctuations to be absorbed without changes in the inter-national value of a country's currency, or which would enable such changes to be made without general and major upheaval, was no part of that system. The decision of the UK to return to the gold standard in 1925 illustrated how the system operated; at the time, almost all expert advice was in favour of the return, with arguments based on domestic as well as external need, and the level of the exchange rate with the dollar to be adopted was hardly examined. Yet by the time we came off gold – six years later – it had become clear that it was the rate adopted, rather than the return itself, which had the most serious consequences.

The experience of the slump quite literally brought home the consequences of this system, with the spread of recession and unemployment from one major trading country to another. Economic theory developed methods of dealing with these problems, and brought out the importance of international economic co-operation. Governments came to accept the need for more intervention in the economy – essential for the orderly adjustment of domestic economies to remove international imbalances.

The fruit of this experience is the now highly developed system of international monetary co-operation. It is worth briefly describing the growth of this system, to show its extent and the diplomacy involved in its creation and development. Coming after the depression of the 1930s, the second world war provided occasion for international planning between the Allies, and indeed the will to accept some of the necessary domestic implications of effective international co-operation. The Atlantic Charter of August 1941 not only laid down principles later embodied in the United Nations; it also proposed commercial and economic international co-operation. With fresh memories of the slump and its consequences, work to implement these ideas proceeded fruitfully, with the primary aim of providing for post-war reconstruction. Plans for international institutions for financial co-operation were drawn up and discussed both in America and Britain. The result, in July 1944 at Bretton Woods, was the Monetary and Financial Conference of the United Nations – political and economic co-operation had advanced together – when, after a month of negotiation between 44 countries on the detail of the final plans, it was agreed to establish the International Monetary Fund (IMF) and the International Bank for Reconstruction and Development.

The basic framework for international financial co-operation was thus established. But it did not become really effective for a decade. The IMF had been designed to help the workings of a system of general convertibility (providing for the free exchange of currencies at or very close to fixed rates) which the wartime planners had hoped to re-establish quickly. In the event, this was not possible : the UK restored convertibility in 1947, but had to suspend it after only six weeks. A period of bilateral controls on trade and on payments followed, while the war-damaged countries rebuilt their economies.

But while truly international co-operation did not develop, regional collaboration did, particularly in Europe. The problems of administering Marshall Aid led to the creation of the Organisation for European Economic Cooperation (OEEC) in 1948. This collaboration led to closer financial co-operation in the European Payments Union set up in 1950, under which restrictions on trade and payments between participating countries – all European – were relaxed. In addition, the countries of the Six had a strong political desire for supranational collaboration, a desire not shared by the UK. This helped the emergence of more lasting institutions. First came the European Coal and Steel Community in 1952, and then in 1957 the European Economic Community. The UK stood apart from both, and instead proposed a looser form of purely trade grouping. From these ideas developed the European Free Trade Association (EFTA) in 1959.

Europe's growing prosperity made it possible to reduce currency controls in the mid-1950s (before formal restoration of convertibility of sterling and many other currencies at almost the same time in 1958). In these freer conditions the system of international financial co-operation began to develop further. In 1956, coincident with the appointment of Per Jacobsson as Managing Director, the Fund became an active supplier of credit (the annual average of drawings from the Fund from 1947 to 1955 was only $135 million; over the period 1956 to 1970 the average was $1386 million). It rapidly became clear that the Fund needed greater resources than had been planned in 1944 : in 1959 the Fund's members decided on a 50 per cent rise in quotas (there have been further increases in 1965 and in 1970), and in 1962 10 major industrialised countries (the Group of Ten) came together to establish the General Arrangements to Borrow (GAB) under which the Fund could be provided with yet further funds of up to $6000 million. As well as these resources, the US also undertook to provide further funds under the 'swap' network of central bank assistance provided by the US Federal Reserve Bank. In parallel, regular contact and discussion between financial experts about common problems – for example the growth of export credit, as well as the major countries' economic prospects –

became established in the Economic Policy Committee (and even more frequently in its Working Party No 3) of the Organisation for Economic Cooperation and Development (OECD) – the successor to the OEEC, established in 1960, and expanded to include non-European industrialised countries. In addition the Group of Ten (which is almost the same as Working Party No 3 though with a different chairman and different terms of reference) meet from time to time to discuss and sometimes to take a common position on important developments in the international financial field, e.g. the creation of Special Drawing Rights.

The way in which this highly developed system of international financial co-operation works is well illustrated by British experience in the last decade. Between October 1964 and the autumn of 1969 the United Kingdom experienced a long series of economic difficulties, all marked by severe pressure on the reserves. Throughout that period the British Government was assisted by the international financial community. Britain's largest single source of funds was the IMF : between December 1964 and March 1970, total drawings of $4922 million were made, though because of repayments outstanding debt never rose beyond $2908 million. These drawings involved discussions with the Fund of UK economic policy, under the Fund's normal rules. Moreover, since borrowing from the Fund was in part financed by the GAB, the members of the Group of Ten wished to express their views on the economic policies of the UK and of other countries whose interests might involve calls on the Fund. This wish was met by development of the system of 'multilateral surveillance' in which there is discussion of major countries' economic performance both in Working Party No 3 of OECD and by central bank governors at the BIS. In addition, the UK at various times used its swap facility with the Federal Reserve Bank of New York (which at present totals $2000 million) and other central bank facilities.

The causes of all these events are a matter of controversy. There are those who regret that so great volume of borrowing should have been accepted. It has to be serviced, and its repayment limits subsequent freedom of manoeuvre. There are those who advocated different policies in 1968 in order to avoid the further large increase in the debt during that year (when it rose by $3110 million to a peak of $8071 million at 31 December

1968). But the readiness of the international community to grant such credits is a not insignificant measure of the strength of the machinery that had been built up.

On the other hand, the whole structure of international financial and economic co-operation is based on the belief that national objectives which include a satisfactory level of activity are not attainable save in an appropriate international environment. This cannot be achieved and maintained unless the main members of the international economic community are ready to have regard to the international consequences of their own domestic policies. There are some rules that have been accepted by all; even more important is the framework of consultation and co-operation. This is an enterprise built up entirely on enlightened self interest. Because it appears from time to time to be venturing into delicate areas of policy, tact is needed by all concerned. The international community has a legitimate interest in the domestic policies of its main members. It has to find means of expressing that interest which do not embarrass or make more difficult the task of the Governments of those members.

It is the general belief, shared by those who take part in these international operations, that the consequence of this self interest has been a massive rise in world trade, by 400 per cent over the last two decades. This has brought with it a great increase in the prosperity and economic strength of the western world. It has been a primary purpose of British external economic policy for the last twenty-five years to build up this machinery, to ensure that nothing be done to damage it, and that it is continually nourished and improved. The creation of Special Drawing Rights is a major step forward; their main purpose is to provide liquidity lest further expansion in world trade should be hindered by lack of funds, and to help the stability of the international monetary system generally by establishing a rational and controllable expansion in liquidity as circumstances demand. No doubt in the future new problems will require further development of the machinery of co-operation. The interdependence of the modern economic world is monthly seen to be becoming more far reaching.

Although the consequences of these developments are of major political importance, their substance has been financial. They have been generally handled by economic experts both from the

UK and from other countries. Thus the Treasury has been directly involved in developing the present system of financial collaboration and is concerned with its future : this gives the department a continuing central and positive role in the management of the UK's external relations.

RESTRAINING EFFECT OF THE UK'S ECONOMIC SITUATION

The Treasury has however also been concerned with the limiting effect of economic factors on other aspects of external relations.

Over the post-war period, the UK economy has grown overall at a slow rate compared to growth in other countries. An important limitation on the UK's expansion has been the balance of payments. It has therefore been a continuing policy aim to increase balance of payments earnings and to reduce costs. It is wrong to attribute the poor performance on balance of payments to any particular type of transaction. On the capital account particularly there are many different kinds of inflow and outflow, and it is artificial to single out a particular flow as the 'cause' of the overall deficit in any bad year. However on current account, important both in itself and because of its effect on confidence, it is clear that private trade and private invisible transactions have regularly produced a net inflow, offset by the payment of interest on the sterling balances and on UK official debt long and short term (this payment was of over £350 million in 1969), and by Government expenditure overseas. This expenditure is mainly the cost of a foreign military presence, and of aid. After rearmament at the time of the Korean war and the end in 1955 of German payment of the stationing costs of UK troops in Germany, defence costs abroad began to increase rapidly; from £158 million in 1952 they rose to £181 million in 1958 and £306 million in 1964. This also reflected the expense of maintaining wholly professional troops abroad, often with their families. Over the same period, aid payments were a further appreciable and mounting balance of payments cost; expenditure rose from £52 million in 1952–53 to £88 million in 1958–59 and £190 million in 1964–65. These are gross figures. They are not an accurate measure of the foreign exchange burden either of aid or of a military presence overseas, but it is certain that as the gross cost rose so did the net burden.

This, and the very much larger total spending on defence, was the background to the many decisions which had to be taken affecting the extent of the UK's external relations. At the end of the war, the UK had extensive foreign commitments reinforced in the following years by the confrontation with Russia in Europe and the Korean war. This role was confirmed by the commitment in 1954 to maintain an army of four divisions with supporting air strength on the Continent, the earnest of the UK's support for her European allies which was offered as part of the establishment of the Western European Union. Elsewhere in the world, UK troops were involved in Malaya, in Cyprus, in Kenya and later in the confrontation between Malaysia and Indonesia, while many bases were maintained around the world, of which the largest were in Singapore, Aden and the Mediterranean.

Some reductions in the UK's military presence abroad came about for political reasons – for example withdrawal from the Middle East. But much retrenchment was due to repeated cuts in defence expenditure as part of reductions in public expenditure as a whole. This was the economic motive for the Conservative Government's plans announced in 1957 to reduce the Armed Forces from 690,000 to 375,000 in 5 years, with reliance on nuclear forces as the main means of defence. Later, the Labour Government cancelled expensive defence projects, for example the development of the TSR-2, and subsequently the purchase of its replacement, the American F-111. Moreover in 1966 the Government announced its intention to withdraw from Aden, in 1967 from the Far East by the mid-1970s, and in 1968 from East of Suez by the end of 1971. These cuts necessarily affected the UK's external relations in the defence field. There were also more general consequences; for example, the reduction of our military commitment in the Far East was a further factor tending to weaken ties with Australia.

The purpose of these cuts was not mainly to save foreign exchange, but to release resources in the UK which could be used to produce exports. Nevertheless, foreign exchange costs were necessarily given attention. This was particularly so in the case of the foreign exchange costs of British troops stationed in Germany. These costs to the UK were of course foreign exchange receipts for Germany, though for both parties the true net cost or advantage was less than the gross cost or receipt. Negotiations with Germany have continued throughout the period since the formation of the Western European Union. Ten separate formal agreements have been reached in the sixteen years from 1956 to 1971. The results of these arduous negotiations have been of some benefit to the UK. But it is clear from the published agreements that as time passed more and more items were brought within the 'offset' calculations, and as this happened it became increasingly doubtful whether these items brought the UK balance of payments a benefit which would not have happened anyway. It is welcome that, in the most recent agreement of 1971, the important principle of a budgetary contribution from Germany to the UK (the sole certain completely offsetting payment) has been conceded for the first time since 1961, albeit only for a modest amount.

A major political effort was required to secure even these uncertain benefits. Frequently the negotiations were conducted by ministers, and the involvement of heads of government was by no means uncommon. 'Offset' became an important domestic issue in Germany. There can be little doubt that as a result Anglo-German relations in general were damaged, at a time when development of European institutions made good relations with Germany particularly important.

The Treasury necessarily plays a large part in the examination of any proposals involving external costs or designed to produce external savings. To take defence expenditure as an example, the Treasury determines totals for defence expenditure with the Ministry of Defence; it discusses with the Ministry proposed new commitments; and it pays particular attention to the foreign exchange costs of defence procurement. In another field the Treasury took the lead in German offset negotiations until after the 1967 Agreement, when responsibility passed to the FCO.

There is one problem peculiarly the responsibility of the Treasury which is worth separate examination – sterling. The international use of Britain's currency is sometimes mentioned as an important determinant of British external policy. We must be precise as to what is meant. As already noted, the balance of payments cost of servicing the sterling balances is great, and has contributed to the UK's balance of payments difficulties. Moreover the need to maintain confidence in sterling's parity to avoid the possibility of a run on sterling is a constraint on general economic management. But neither of these aspects has in general been important in determining major objectives of external policy.

There is of course an exception. A run on sterling was a decisive factor leading to the declaration of the Suez 'cease-fire' in November 1956. Heavy sales of sterling occurred following the start of fighting, and the US – opposed to the British and French action for other reasons and anxious to stop hostilities – used the UK's need for immediate financial support either from the US themselves or from the IMF as an additional lever to impose their will. But as Macmillan (then Chancellor and responsible for seeking this support) has said, this was only one of several vital influences which all pointed the same way. On another occasion, in 1967, some Arab countries withdrew part of their sterling balances in protest against alleged UK participation in the June War. The reserves fell to some extent, but much of the money withdrawn found its way back to London of its own accord.

While these aspects of sterling have not greatly affected external policy, the existence of the sterling area has been very important. When, after the war, Britain was faced with the problem of rebuilding her world trade and financial business, the Government attached importance to restoring sterling's place in the international monetary system and with it the sterling area. This was for several reasons : before the war the sterling area – then informal – had been an important source of the UK's wealth as a financial and trading centre; much of the UK's overseas investments were in sterling area countries; Britain had political ties with the countries of the sterling area, which had been re-inforced by the part played in the war both by the dominions and by the colonies; it seemed that only by strengthening the sterling area could the UK hope to defer if not remove the problem of repaying the sterling balances which had accumulated during the war. A major consequence of this interest in re-establishing sterling as a world currency was British reluctance in the 1950s to favour schemes for European collaboration. Thus the UK stayed out of the European Coal and Steel Community, and pressed her interest in convertibility in advance of that of European countries at the expense of some strain in the European

Payments Union. There were other reasons for this attitude. But the international role of sterling did tend to diminish the interest of successive British Governments in regional solutions.

However, it is clear that sterling's position has now changed fundamentally. For most sterling area countries trade with the non-sterling area has grown more than trade within the sterling area. London's prosperity as a financial centre no longer depends on the use of sterling as an international currency – London has shown great ability in drawing to itself the development of the Euro-dollar market, while other important invisible earners, for example insurance, do not depend on sterling. The close economic cohesion of the sterling area at the time of the 1949 devaluation, when virtually all member countries followed the British lead, had greatly diminished by the time of the 1967 devaluation; then response to the UK devaluation was very varied. Neither the UK nor the members of the sterling area gain the same advantages as before from the area's existence, although important aspects of the sterling area, in particular the sterling balances, still remain.

At the same time as these facts came to be appreciated, economic thought in Britain gave increasing weight to the importance of scale of industrial production and the size of home markets. This provided the economic arguments for collaboration with Europe in the development of which the Treasury played an important part : both the more limited objectives of the free trade area in the late fifties and the effort to join the EEC from 1961 onwards owed a great deal to successive Chancellors and their official advisers. It is now clear that the UK wishes to join Europe, while it is content to see sterling's international role decline.

Nevertheless the sterling balances still claim attention. A substantial fall in the balances of official holders in the sterling area in the second quarter of 1968 (after UK devaluation and the monetary uncertainty which followed) led to the arrangement of September of that year to stabilise the balances. These arrangements are a good example of international monetary co-operation to protect the financial system; twelve major industrialised countries and the Bank for International Settlements provided a line of credit on which the UK could draw if necessary to cover falls in the sterling balances; virtually all sterling area countries undertook not to diversify further out of sterling; the UK provided a dollar-value guarantee on the bulk of official sterling holdings. The aim of these tripartite arrangements was not to build up sterling's role, but to avoid a sudden collapse. In this they were very successful. For the future, a more durable solution is needed to remove a possible source of instability from the international monetary system. While the sterling balances are a liability of the UK, they have also for the last twenty years been an important store of world liquidity and a convenient form of reserve asset. A long-term solution may lie in replacing the balances by some other acceptable asset without imposing an intolerable burden on UK current earnings, so that Britain's reserves are not threatened by confidence movements. But whatever form the solution takes, clearly it is a major issue for future financial diplomacy.

BIBLIOGRAPHY

The Rt. Hon. Lord Bridges : *The Treasury* (London 1964).
S. Brittan : *Steering the Economy* (London 1969).
M. Camps : *Britain and the European Community, 1955–63* (London 1964).
S. V. O. Clarke : *Central Bank Cooperation, 1924–31* (Federal Reserve Bank of New York).
J. C. R. Dow : *Management of the British Economy, 1945–60* (Cambridge 1964).
R. N. Gardner : *Sterling-Dollar Diplomacy* (New Edition, New York 1969).
D. E. Moggridge : *The Return to Gold, 1925* (Cambridge 1969).
G. L. Rees : *Britain and the Postwar European Payments Systems* (Cardiff 1963).
A. Shonfield : *British Economic Policy since the War* (Harmondsworth 1959).

7 Trade and Commerce in External Relations

PETER BYRD

WHY THE GOVERNMENT IS INVOLVED

BRITAIN is the third largest trading nation and, *per capita*, easily the largest. Exports are dominated by manufactures (about 85%), particularly engineering products (about 45%). Nearly all industrial raw materials must be imported. In addition about half the national consumption of foodstuffs is imported.

Since the industrial revolution imports have usually exceeded exports in value. This deficit has generally been compensated for by 'invisible exports' (see table 1). National prosperity depends on the export of about 15% of the Gross National Product. Since the second world war Britain has suffered from a chronic balance of payments problem, caused partly by the realisation of many overseas assets during the war and partly by much greater competition in many traditional markets since the war. The determination of successive Governments to maintain the Pound as an international currency has demanded a payments policy aiming at producing a surplus in order to build up reserves capable of cushioning the Pound against periodic foreign pressure. The large debts incurred during the period 1964–68 in defending the Pound must also be repaid from payments surpluses.

Britain's foreign trade is mostly conducted by private agencies without government interference. But the Government is vitally interested because trade performance is crucial to national prosperity. Three main strategies have been open to Government in approaching the payments problem :

1. *Deflation* of the British economy through credit, taxation and incomes policies, which reduces the value of the British market to domestic and foreign manufacturers, concentrates the efforts of domestic industry on exporting and contributes to the competitiveness of exports.

2. *Devaluation* of the Pound which reduces the price of exports and increases the price of imports. This strategy has been shunned for political reasons.

3. *Commercial Policy* which involves the manipulation in Britain's favour of the 'rules of the game' of international trade.

TABLE 1. BRITAIN'S INTERNATIONAL FINANCIAL POSITION IN 1969 [1]

		£m	
A	*Balance of Payments*		
	1 Exports	7061	(manufactures 85%)
	2 Imports	7202	(foodstuffs 23%, basic-raw materials and semi-manufactures 37%, petroleum 11%, manufactures 22%)
	Deficit	141	
	3 Invisible Trade	+557	
	Current Balance	416	
B	*Invisible Trade Analysis*		
	1 Private services and transfers	+564	(shipping and aviation £86, banking £46, insurance £150, other finance £86, construction work abroad £55, tourism and spending in UK £90)
	2 Private interest and investment	+780	(interest on investments abroad)
	3 Government services and transfers	−458	(expenditure on troops abroad, diplomatic representation, aid to developing states)
	4 Government interest	−329	(Interest payments on foreign debts)
	Total Invisible Trade	+557	

C *Overall Position*

In 1969 the total *currency flow* into UK was £743 m. The difference between the current balance and this figure is made up by long-term investment in UK, increase in sterling balances held in London, etc. £699 m of the total currency flow was used to repay international debts, leaving £44 m to supplement the reserves.

The administration of commercial policy is the subject of this article.

The need to acquire and retain markets, and the threat to trade posed by threats to peace, has moulded the general strategy of Britain's external policy. Foreign policy before 1939 for instance must be seen against the background of a commercial policy of protectionism and imperial preference which contributed to the failure of the Foreign Office to persuade the Cabinet to implement a concerted policy towards Nazi Germany.

During and after the second world war restrictive and autarkic trade policies were criticised for contributing to the break-down of international order during the 1930s. Britain became a leading advocate of international agreements to liberalise trade. Within this general framework, the search for increased participation in the economic recovery of Europe has, from the middle 1950s, gradually come to dominate British foreign policy. Since 1961 policy has been based on the assumption by government that entry to the European Economic Community offers the greatest economic and political opportunities.

HOW THE GOVERNMENT IS INVOLVED: THE POLICY PROCESS

The formulation and administration of commercial policy is chiefly the responsibility of four Departments: the Department of Trade and Industry, the Foreign and Commonwealth Office, the Treasury and the Ministry of Agriculture, Fisheries and Food.

(a) Promoting Trade Abroad

The aim of British commercial policy abroad is to reduce tariffs and remove non-tariff barriers, such as quota restrictions, in order to open up markets, and to assist industry to exploit fully opportunities in foreign markets. The chief instrument of multilateral tariff negotiation is the General Agreement on Tariffs and Trade (GATT) of which Britain was a founder member in 1947. Under the aegis of GATT there have been several sets of negotiations, the last of which (the 1963–67 Kennedy Round negotiations) reduced tariffs on manufactures by up to 50%. The Board of

TABLE 2. COMMERCIAL POLICY ORGANISATION OF THE DEPARTMENT
OF TRADE AND INDUSTRY [2]

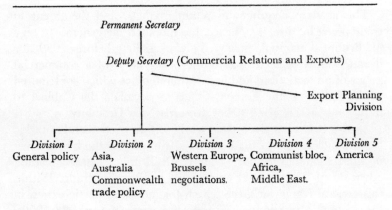

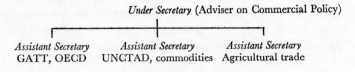

Trade took the lead within Whitehall in the formulation and
administration of policy at GATT until 1970 when it became
part of the Department of Trade and Industry. Multilateral
trade negotiations are handled by Commercial Relations and
Exports division 1, the Under Secretary of which has the title of
'Adviser on Commercial Policy'. An Assistant Secretary specialises
in GATT questions. (See table 2.)

The President of the Board of Trade, Reginald Maudling, took
the lead in the abortive negotiations 1956–58 to establish an
industrial free trade area between the members of the Organisation for European Economic Co-operation [3]. These talks, which
represented an intensification within Europe of the general policy
of trade liberalisation, broke down because of the opposition of
the six Rome Treaty states. The Board of Trade succeeded in the
Stockholm Convention of 1959 in establishing a free trade agreement with six of the OEEC states. These negotiations represented
a partnership between the Board and the Federation of British
Industries, which had established close contact with its European

counterparts. The Foreign Office took little active part in these developments.

The Department of Trade and Industry also attempts by bilateral negotiation to remove restrictions on Britain's exports. There are four Commercial Relations and Exports divisions, each headed by an Under Secretary, organised on a geographical basis.

The activities of British companies operating abroad are also important, in the case of the oil industry vitally important. The oil industry maintains constant liaison with its *sponsoring divisions* in the Department of Trade and Industry which advise Ministers on national fuel policy. In addition the Foreign and Commonwealth Office has an Oil department to inform companies on current government policy as it may affect overseas operations, and to advise on developments in oil-producing states. Oil is the chief element of Britain's relations with the Persian Gulf states, and the Government therefore wishes to be kept informed of current developments in relations between the companies and the producer states. The needs of the companies are of national importance. Thus the companies were consulted on the question of military withdrawal from the Gulf – which does not mean that their views were in fact implemented. British Petroleum's attempt in 1970 to break into the American oil retail business received Government support. BP's shares are 49% Government owned, but the Government does not interfere with its commercial management, and BP, like other companies, likes to be seen as independent of Government. The oil companies' policies may occasionally embarrass the Government, as for instance during the early stages of the Nigerian Civil War when they followed a pro-Biafra policy.

The Government actively assists industry to exploit to the greatest advantage opportunities in foreign markets. The services which, according to a survey taken by the Duncan Committee, industry found most valuable were :

1. Assistance in making contact with foreign firms.
2. Assistance in finding suitable agents.
3. Information on foreign firms.
4. General background market information.
5. Assistance with participation in joint ventures.

The least used services were :

1. Assistance in making contact with foreign governments.
2. Advice on business methods in foreign countries.
3. Information on market opportunities and investment opportunities.
4. Assessments of the firm's own export efforts [4].

The overseas work of export promotion is the responsibility of
British diplomats. From 1945 the Foreign Service acknowledged
export promotion as a legitimate function of diplomatic representation.* The Plowden Committee in 1964 considered that,
'The work of our representatives overseas must be increasingly
dedicated to the support of British trade. . . . It must be regarded
as a first charge on the resources of the overseas Services'[5].
Commercial work, including negotiation with governments and
promotional work, can involve all members of a mission, but is
mostly performed by officials who specialise in commercial work
and who are posted as 'First Secretary (Commercial)', 'Counsellor
(Commercial)', etc. In 1968 24% of United Kingdom based staff
(392 officials) and 14% of locally engaged staff (302 officials)
were engaged full time on commercial work. Since 1958 the
number of officials in the representational grades, the present
grade 8 and upwards, had increased by 20%, and most senior
officials were at Counsellor rather than First Secretary rank. The
proportion of executive class to administrative class officials in
commercial work had increased however from 63:37 in 1963 to
70:30 in 1968.

The Plowden Report recommended several improvements to
the performance of commercial work. Most were repeated in
1968 in a report of the House of Commons Estimates Committee
[6] and again by Duncan. The recommendations fall into five
main areas concerning :

1. Provision of more and better training.
2. Increased secondments to and from industry and other
   Government Departments.
3. Longer postings in order to increase local expertise.

---

* Until the amalgamation of the Commonwealth and Foreign Offices,
expert promotion in Commonwealth countries was the responsibility of the
Trade Commissioner Service of the Board of Trade (ed).

4. Improvements to the conditions of service of locally engaged staff.
5. Increased concentration of effort.

The Export Promotion Department of the Foreign and Commonwealth Office has been following up these recommendations, the fifth of which is particularly difficult to implement because it involves paying more attention to some firms than to others, which may incur charges of favouritism. Duncan also recommended that in the advanced market economies of western Europe and north America officials should concentrate on seeking out specific market opportunities. In other areas they should continue to concentrate on answering requests for information. The value of this distinction is questionable, and Duncan itself found that the provision of individual export opportunities was among the least used export services.

Export promotion at the home end is the responsibility not of the Foreign and Commonwealth Office but of the Department of Trade and Industry which acts as the link between industry and FCO posts abroad. The Commercial Relations and Exports divisions assist with large contracts, contracts with governments and contracts which run into political problems. Day to day promotion work is performed by 3 divisions under the Deputy Secretary for Export Development and Services. (See table 3.)

Export Services division is the work-horse of the machine, employing about 900 officials, mostly executive and clerical officers, transmitting the information received from missions abroad to industry, and supplying the other basic export services, such as advice on obtaining agents. Hard information about specific export opportunities is processed in a computerised system which allows firms to state the specific markets in which they are interested.

Overseas Projects Group, a much smaller division, assists industry to obtain large investment contracts, such as transportation equipment or power stations, which are usually placed by public authorities.

Export Planning and Development division is responsible to the Deputy Secretaries for export promotion and for commercial policy. It has the task of co-ordinating export promotion with commercial policy thereby producing a coherent export strategy.

It must ensure that promotional ventures such as British Weeks, employ resources of money and officials to best advantage. This division works closely with posts abroad and the unofficial export promotion organisations of the Chambers of Commerce, Confederation of British Industries, etc.

TABLE 3. EXPORT PROMOTION ORGANISATION OF THE DEPARTMENT
OF TRADE AND INDUSTRY

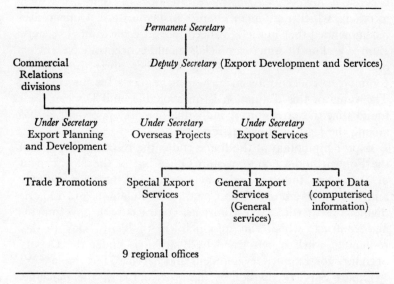

Export promotion contributes probably only a marginal increase in total exports although, as the Duncan Report pointed out, only a marginal increase in exports over imports is required to ensure that Britain stays safely in the black. Industry welcomes the service but wants above all a secure and expanding domestic market as the best basis from which to launch into exporting. Export promotion can perhaps be considered as an internationally acceptable form of subsiding exports to the tune of about £20 million a year.

Probably the most valuable government service to exporters, namely credit insurance, has received least attention. Exporters must often raise credit in order to fulfil a contract. To an increasing extent, buyers expect potential sellers to offer credit, the length and cheapness of which may decide who gets the order. The Export Credits Guarantee Department insures the credit involved in about 35% of all Britain's exports. The Department is a subsidiary department of the Department of Trade and Industry, with whom it works closely. Its operations are run on a commercial basis; the premiums it charges involve no element of government subsidy except for the actual running cost of the department. During the 1960s Britain gradually moved into the lead in the international credit race, and the rate at which exporters could borrow money, guaranteed by the Government from the banks, fell below current credit charges. In October 1970 the Government increased the normal interest rate on these loans from $5\frac{1}{2}$% to 7%. This may significantly reduce competitiveness in obtaining large overseas contracts.

The chief area of contention in export policy has concentrated on the export of armaments. This aspect of commercial policy requires close integration with overall external policy, although some cases of arms exports, particularly to the Middle East, seem to have run counter to Britain's overall diplomatic effort. The Government both promotes and controls the export of armaments, which amount to over £155 million a year. In many British Embassies the Service Attachés have a sales role. The Defence Supply Attachés in Washington, Bonn, Paris and Ottawa have an explicit sales job. The Ministries of Technology and Defence established in 1964 a joint 'Defence Sales Organisation'. The firms with important export capability maintain close relations with the Government because they rely on the Government for their domestic sales. This facilitates control of exports. The regular meetings of the Export Licensing Board, on which the Foreign and Commonwealth Office is represented, keep a standing watch on the political implications of sales. Inter-Departmental committees scrutinise more important or difficult cases, and the large or really contentious cases probably always require Cabinet sanction.

Export of armaments and strategic material to Communist countries is prohibited by the NATO strategic blockade and the British embargo list. The embargo list of exports to the Soviet Union and eastern Europe has been relaxed under pressure from industry. The question of resuming arms sales to South Africa was widely reported to have divided the Cabinet in December 1967, although apparently along political rather than departmental lines. Prime Minister Heath's decision in 1970 to resume sales was reported to have been taken against official departmental advice. The Foreign and Commonwealth Office must balance relations with South Africa against possible repercussions in Black Africa and the Commonwealth. In 1967 the Commonwealth Office existed to put the latter case, whereas the Foreign and Commonwealth Office can now assess interests on a global basis, including of course relations with the Commonwealth. The Board of Trade, and now the Department of Trade and Industry, has had to balance the value of arms sales, within the context of Britain's commercial relationship with South Africa, against possible damage to trade and investment in Black Africa and the Commonwealth. The Ministry of Defence must balance any strategic gains in maritime defence accruing to Britain against possible increases in Communist influence in other parts of Africa. Moreover Zambia, one of the leading Commonwealth opponents of the Conservative Government's policy, supplies 37% of Britain's copper, an important strategic material. The Home Office must consider the impact of selling arms on the immigrant population in Britain. The South African arms question dominated the 1971 Commonwealth Conference in Singapore.

(b) Protecting Industry at Home

Industry wants sales abroad but naturally wishes to maintain its share of the domestic market against foreign competition. Commercial policy aims to increase export potential without sacrificing an unacceptable share of the domestic market. Commercial policy involves close liaison between Government and Industry, and may produce a tension between the two. It illustrates well the intimacy, though not necessarily cordiality, of relations between Government and Industry. Important industrialists may be on close personal terms with Ministers, particularly Conservative Ministers. At official level there is constant informal communication between industry and its sponsoring Departments in addition to formal consultation. Government is well informed of industry's needs. During one stage of the Kennedy Round negotiations, executives from the chemicals industry gave the official delegation first-hand advice on the implications of proposals under discussion.

The tension between the demand for export markets and the reluctance to sacrifice the home market, often originating between different industries, has been reflected in the Government's organisation of its relations with industry. Until 1964 the Board of Trade was responsible for commercial policy and Government relations with industry. Between 1964 and 1970 these responsibilities were divided, mostly between the Board of Trade and the Ministry of Technology. At first the Board of Trade was responsible for commercial relations, export promotion and most industrial sponsorship. The Ministry of Technology concentrated on active promotion of technologically advanced and potentially export-orientated industries. Its functions were continually expanded however until, by 1970, it was responsible for sponsorship of nearly all manufacturing industry. It thus assumed through a policy of active involvement in industry a dual role of promoting young and vulnerable industries and propping up old and inefficient industries. Both types of industry wanted protection from foreign competition. At the same time the Board of Trade became a 'Ministry of Exports', dominated by the outward-looking Commercial Relations and Exports divisions, whose traditional attitude to the balance of payments problem was to promote exports rather than restrict imports [7].

Industries which have been practically squeezed out of the export market, and are chiefly concerned with defending a domestic market, may seek tariff protection from foreign competition. The cotton textile industry waged a long struggle, through the Cotton Board, with the Board of Trade for protection from cheap Commonwealth imports. In 1966 import quotas were imposed. The industry then concentrated on obtaining tariff protection. In 1969 sponsorship of the industry was transferred from the Board of Trade to the Ministry of Technology. Thus a potential conflict between the sponsoring divisions and the commercial policy divisions within the Board of Trade became a potential inter-Departmental conflict between the Ministry of Technology and the Board of Trade. Such a policy decision involves of course the Foreign and Commonwealth Office, because of the threats it poses to Britain's relations with Commonwealth textile producers, especially India.

The attitude of the Foreign and Commonwealth Office to import policy is similar to that of the commercial policy divisions of the Department of Trade and Industry. Restrictive or discriminatory tariff and industrial policies adversely affect its general role of promoting British interests through good relations with foreign states. But unlike the Department of Trade and Industry, the Foreign and Commonwealth Office has no powerful constituency from whom to draw support for its policies. It does seek the support of certain interest groups, like the British Council for the European Movement which it subsidises, but in one sense foreign states represent the constituency of the Foreign and Commonwealth Office.

The British Government, in common with other Governments, has deliberately fostered the nuclear energy industry. In 1969 the Ministery of Technology concluded an agreement with the Netherlands and West Germany for production of enriched uranium in an attempt to lower the price to the level of the American product. This agreement involved the Ministry of Technology in complex diplomacy, during which the Foreign and Commonwealth Office appeared to be a mere by-stander.

During its short history the Department of Economic Affairs was also involved in commercial policy. From 1965–67 it acted as a co-ordinating department in international economic policy, including relations with the European Economic Community. The Industrial Policies Division acted as sponsor of the National Economic Development Council and Office and the Economic Development Councils established for particular industries. The Councils were instructed to examine the reasons why their industry's products were imported into Britain in preference to the domestic product. The growth of manufactured imports which was running at 10% a year, and in engineering products at 15% a year, was of great consequence in the attempt to produce a balance of payments surplus. The Department pursued a policy of economic expansion to deal with the balance of payments problem. In December 1966 the Industrial Reorganisation Corporation was established to promote effective rationalisation of industry, and in 1967 grants to industry for capital investment were introduced. In both cases the contribution which the industry could make towards improving the balance of payments was a criterion of eligibility for assistance. This policy was continued and extended in the Industrial Expansion Act of 1968. The Government also sought to lessen dependence on imports of refined raw materials by encouraging refining in Britain. In 1968 an aluminium smelter programme began with government assistance to establish three large smelters at Invergordon, Anglesey and Lynemouth. These plants will be able to produce aluminium at competitive rates *vis-à-vis* imported aluminium, because the Government, in addition to offering loans, is making available the necessary supplies of cheap electricity.

Manufacturing industry during this period looked to several departments for support, and Government's relations with industry were conducted through several departments. Industry could lobby one Department about its export opportunities and another about the extent to which its domestic market was threatened by foreign competition. The Department of Trade and Industry now performs all these functions, although of course within such a huge Department there are distinct divisions of responsibility, and perhaps distinct policies being pursued. Manufacturing industry is the clientele or constituency which lobbies the Department of Trade and Industry and to which the Department of Trade and Industry looks for support in its attempt to reduce trade barriers abroad. Manufacturing industry is also the constituency to which it must defend its policies when they involve concessions affecting the British market. It remains to be seen whether the Department will continue the traditional Board of Trade policy of liberalising trade. That policy went hand in hand with a non-interventionist attitude towards industry.

The institutional framework must be seen of course in the context of the present Government's expressed intention to 'disengage' from active intervention in industry. The intimacy of relations between the Government and industry, and the difficulties confronting a policy of disengagement are illustrated by the aerospace industry. A separate Aviation Ministry was maintained until 1967 when it amalgamated with the Ministry of Technology, reappearing briefly as the Ministry of Aviation Supply in 1970. The aerospace industry is almost entirely dependent upon government support for its existence. Moreover the development of aircraft has become so expensive that international co-operation has become necessary in order to share research and development costs. Projects such as the Anglo-French Concorde and Jaguar and the Anglo-German-Italian Multi-Role Combat Aircraft are the results of a new diplomacy of technology in which the Ministry of Defence, the Ministry of

Aviation and its successors, the Treasury and the Foreign and Commonwealth Office are all involved.

The decisions in 1970 whether to re-enter the European Airbus project or to fund a separate British Aircraft Corporation project involved several Departments. The British Aircraft Corporation strongly lobbied the Ministry of Technology and later the Minister of Aviation Supply which was in a weak position to resist this sort of pressure because it was a one-industry Ministry. The Foreign and Commonwealth Office strongly favoured the European project as an outward and visible sign of Britain's commitment to Europe, especially as a British airbus would compete directly with the European airbus. The Treasury of course was involved and the final decision, taken by the Cabinet, rejected both projects as likely loss makers.

The Government decided however to fund the continued participation of Rolls-Royce in the American Lockheed airbus, a contract which the Ministry of Technology had helped Rolls to obtain in 1968. The cost to Rolls of continuing the contract precipitated the firm's bankruptcy in February 1971, with the result that the Government was forced to step in and nationalise the company's aerospace division. The attempt at disengagement in this industry resulted therefore in direct Government responsibility for the industry and negotiations with Lockheed for a new contract.

(c) *The Problems of Agriculture and Fisheries*

Agricultural policy is important because of Britain's reliance on imported foodstuffs. It illustrates also a further aspect of the extent to which commercial policy involves wider considerations than tariffs. Trade in agricultural commodities is notoriously difficult to liberalise because most industrial states protect and subsidise their agricultural industries. British agriculture has been protected by production grants (subsidies) and deficiency payments (guaranteed prices), with tariff protection for the horticultural industry. Most of the work of the Ministry of Agriculture, Fisheries and Food has therefore *direct* international implications. The Ministry has an External Relations Group to advise the specialist commodity divisions on the international implications of their policies, and to represent the Ministry on inter-departmental discussion of international questions. (See table 4.)

TABLE 4. EXTERNAL RELATIONS GROUP OF THE MINISTRY OF
AGRICULTURE, FISHERIES AND FOOD

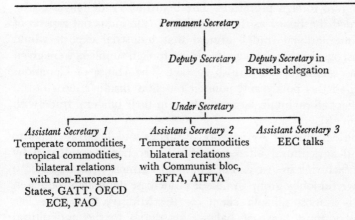

Permanent Secretary

Deputy Secretary   *Deputy Secretary* in
Brussels delegation

Under Secretary

Assistant Secretary 1	*Assistant Secretary 2*	*Assistant Secretary 3*
Temperate commodities, tropical commodities, bilateral relations with non-European States, GATT, OECD ECE, FAO	Temperate commodities bilateral relations with Communist bloc, EFTA, AIFTA	EEC talks

Detailed organisation of division 1

Assistant Secretary 1

Principal	*Principal*	*Principal*
GATT, tariff policy	OECD, ECE, FAO	Commodities, bilateral relations

Britain's agricultural output is restricted by agreements which guarantee foreign producers liberal access to an agreed share of the British market. Commonwealth trade agreements, the Anglo-Irish Free Trade Agreement and other trade agreements contain provisions relating to most temperate agricultural commodities. British bacon production for instance is limited by the Bacon Market Sharing Understanding of 1969 which guarantees foreign producers an agreed share of the British market. In 1969–70 the British share of production was 35%; the Ministry of Agriculture, Fisheries and Food negotiated an increase on this figure to 41% for 1970–71.

These agricultural agreements are part of Britain's overall commercial policy, in the formulation of which the Ministry of Agriculture, Fisheries and Food plays only a relatively unimportant role. The only justification for such agreements is that in return for the self-denying ordinances on behalf of British agriculture, counter-advantages will accrue to Britain's industrial exports. The two reports of the House of Commons Select Committee on Agriculture reveal the objections held by the Board of Trade to expansion of British agricultural production at the expense of foreign producers. The Board of Trade officials, who regarded the Board as the custodian of 'the industrial aspects of our international trade', argued that industrial exports would suffer considerable damage if existing foreign suppliers were given smaller shares of the British market. The House of Commons criticised this policy and pointed out that Britain's agricultural suppliers all maintain large surpluses in their bilateral trade with Britain [8].

The Ministry of Agriculture, Fisheries and Food attempts to defend agricultural interests within an economy dominated by manufacturing industry. The National Farmers' Union has been a powerful lobby group in favour of increase domestic production and is a most difficult client for the Ministry to satisfy. The Ministry must however balance its duties to the agricultural industry against its duty to ensure that the consumer, its other client, has adequate supplies of food. Britain's traditional cheap food policy has relied on imports of food from countries like New Zealand where production costs are cheaper than in Britain.

The Foreign and Commonwealth Office is closely, if indirectly, concerned with agricultural policy. Its view, which is put by the Commodities department, corresponds with that shown by the Board of Trade. Trade in agricultural commodities is an important element in Britain's relations with certain states, and a change of agricultural policy in Britain will have repercussions on those relations. More important than the Foreign and Commonwealth Office attitude is the Treasury attitude. Agricultural policy involves both aspects of its management of the economy : supervision of Government expenditure and control of financial policy [9]. Agricultural production incurs Government expenditure but reduces the level of imported foodstuffs, thereby assisting the balance of payments. The Treasury has generally shown itself much less reluctant than the Board of Trade to pursue policies which restrict imports. During the period of the Labour Government consideration of the balance of payments predominated and an important selective expansion programme in agriculture was introduced.

The Conservative Government, which has inherited a healthy payments surplus, is giving greater weight to reducing Government expenditure. The Government hopes to assist farmers by raising market prices by means of a levy on imported foodstuffs. This involves a massive shift of policy away from guaranteed prices and cheap imports towards the Common Market system of agricultural finance. Existing trade agreements may require renegotiation. This is part of the price of entry to the Common Market.

The Ministry of Agriculture, Fisheries and Food takes the lead within Whitehall in the negotiation and administration of international agreements relating to trade in agricultural commodities which are designed to give stable prices and production. Britain relies, of course, totally on imports for tropical commodities.

There are additional, and more generous, agreements with Commonwealth producers. Perhaps the most important is the Commonwealth Sugar Agreement, which guarantees Commonwealth producers access to the British market at a price considerably higher than that otherwise obtainable. The future of this agreement became important in the Brussels negotiations, because Common Market producers of beet sugar wanted to replace Britain's Commonwealth imports.

Fisheries policy involves similar inter-departmental co-operation. During the 1950s the Foreign Office tried to obtain international acceptance of a limit of three miles on territorial waters, chiefly in order to protect the British deep-sea trawler fleet which fished the coasts of Norway and Iceland. Those two countries have very important fisheries industries and unilaterally extended their fishing limits against foreign boats to twelve miles. Two international conferences under United Nations auspices proved abortive. The Foreign Office was thereafter forced, on behalf of British fishing interests which looked to the Ministry of Agriculture, Fisheries and Food for support, into coping with a severe breakdown in Britain's relations with two NATO allies. The dispute with Iceland involved a limited use of force. The Foreign Office rapidly withdrew from its exposed position, concluded bilateral agreements which recognised the twelve mile limit, and in 1964 obtained general European consent to this figure. The Foreign Office frankly admitted that the fisheries interest in Iceland and Norway was greater than in Britain.

The whole fishing industry (deep-sea and inshore) argued that Britain's liberal fish import policy pursued within EFTA had sacrificed fishing interests to Norway. The Foreign Office replied that manufactured exports to Norway benefited by a considerable, although unquantified, amount [10]. A measure of protection for the domestic market has in fact been restored.

The problem of the extension of fishery limits has been replaced by the problem posed by the policy of the Common Market states, who possess no important inshore fishing grounds, to abolish territorial restrictions upon member states. The British inshore fisheries industry, which flourished as a result of the 1964 agreement, fears that its interests are considered expendable in face of the needs of industrial exports. Fisheries policy thus became the subject of negotiation at Brussels.

The Fisheries Department of the Ministry of Agriculture, Fisheries and Food, headed by an Under Secretary, deals directly with other Government Departments on fisheries questions. There is a separate Department of Agriculture and Fisheries for Scotland, for whom the Common Market fisheries policy is of particular significance because of the local importance of the inshore fishing industry as an employer of labour. Within the Foreign Office fisheries questions are dealt with by the Marine and Transport department. Fisheries, like oil and agricultural imports, constitute an important element in Britain's relations with a few states.

The discovery and production of oil and natural gas around the British coast has added a new dimension to the question of territorial limits. The Continental Shelf around Britain is in the process of being divided into areas in which the adjacent state can control the activities of the exploring and producing companies. There exists already some agreed but inadequate international law with regard to the Continental Shelf. Exploration of the high seas will pose new problems, particularly for states like Britain with a great stake in the freedom of the high seas.

The Foreign and Commonwealth Office is concerned to promote the development of international agreements and law in this sphere. The Marine and Transport department deals with these problems.

(d) The Co-ordination of Interests

Britain's commercial policy, in the wide sense in which it has been discussed, is affected by diplomatic considerations and forms an important part of Britain's foreign relations. Thus as part of a general policy of assisting the under-developed states, Britain has been active as a member of the United Nations Conference on Trade and Development (UNCTAD) in the negotiation of an important scheme for the rich western states to grant preferential treatment to the export by developing states of manufactures and processed food. Britain's UNCTAD policy involves several Departments. When UNCTAD was established the Board of Trade took the lead within Whitehall. An Assistant Secretary in the Commercial Relations and Exports division 1 specialises in UNCTAD and commodity questions, which greatly concern developing countries. Within the Foreign and Commonwealth Office, the United Nations Economic and Social department is concerned with the detailed administration of Britain's policies at the United Nations. The Trade Policy department is concerned with the commercial and thus the political alignments of the developing countries. These functional departments liaise closely with the respective geographical departments. UNCTAD also involves the Treasury and the Ministry of Agriculture, Fisheries and Food. The Ministry most concerned was Overseas Development. In 1970 it was demoted to the status of an 'independent wing' of the Foreign and Commonwealth Office under a Minister of the Office. This may affect its role as the Department responsible for formulating and administering the aid programme. British commercial relations with the poorer under-developed countries were dealt with by the Ministry of Overseas Development as well as by the Board of Trade, because the relationship was one of aid rather than commerce.

Policy at UNCTAD also raises the general question of preferential treatment of the Commonwealth. The general UNCTAD preference further diminishes the value of Commonwealth preference, already greatly diminished and now comparatively insignificant. It does represent however the special status accorded to relations with the Commonwealth. That status no longer merits a special external relations ministry. But within the Foreign and Commonwealth Office some departments, such as the Commodities department, can put the Commonwealth 'case' when formulating commercial policy.

Bilateral commercial relations reflect the various elements which, together, make up British commercial policy. The Depart-

ment of Trade and Industry is responsible for the conduct of
bilateral relations, along lines agreed with the Foreign and
Commonwealth Office. Concessions are negotiated for British
exports at the cost of counter-concessions in the domestic market.
This process requires a balancing of interests in which other
Departments may have to be consulted. In addition Britain has
commercial treaties or Commonwealth agreements with many
states. These require interpretation, administration and periodic
renegotiation. There is a vast amount of day to day work, much
of it of a relatively minor nature. For instance Anglo-Canadian
commercial relations have recently involved problems such as :

> Canadian complaints about the subsidies involved in British
> aluminium smelter policy.
> British complaints against discriminatory provincial legislation
> affecting whisky exports.
> Canadian allegations (and the denials of the British industry)
> about dumping of heavy electrical transformers.
> Canadian complaints about British apple import quotas.

The Department of Trade and Industry leads the British delegation in a joint annual Anglo-Canadian trade review. The
administration of these relations is based upon the complaints,
grievances and demands of British industry channelled through
trade associations, Chambers of Commerce, and the Confederation of British Industry or raised by individual firms. During 1970
the most important development in bilateral commercial relations
was undoubtedly the threat to British exports posed by protec-
tionist trends in United States' tariff policy, which threatened to
spark off a general tariff war. The Permanent Secretary of the
Department of Trade and Industry represented Britain in talks
at GATT headquarters on this problem.

In London, the Department of Trade and Industry often deals
directly with foreign diplomats, always keeping the Foreign and
Commonwealth Office informed. In negotiations abroad it relies
usually on the diplomatic mission to act on its behalf.

The management by the Foreign and Commonwealth Office
of bilateral diplomatic relations is affected by similar lobbying.
For instance, industries with interests in Greece may lobby the
Foreign and Commonwealth Office in favour of a conciliatory
attitude towards the Greek regime. Commercial relations are an

important factor which the Foreign and Commonwealth Office must always assess when advising on overall foreign policy.

The question of British entry to the Common Market has involved the whole range of inter-departmental consultation by officials and Ministers within a policy area extending far beyond commercial policy. The 'rules of the game' of the Common Market potentially affect practically the whole range of Government activity.

The Board of Trade continued after 1959 to bear chief responsibility for relations with EFTA. The decision to apply for membership of the European Economic Community involved from the beginning much wider questions of national policy, including the adoption of a common external tariff. During the first application (1961–63) the Treasury acted as the chief co-ordinating Department in Whitehall. Sir Frank Lee, the joint Permanent Secretary to the Treasury, was closely involved in the decision to apply for membership. During the second application in 1967 the Department of Economic Affairs acted as chief co-ordinator. In the negotiations which began in 1970 the Cabinet Office was given this role. The European Integration department of the Foreign and Commonwealth Office is responsible for day-to-day organisation. The Foreign and Commonwealth Office, the Department of Trade and Industry, the Treasury and the Ministry of Agriculture, Fisheries and Food, each have a department or division primarily concerned with the negotiations. They are each represented at Deputy Secretary level on the official negotiating team, which is led by Sir Con O'Neal of the Foreign and Commonwealth Office.

The Foreign and Commonwealth Office and the Department of Trade and Industry (and its predecessors) have appeared enthusiastic for entry. Ministers and officials of the Ministry of Agriculture, Fisheries and Food have appeared more reluctant. Sir John Winnifrith, the Permanent Secretary during the 1961–63 and 1967 talks, became a leader of the campaign against entry. The Treasury has had to assess the impact on the balance of payments of contributing to the Community's budget, especially the cost of financing the Common Agricultural Policy. Freedom of capital movement within the market could also adversely affect the balance of payments. Potential long-term benefits have had to be weighed against likely short-term costs. In recent years the Treasury's management of the economy was characterised by an emphasis on short-term manoeuvres. The Common Market question required a more strategic approach [11].

All commercial policy must be decided within parameters acceptable to the Treasury. The Treasury is not always an active participant in the process, the detailed administration of which is the responsibility of the Department of Trade and Industry. In export policy the Treasury interest chiefly involves the expenditure to be devoted to export promotion and the price of credit available to exporters. In the balance of payments the Treasury is concerned with all aspects of import policy and can, virtually unilaterally, alter commercial policy. In 1964 the Chancellor of the Exchequer imposed a 15% additional tariff on all manufactured imports, regardless of origin. This decision was particularly embarrassing to the Board of Trade, whose President had great difficulty in calming irate EFTA partners. Throughout the 1960s the Treasury pressed West Germany to conclude agreements to off-set the foreign exchange cost of maintaining British troops in Germany. At the same time the Foreign Office was cultivating Germany as an ally in the Common Market negotiations.

An increasingly important phenomenon is the growth of large transnational or multinational firms, whose intra-company transactions constitute an increasing share of Britain's foreign trade. This development sets new problems in the management of national economies. The Treasury is responsible for considering foreign investment in Britain (to which its attitude has been generally favourable) and to British investment abroad (to which its attitude has been generally less favourable). But control over, for instance, the investment policy of established transnational firms is much more difficult to establish. The Ministry of Technology became seriously concerned about this problem which may become of great importance during the 1970s.

The administration of commercial relations, demonstrated by the problems posed by accepting the 'rules of the game' of the Common Market, involves consultation and co-ordination between Departments whose exact spheres of authority cannot be clearly defined because responsibilities overlap.

Between Departments there are well-defined channels of communication, official and Ministerial, to allow continuous informal consultation by telephone and personal contact. Despite informal consultation and the use of 'tacit committees' (organised circulation of papers for minuting), formal committees remain an important part of the machinery of co-ordination at all levels. Above the official committees, the Cabinet maintains a Defence and Overseas Policy Committee, an Economic Policy Committee and an Agricultural Policy Committee. There is a constitutional reticence about admitting the existence of these committees.

The process of co-ordination depends upon willingness to act on behalf of the 'national interest'. It is not always easy to define that interest. The Permanent Secretary of the Ministry of Agriculture, Fisheries and Food explained to the Select Committee on Agriculture when questioned on the prospect of securing agreement on an import saving agricultural expansion that he felt, ' bit embarrassed about this . . . as long as I can remember this has always been a point of conflict.' When legitimate interests appear to conflict, Ministers must decide.

Officials usually remain within one department; secondments between departments are a valuable means to promote a common identity. Adjustment of departmental responsibilities is another solution to the problem of co-ordination. The amalgamation of the Board of Trade with the Ministry of Technology, the Foreign Office with the Commonwealth Office and the Foreign and Commonwealth Office with the Ministry of Overseas Development may have facilitated the decision-making progress, in that questions formerly decided between departments are now decided within departments. But the separation of distinct points of view and responsibilities between departments can promote a thorough analysis of policy from all angles, and may result in decisions being taken by Ministers rather than by officials within one Department. Policy represents a compromise between different interests of varying strengths. Between Ministers there is, Patrick Gordon Walker has written, 'a community of party interest. . . . It enables deadlocks to be broken, compromises to be made, co-ordination of departments to be achieved' [12]. This is perhaps an optimistic view, and new Ministers may be shocked at having to defend purely departmental briefs. Prime Ministers can, if they wish, deliberately organise responsibilities so as to encourage tension between Departments.

A NEW DIPLOMACY?

Between the advanced industrial states increased economic integration is fusing the national political process with the international process. Government management of national economies is paralleled by international agreements and co-operation in fields of activity hitherto contained within the state. The conduct of international relations is increasingly entrusted to specialist officials or Ministers from 'domestic' departments of government [13]. In 1965 for instance, officials from the Ministry of Agriculture, Fisheries and Food, paid seventy-nine separate visits to Paris.

The 'new diplomacy' is often conducted multilaterally. This is well demonstrated in the proceedings in Paris of the Organisation for Economic Co-operation and Development, whose membership consists of the rich industrial states. Committees and sub-committees of the Council investigate and act on detailed problems of international finance, trade, economic co-operation, agriculture, fisheries, transport, etc. Officials from London also attend sessions of many other international organisations, but the new diplomacy is seen in its most extensive and developed form at OECD and of course at Common Market headquarters where relations between the members are rapidly fusing into a type of 'domestic' politics.

Thus as the Foreign and Commonwealth Office has been drawn into an increasingly wide range of activities its competence to manage the full range of inter-state relations has diminished. In many areas of Government activity which involve international action or reaction, the Foreign and Commonwealth Office is not the co-ordinating Department but one extra Department to be co-ordinated. Its role could decline to that of a post office for specialist departments, with diplomats abroad acting as door-openers for the men from London. The Duncan Committee considered this question and concluded that, 'the Foreign and Commonwealth Office is in this respect a co-ordinating Department. We see every reason for it to continue to perform this co-ordinating function'.

This analysis ignored two factors. Firstly, it saw co-ordination almost entirely in terms of Foreign and Commonwealth Office

TABLE 5. REPRODUCTION OF 65 OF THE DUNCAN REPORT

The division of responsibility between the Board of Trade and Foreign and Commonwealth Office on commercial and economic work.

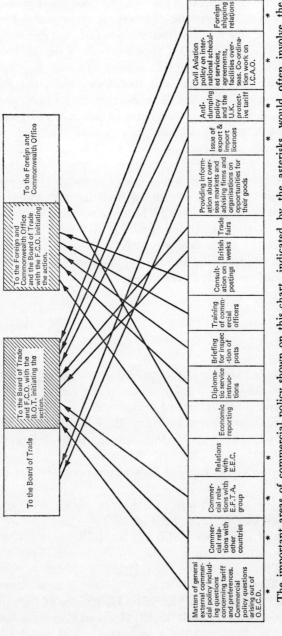

The important areas of commercial policy shown on this chart, indicated by the asterisks, would often involve the Treasury and the Ministry of Agriculture, Fisheries and Food. When Duncan reported the Ministries of Overseas Development and Technology were also involved. Since 1970 the commercial policy divisions and the sponsoring divisions of the Department of Trade and Industry have been concerned in the commercial policy process. Other Ministries – such as Transport Industries – may be involved in some decisions.

relations with the Board of Trade and ignored the Treasury, the Ministry of Technology, the Ministry of Agriculture, Fisheries and Food and other Departments. (See table 5.) Secondly, the Foreign and Commonwealth Office lacks one of the chief tools of co-ordination, namely financial control. In one key area of external relations, financial and monetary policy, the Foreign Office was never sovereign. The Foreign and Commonwealth Office must deal in the soft currency of international good-will, which must often take second place within Whitehall to the harder currency of finance.

Judged solely from the point of view of economic relations the long-term rôle of the Foreign and Commonwealth Office appears unclear. Will there be a continuing need for a vast diplomatic apparatus at home and abroad? More important, is there likely to be a continuing need for retaining a foreign civil service distinct from the home civil service? Problems in the economic field suggest the need for an amalgamated service within which specialist skills can be fully developed.

REFERENCES

[1] *Economic Progress Report* published by the Treasury.
[2] Tables drawn from information in the *Imperial Calendar* and with the assistance of civil servants.
[3] See memorandum of February 1957 by the Chancellor of the Exchequer and the President of the Board of Trade, Cmnd. 72.
[4] See report of the Duncan Committee, pp. 68–9 and 192–4, Cmnd. 4107, 1969.
[5] See report of the Plowden Committee, paragraphs 7–27 and 233–55, Cmnd. 2276, 1964.
[6] House of Commons, 1967–68, No. 365.
[7] See Board of Trade evidence to the Select Committee of Agriculture given June 1968. House of Commons 1968–69, No. 137, questions 911–921.
[8] See the two reports of the Select Committee of Agriculture, Fisheries and Food of 1966–67, House of Commons No. 378 (on agriculture and the Common Market) and 1968–69,

House of Commons No. 137 (on a programme of agricultural expansion).

[9] See Treasury evidence on expanding agricultural production, in House of Commons, No. 137, 1968–69.

[10] See the report of the Estimates Committee on 'Assistance to the Fishing Industry', particularly the Foreign Office evidence. House of Commons 1966–67, No. 274. Also Select Committee on Agriculture, 1966–67, No. 378.

[11] See 'Britain and the Economic Communities: An Economic Assessment', February, 1970. Cmnd. 4289.

[12] Patrick Gordon Walker: *The Cabinet* (London, 1970) p. 44. See also pages 28, 40, 110 and 117.

[13] See the Duncan Committee report, p. 59. The committee was generally critical on grounds of cost to the practice of attaching home civil servants to missions abroad. It recommended that most *reporting* could be done by diplomats, with *negotiations* performed by officials sent from London. See Duncan, page 135.

BIBLIOGRAPHY

1. Plowden Report (Cmnd. 2276, 1964) and Duncan Report (Cmnd. 4107, 1969).
2. The two reports of the Select Committee on Agriculture, House of Commons 1966–67, No. 378 and House of Commons 1968–69, No. 137, give a good picture of the decision-making process in one area of commercial policy.
3. Max Beloff, *New Dimensions in Foreign Policy* (London, 1961) and *The Future of British Foreign Policy* (London, 1969). In the first book he argues against amalgamation of the home and foreign services. In the second book he argues the opposite case.
4. Harry G. Johnson (ed.), *New Trade Strategy for the World Economy* (London, 1969).
5. Hugh Corbett (ed.), *Trade Strategy and the Asian-Pacific Region* (London, 1970). This book and No. 4 both argue in favour of free trade, and against the Common Market.
6. Volumes of the New Whitehall Series, on the Treasury, the Foreign and Commonwealth Office, and the Ministry of Agriculture, Fisheries and Food.

8 The Aid Programme

ANDRZEJ KRASSOWSKI

THE ORIGINS OF BRITISH AID

THE IDEA that the British Government should provide regular financial assistance to overseas countries was first accepted in 1929. With the passing of the first Colonial Development and Welfare Act [1] in 1940, the principle that colonial territories should rely on their own resources was abandoned; Britain accepted explicitly that many of them needed outside help with their development. The 'Statement of Policy' accompanying the Act stressed the importance of social development, especially education, and the need for research and planning. It committed the Government to an annual allocation of aid on a much larger scale than before, to be used for a very wide range of purposes, including recurrent as well as capital expenditure. This commitment was made for a period of ten years ahead to encourage long-term planning. It was enlarged, and extended for a further five years, in 1945. At the same time, regular financial assistance to independent countries, both inside and outside the Commonwealth, was not contemplated, although exceptions could be made in special circumstances. In the post-war years such emergency aid in fact took up a large proportion of the total amount made available: between 1945 and 1949, two-thirds, and between 1945 and 1954, 42% of total aid went to independent countries and multilateral institutions.

Despite this significant flow of aid to non-colonial territories, the orientation in aid-thinking was predominantly 'colonial'. The objectives and nature of colonial aid were shaped by the then prevailing view on the political future of colonies. It was anticipated that all colonies would, sooner or later, follow the path of the Indian subcontinent, which had attained independence in 1947. Progress towards political independence would require parallel progress towards economic independence, and the latter was to be supported by a development aid programme. On this reasoning, once a country had achieved political independence – and by implication also economic independence – aid would no longer be required [2].

A not inconsiderable effort went into improving and refining the system of colonial aid, so that by the mid-1950s an integrated programme, impressive in its quality even by today's standards, had been built up. There were shortcomings of course, the most obvious being the small volume and the lack of a clear rationale for its apportionment between colonies; but on the whole the programme was capable of serving major development needs. The system was made up of five inter-linked parts. Colonial territories not able to balance their current budget qualified for special grants-in-aid. Colonial Development and Welfare funds were available to help with the financing of public sector investments. The CD and W scheme was especially useful : aid was almost entirely in grant form; free from procurement-tying restrictions; committed for long periods ahead; available for a wide range of purposes, including agricultural schemes; and very simple to administer. In addition, colonies had privileged access to the London Capital Market; amongst other things, their debts were fully guaranteed by the British Government. After 1948, finance from the Colonial Development Corporation (CDC) was made available for investment in productive enterprises, often in association with local or expatriate private capital, where high risks may have discouraged unaided private efforts. Finally, to back up financial aid, there was a network of British, or British financed, training and research institutions covering a wide spectrum of activities : surveying and mapping; disease and pest control; cultivation, storage and use of tropical products; building and construction; and tropical medicine.

In 1957, when Ghana and Malaya became independent, it was still official policy not to make further aid commitments after independence. A year later, this policy was reversed and for the first time former colonies became eligible for regular assistance. New commitments increased sharply, and between 1957 and 1962 the aid programme doubled – from £80 million to about

£160 million – with the bulk of the increase going to independent Commonwealth countries.

The rapid increase in the volume of aid was not matched by improvements in its quality. Indeed there was some deterioration in this respect. While colonies continued to have access to broadly the same facilities as before, the forms of aid to independent countries were, with one or two exceptions, much less appropriate. A series of hurried *ad hoc* measures had been devised for helping them, and there was a conspicuous lack of effort to build up a comprehensive programme based on the lessons learnt in administering colonial aid – a failing that brought sharp criticism from Parliament [3].

For independent countries the colonial system of aid had been replaced by three new provisions: the so-called 'golden handshakes', Board of Trade (ECGD) loans, and the Overseas Service Aid Scheme (OSAS). The 'golden handshakes', or lump sum independence settlements, varied in generosity, taking into account not only the needs of the recipient but also the difficulties surrounding the independence negotiations, and other factors, such as British strategic interests in the area, the British balance of payments situation at the time of settlement, and, not least, the attitude towards Britain of the political leaders of the emergent countries concerned [4]. The main new form of financial aid (ECGD loans) had three major disadvantages compared with colonial financial aid: commitments were made for only short periods in advance; high interest loans replaced grants; aid was tied to British goods and services, and could not be used for recurrent or local costs – a restriction especially onerous for most African countries [5]. In addition to financial aid provided under the two headings mentioned, Britain signed technical assistance agreements with most newly independent Commonwealth countries, the most important one being OSAS [6]. Under this scheme skilled British personnel formerly in the Colonial Service were to be induced, with British financial help, to stay on to serve the newly independent countries. It also made provisions for attracting new recruits for such service. OSAS was able to arrest the rate at which skilled colonial officers were leaving the developing countries, and although it subsequently attracted many new recruits, the scheme was not an effective substitute for a career service in development work.

As the inadequacies of the new measures became apparent, various minor improvements were introduced : loan terms and some tying restrictions were eased, for example, and the CDC was empowered to operate in newly independent countries as well as in colonies.

THE EMERGENCE OF A DEVELOPMENT POLICY

In the early 1960s the 'aid programme' was no more than an amalgam of measures, prepared and administered by different Government departments according to widely varying criteria. The prime responsibility for 'aid' rested with the appropriate external relations department – the Foreign, Commonwealth Relations and Colonial Offices – although the Board of Trade, and, in a minor way, a number of other Ministries also had a hand in policy or administration. Funds for aid were authorised by Parliament under five separate Votes in the Annual Estimates, and five specific Acts of Parliament for expenditure falling 'below the line' in the Budget accounts.

The origin of British aid to non-Commonwealth countries can normally be traced to direct foreign policy interests : these are most clearly discernible in the case of aid to Turkey, Jordan and Libya. Isolated grants and loans made in the 1940s and the 1950s to Burma, Greece, Iran, Iraq, Syria and Yugoslavia were also of a direct political or strategic nature, while similar loans to Argentina, Brazil, Bolivia and Chile were prompted either by the desire to protect British-owned enterprises abroad from financial embarrassment, or to allow foreign countries to meet their debt obligations to British firms. The first big loan to Pakistan, the first ever to an independent Commonwealth country, was no less motivated by strategic considerations; in addition, the British Government found itself pressed into a multinational rescue operation by the United States, which viewed an impending balance of payments crisis in a country of such central strategic importance with considerable misgivings. Similar circumstances arose also in the case of India, inducing Britain to join in the World Bank's aid consortium for that country [7].

It was mentioned earlier that aid to colonial territories consisted of a reasonably well-designed package for furthering economic and social development. But even here, where the purpose of aid has always been primarily developmental, the circumstances in which it arose, and the precise motives in any single case, are difficult to disentangle. While there is little doubt that an increased feeling of responsibility for the welfare of colonial territories reflected the growth of communal responsibility within Britain for the individual's welfare and for the health of the economy as a whole – it is no coincidence that three pioneering Acts of colonial aid owed their place on the Statute Book to Labour initiatives – political expediency was also much in evidence.

The 1940 Colonial Development and Welfare Act owed a great deal to the pre-War unrest in the West Indies, and the high allocation of funds to the islands reflects the recommendations of the Moyne Commission which investigated their problems. Later, as CD & W funds increased, no clear developmental rationale for their distribution was discernible, and colonial aid generally favoured countries in which there was a clear political threat, as in the case of Malaya and Kenya, or direct British strategic interest, as in Malta. Moreover the very principle, upheld until 1958, that colonies ceased to be eligible for financial aid on independence, implied, even if this was not deliberately intended, some penalty for those choosing independence.

This principle was abandoned largely as a result of two important developments which were altering the international political climate. More than half of Britain's remaining colonial empire was on the verge of independence; self-government in Africa and the Caribbean was no longer the distant possibility it had seemed : Ghana's independence had been secured already, while that of Nigeria and others was in sight, and they were all much poorer and less well prepared than Ghana. At the same time, interest in development was increasing rapidly throughout the world, with aid edging into a prominent position in dealings between developed and less-developed nations. Henceforth, aid assumed political importance at two levels. At one level, it remained an instrument of British foreign policy, in both the political and commercial spheres, to be used when the national interest seemed to warrant it. In the case of newly independent Commonwealth countries, especially those least prepared to fend for themselves, aid seemed an ideal instrument for smoothing their transition from colonial status, for maintaining good-will, stability and commercial interests, and for promoting a host of other desirable objectives. Superimposed on this, an 'aid programme' became an international obligation, a political necessity for a developed country wishing to maintain a decent posture in a development-conscious world; proof, almost, in the eyes of the developing world, and, more and more, also in the eyes of other advanced countries, of responsible behaviour.

The underlying causes of this growing development conscious-ness provide an interesting subject for enquiry in themselves. The only point that need be noted here is the changing complexion of international organisations, reflecting the growing numbers of poor, ex-colonial territories, and the rising importance of this non-industrial bloc – or Third World as it came to be known – in the rivalry between the big Western and Eastern 'alliances'. For this new force in international politics development and aid became central concerns, while the advanced countries took up defensive positions, with increased aid as one of their more positive responses.

The deliberate use of aid to promote short-term political, strategic or commercial donor objectives came under criticism, initially most strongly in the United States [8]. By the early 1960s, the limitations of aid as a short-term policy tool were increasingly recognised, while at the same time both political and academic groups in developed countries joined international organisations and the representatives of developing countries in calling for aid which was primarily addressed to long-term development needs. Within Britain the 'Left', though by no means exclusively, was in the forefront of this movement, and British aid came under increasing attack for its political, strategic and commercial self-interest content.

In the early 1960s the British 'aid programme', seen as an entity, was not developmental in design, nor indeed could it be described as a 'programme'. Apart from the fast-dwindling colonial programme, in which the developmental element was strong, aid was, as has been shown, little more than a series of by-products of Britain's vast international interests and respon-sibilities. While it was not developmental in its primary intent, neither was it consciously designed to push particular British interests. It grew, rather, in the way described, through a succession of responses to requests, crises, pressures (both foreign and domestic), problems and the changing international situation. Once the international practice of publishing donor aid efforts had become established [9], the British Government felt obliged to make its performance look as credible as it could; expenditures on a variety of programmes, lumping together anything that could conceivably qualify as 'aid' by dint of its *prima facie* destination to a developing country, were added together, and this sum became the British 'aid programme' [10]. Some degree of central direction, or co-ordination of various aid measures, was achieved through the normal inter-departmental channels, and major conflicts were resolved, or new initiatives taken, through consultations at the political level. Effective overall control remained with the Treasury, as part of its normal survcillancc of public expenditure, and major policy decisions affecting financial provisions emanated from the Treasury; it was this department, also, which was responsible for drafting the 1957 and 1963 [11] White Papers on aid, and for placing them formally before Parliament.

The attack on Britain's so-called aid programme, noted earlier, was three sided. On the one side there was dismay with the lack of central direction and absence of clear objectives. Next, there was the haphazard manner in which aid seemed to be allocated, with no clear developmental guidelines. Finally, the composition of the programme came in for severe critcism : the terms, conditions and uses of aid seemed in many cases not to accord with development needs or priorities.

Some of these criticisms were taken to heart, to judge by the improvements mentioned in the previous section. In addition to those, steps were taken to improve administration; in 1961 the then Conservative Government, seeing the need to centralise aid operations, set up the Department of Technical Co-operation, and this brought together the bulk of technical assistance under one roof. In 1964, the newly-elected Labour Government carried this centralisation much further by establishing a new and separate ministry, the Ministry of Overseas Development (ODM), to administer both capital aid and technical assistance. The prime responsibility for most of Britain's aid was brought together under one Minister, and, by virtue of the Minister's membership of the Cabinet, aid was given not only an identity but also an enhanced status. In a White Paper published in 1965 [12], the Government made it clear that it 'recognises the need to make our full contribution in the co-operative effort to promote development of the poorer countries' and that the 'prime objective of the British aid programme is to help developing countries in their efforts to raise living standards'. The White Paper went on to say that aid should not be thought of as a means of winning friends; nor should aid be used to secure Britain's economic advantage, unless it was clear that this did not conflict in any way with the primary objective of development.

Since then the Minister of Overseas Development has lost his place in the Cabinet, and indeed the Ministry has lost its status as a separate department. But it continues to have a separate identity within a unified external relations department; as the Overseas Development Administration (ODA) within the Foreign and Commonwealth Office, it retains its own representation on inter-departmental committees, and its own cadre of professional aid administrators and specialists with a Minister as its political head. Since 1964 a large number of internal administrative and procedural changes have been made and these have gone a long way towards making possible the early realisation of the objectives set out in the 1965 White Paper. The more important of these were that aid should be made into an effective instrument for promoting development, and that the criteria for allocating aid should be rationalised. Most important, the basic rationale for aid put forward in the White Paper, that aid should be used primarily to promote the recipient's development, has become firmly established in principle, even though the principle has not yet managed to impose itself in practice with the force its protagonists would have liked.

British aid has a clearer purpose now than it had ten years ago; it is also better planned, more expertly managed, and pound for pound, better value. There are, however, two drawbacks: its allocation between countries is no less chaotic than before, and in overall volume it has hardly risen; indeed, as a proportion of Britain's wealth, the net allocation to aid is now less generous than a decade ago [13].

THE PRESENT SYSTEM : PLANNING AND ALLOCATION

Before the setting up of ODM, individual requests for aid were considered in isolation by different departments and the expenditures arising from any commitments entered into were added up to produce an overall figure for aid. In 1964 an aid 'ceiling' was introduced, fixing the total amount that could be made available during the year ahead. Although introduced primarily as one of the Government's measures for restraining the growth in public expenditure, the move had the longer-term effect of encouraging a more deliberate process of allocation of aid between competing claims, and hence closer attention to the overall context of individual decisions.

The 'ceiling' refers to annual expenditure, and as there are always delays, of varying periods and varying degrees of predictability, between commitment and disbursements, ODA has to enter into commitments at such a time and rate that the eventual disbursements arising from them add up to the total funds allocated for disbursement in any given year. Because disbursements arise largely from commitments entered into in previous years, the scope for taking new initiatives in any one year is limited. As long as the ceiling was fixed for one year ahead, the inhibition on new initiatives was particularly severe. Since 1969 however the ceiling has been fixed for four years ahead, and in addition an annual increment in aid funds has been allowed. This has introduced needed flexibility, and in future it should be easier to re-direct the aid programme in accordance with evolving ideas on needs and priorities. In particular, there should be greater scope for using imaginatively two important tools of policy planning : the 'Aid Framework' and the 'Country Policy Papers'.

The 'Aid Framework' is an annual exercise under which projected aid disbursements – over the four years covered by the current Public Expenditure Review – are broken down into a number of broad categories, for example bilateral capital aid, multilateral aid, technical assistance etc.; these broad categories are then subdivided further. The initiative for producing this breakdown comes from ODA, and the work is based on expenditure forecasts made by the various departments in ODA, reflecting the programmes which they wish to put into effect. The departmental proposals are consolidated by the Finance Department of ODA in line with general policy as set down by the Government, and the final document is then agreed to with other Whitehall Departments. Disputes are settled, if necessary, at Ministerial level. The Country Policy Papers bring together proposals for aid in a particular country, covering also a period of four years. A paper is prepared for each of some 40 recipients, varying in detail according to the degree of British interest in the country and the size of the aid programme, but always aiming to provide a brief analysis of the country's problems, needs, efforts and aid use. In addition, the papers set out the aim and objectives of current British aid, and provide a rationale for future aid in the context of an assessment of development priorities, as well as general political, commercial and other British interests in the country. As with the 'Aid Framework', each Country Policy Paper is initially prepared in ODA and then discussed with other Whitehall Departments as well as diplomatic posts, and agreed by them jointly.

The significance of these two instruments lies in their requirement to make policy aims explicit at the global, sectoral and country levels. This is both essential for the preparation of a coherent policy within ODA, thereby facilitating the development of more appropriate aid terms, conditions, projects and so on, and for considered appraisals of recipient requests and performance. At the same time, by getting other departments to understand ODA's thinking in relation to particular problems or countries, and getting formal commitment from them to a stated policy in which ODA has played a large, possibly major, part in preparing, the developmental orientation of the aid programme as a whole is likely to be secured more readily.

It is worth noting that in the preparation of the 'Aid Framework' and Country Policy Papers, ODA must seek not only formal approval within the consultations procedure just described, but that the initial ODA proposals are already framed with the likely reactions of other departments in mind. In view of this double check on ODA, it may be thought that its final influence on matters of substance will be small as compared with more prestigeous and more weighty departments, such as the FCO or the DTI. This may appear to be so, but there is already evidence that despite its relative weakness, ODA has a disproportionate strength in aid matters by virtue, on the one hand of its professional expertise, and on the other of the marginal importance of aid to the interests of the other departments. ODA's growing strength is already being reflected in a greater developmental orientation in British aid; even the FCO is no longer willing to dispute that the development objective has a major claim, and it has conceded the principle, grudgingly no doubt in some quarters, that aid for oiling the political wheels should properly give way to development-oriented projects. ODA's hand will be strengthened further if, as it is hoped, the Treasury can be persuaded to authorise expenditure on the basis of the Country Policy Papers, leaving ODA free to make the detailed decisions within the agreed policy outlines.

The present pattern of distribution of aid has not altered significantly from that laid down in the late 1950s and early 1960s. The political considerations and historical obligations which had helped to form the pattern in the colonial and immediate post-colonial period still exert a predominant influence. Important changes in allocation, when they have occurred, have also tended to follow on major political events : Zambia and Singapore, for example, have been given increased allocations to compensate them for losses suffered as a result of specific foreign policy moves by Britain [14]; the re-entry of Ghana and Indonesia into the aid fold also followed closely on the downfall of Nkrumah and Sukarno, and although both countries were deserving cases, temporarily barred from aid by the extravagances of their rulers, the move to restore aid was nevertheless primarily a political gesture. ODA has expressed its wish to make adjustments based on criteria in which developmental considerations are more to the fore, but in the past the stagnant aid budget has been an almost insuperable obstacle to this; it has, indeed, encouraged the reverse trend, since what little scope there has been for new initiative has been preempted by the demands of areas with a strong, immediate political claim.

Although the Country Policy Papers technique, the four-year aid authorisation, the growing total of aid and waning post-colonial responsibility should make it possible to direct aid in the future on more developmental lines, the possibilities will inevitably remain limited. It is in the very nature of aid to be political, however neutral one may wish it to be. In the first place, there will always be occasions when it will seem expedient to offer some financial reward or inducement to an overseas government for any of a number of reasons. Then there are the pressures from various British interests, commercial or other, which cannot be entirely ignored. Other donors are also able to exert influence; inter-donor rivalry, which is not uncommon, and which can arise in many ways, also imposes its own particular regime on the distribution of aid [15]. Then there are the actions of recipient countries themselves, which on occasion make foreign policy and development objectives pull in opposite directions. Many of the actions of developing countries which in the past have prejudiced their claims to British aid have been petty and need not have impeded long-term support for development – the suspension of aid to Tanzania over the pension issue is a case in point. Other actions however could hardly have failed to influence aid decisions; the most clear cut case is provided by Indonesia's hostility towards Britain at the time of confrontation with Malaysia. There have been many more instances where the issues were less clear cut : Nigeria during the Civil War, Pakistan more recently, disputes with the oil states in the Middle East, all raised problems of aid worthiness. Even if ODA can succeed in insulating temporary quarrels from affecting its aid distribution policy in the future, Britain will always be inclined more favourably towards some states than others, because of their importance in political or commercial terms or because of special ties, and this will influence the allocation of aid in both the short and the long-term.

Non-developmental factors cannot disappear altogether, since no politically neutral formula for allocating aid between countries has yet been devised, or is likely to be devised [16]. Moreover the choice of any formula is in itself a political action. ODA has expressed an intention to concentrate aid on countries which use it well; at the same time it recognises the claims of the very poor, or those who find it difficult to keep going unaided. It is difficult to see how aid is to be divided between even these broad, but competing economic claims, without recourse to judgements that are essentially political; or indeed how the claims of relative need or relative performance can be assessed without making subjective evaluations. Without clear cut developmental criteria which can command agreement from all concerned, even within ODA, it is not surprising that non-developmental pressures weigh heavily in the final balance, and will continue to do so.

Similar considerations apply when the specific use of aid within countries comes to be determined. Here however the non-developmental pressures are relatively weaker, and it is also more easy to reach agreement on how best to *use* aid for development than on how to distribute it between countries. ODA has had considerable success of late in ensuring that aid is used for development, whatever the motives might have been for making the original aid allocation.

AID QUANTITY AND QUALITY

Until recently Britain had made it a practice not to become involved in the affairs of independent Commonwealth countries. Like much else in British aid, this philosophy was a legacy of the colonial experience. Thus, once independence was granted, it had to be seen to have been granted; in the aid relationship, therefore, Britain did not take the initiative. It let the recipient make requests and suggest possible uses for aid; British officials then tried to ensure that aid was used for the purposes agreed. Little or no effort has been made until lately to appraise the economic policies or plans of recipients, to suggest uses for aid, or to attach performance (or 'self-help') conditions [17]. This policy has now been reversed (though rather discreetly), since many recipients are felt to be in need of assistance with the formulation of economic policies, the identification of needs, and the preparation and implementation of aid projects. In order to play a more positive role in the direction and supervision of aid in the recipient country, the British Government has already strengthened its aid representation overseas; this trend is likely to continue. Also, the number of operational personnel to be recruited for service within and for recipient governments is being, and will continue to be stepped up.

At present ODA does not maintain its own aid missions overseas. Management in the field is performed through normal diplomatic channels by officials in Embassies or High Commissions. In some countries there are in addition specialist attachés. In the Middle East and the Caribbean, specialists are based in Development Divisions; three more, for East and Southern Africa, and South-East Asia, were set up in 1971. These Divisions manage the British aid programme on the spot and carry out advisory and technical assistance functions on a regional basis.

Improved techniques for selecting projects, speeded up procedures for processing requests, improved field management, and a more professional approach have contributed to improvements in aid giving in recent years. In the future, much will depend on the degree to which field management can be strengthened still further.

It is possible to delegate aid management, as well as decisions on its allocation and use, to one of a number of intermediate international organisations, such as the UN and its agencies, the World Bank or the regional banks for Africa, Asia and Latin America. All British Governments of both political parties have backed multilateral aid, and the 1965 White Paper considered a greater British contribution to be desirable. But while the absolute amounts going to the UN, the World Bank and other international agencies have increased, the share of the total programme has remained fairly constant at 10 per cent for over fifteen years. Arguments have been advanced that multilateral aid is more efficient, as well as politically less sensitive, than direct government to government aid. The efficiency case is by no means proven : multilateral aid in general tends to be more inflexible than British aid, while UN technical assistance is usually much more expensive to the recipient and less efficient than that provided directly by Britain. There may be some political advantages, but these should not be overstated : in many cases bilateral politics are replaced by the political machinations of international organisations, and their development orientation is by no means as impressive as they would suggest. Britain's support for the various agencies is to some extent determined by considerations of efficiency, such as the contribution to the World Bank Group, but in other respects it is itself a political decision taken on general foreign policy grounds.

Since 1958, there has been a tendency to increase the proportion of aid tied to the purchases of British goods and services. At first, tying applied to independent countries, and since late 1962, to colonies as well. At present, a large proportion of aid is procurement-tied. For some recipients, tied aid is not a serious inconvenience, especially if, as in the case of India, much of it is provided for general imports and not for capital goods for specific projects. But for other countries, especially those with rudimentary monetary systems and relying on external aid for a large proportion of total investment requirements, some forms of procurement tying make aid difficult to use and often lower its development effectiveness [18]. Tying, on the other hand, tends to decrease the balance of payments costs of aid to the donor, and may make possible a larger aid flow than if it were all untied. Tied aid, though accepted as inferior to untied aid, will continue pending international agreement to the contrary, which Britain would welcome. In the meantime however ways and means are being explored to reduce the most serious disadvantages of tying to the recipient.

Financial terms, which were generous for colonial territories and later hardened as the aid emphasis shifted towards independent countries, have once again improved. Since the introduction of interest-free loans in the early days of ODM, British aid terms are among the softest. There remains however a considerable backlog of repayment and interest obligations to Britain from loan disbursement made in the late 1950s and early 1960s when interest rates charged to many recipients were at a commercial or near-commercial level.

The main criticism than can be made of British aid in the 1960s, taking the view of recipients as a group, is that it has hardly grown. After the quick upsurge in the late fifties it has risen, in gross terms, from £172 million in 1961 to about £220 million in 1970, and by only £10 million in net terms; if account is taken of interest on past aid loans paid to Britain, the net transfer figure for 1970 came to around £160 million, just higher than it was in the early years of the decade [19].

When the Labour Government came to office in 1964 there seemed to be a good chance that the volume of aid, which for several years had stuck at around the £170 million mark (gross), would resume the upward trend of the late 1950s. The 1965

White Paper beat a dignified retreat from the exposed and untenable position taken by the Treasury in the 1963 White Paper that Government overseas expenditure 'is a massive charge on our balance of payments, and that aid to developing nations is one of the biggest items in the account' [20]. In the National Plan published soon afterwards, however, it was stated that 'aid to developing countries will be restrained', and that 'the size of the aid programme will be reviewed periodically in the light of the progress in overcoming our economic problems' [21]. Throughout the 1960s the balance of payments continued to be put forward as a reason for restraint, despite ODM calculations which showed that the net foreign exchange drain was very small, accounting for no more than about 40 per cent of any additional aid, and much less if the effects of other donors' aid were taken into account [22]. In the end, even a modest increase had to await an improvement in the British balance of payments position. The 1969 Public Expenditure Review provided for an increase in gross aid to £300 million by 1973/4 [23]. This figure was endorsed by the new Conservative Government, which also allowed for a further increase, to £340 million gross, in 1974/5. In net terms, however, the increases are expected to represent something under 0.5 per cent of GNP in 1974–5, giving an aid effort in relation to Britain's wealth lower than that already achieved in the early sixties.

These figures take account of aid provided by the Government. Smaller sums – some £10 million in 1970 – are also provided by the Churches and various private organisations, such as Oxfam, War on Want, and the Freedom from Hunger Campaign. In addition, British companies invest considerable sums in the developing world; although such investment can be a useful source of capital and skills, it is not usual to include it as part of Britain's aid effort. It does count however towards the UN target which asks developed countries to transfer one per cent of their GNP for use in developing countries.

It is becoming increasingly recognised in Britain that the aid programme is merely *one* of the methods by which industrial countries can encourage economic development in poorer countries. Other policies, such as trade or the Government's attitude to overseas private investment, can either reinforce or conflict with the objectives of aid. In some areas, the distinction between aid and other policies is in any case somewhat blurred; aid and trade aspects were blurred for example in the British proposal on 'supplementary finance' made at the UN Conference on Trade and Development in 1964; this is also the case in most commodity agreement schemes. It may be said in conclusion that a clear and comprehensive overseas *development* policy is needed; an aid policy alone is insufficient. The responsibility given to ODA for appraising all British economic policies which affect developing countries is a step, albeit a small one, in the direction of an overall policy on overseas development.

TABLE 1. BRITISH GOVERNMENT AID TO DEVELOPING COUNTRIES, 1945–1970 (£m)

	Total gross	Total net[1]	Net transfer[2]	Net aid as a % of GNP
1945–1955 (annual average)	44	n.a.	n.a.	n.a.
1956–1960 (annual average)	96	n.a.	n.a.	n.a.
1961	173	171	151	0·59
1962	165	154	142	0·53
1963	164	148	128	0·48
1964	195	177	152	0·53
1965	197	173	147	0·48
1966	214	184	156	0·48
1967	208	179	151	0·45
1968	210	178	150	0·42
1969	211	180	149	0·38
1970	219	189	160	0·37

Notes:
[1] Gross aid minus capital repayments
[2] Net aid minus interest payments to Britain arising from past aid loans.
n.a. not available
Sources: Annual Abstract of Statistics HMSO 1961, Table 277; British Aid Statistics, HMSO, 1970.

REFERENCES AND NOTES

[1] *Statement of Policy on Colonial Development and Welfare,* Cmd. 6175, 1940.
[2] See Aid White Paper of 1957 (Cmnd. 237).
[3] See Select Committee on Estimates 1959–60, Fourth Report.

[4] For a list of independence settlements see *British Aid – 2 Government Finance*, ODI, 1964.

[5] See Juliet Clifford, 'The tying of Aid and the Problem of local Costs', *Journal of Development Studies*, January 1966.

[6] For a full explanation of the scheme, which is still an important part of British technical assistance, see *British Aid – 4 Technical Assistance*, ODI, 1964.

[7] For the background to British Aid to India and Pakistan see *British Aid 2*, and John White, *Pledged to Development*, ODI, 1967.

[8] A pioneering work was M. Millikan and W. W. Rostow, *A Proposal: Key to an effective Foreign Policy* (Harper, 1957).

[9] In 1961, as part of the first UN Development Decade activities the General Assembly adopted a resolution to the effect that advanced countries should seek to provide resources for poorer countries amounting to not less than 1% of their combined GNP. Further pressure for publishing donor aid 'performance' came with the setting up in 1960 of the American-inspired Development Assistance Group, which later became the Development Assistance Committee (DAC) of OECD.

[10] The original definition referred to the 'flow of financial resources' rather than aid, since DAC had found it impossible to reach agreement on the criteria for defining aid. The British programme, as those of other countries, included many items which a more strict definition would not have permitted. The definition in use to-day is not much stricter, see, for example, Jagdish N. Bhagwati, *Amount and Sharing of Aid* (Overseas Development Council, Washington).

[11] Cmnd. 237, and Cmnd. 2147.

[12] Cmnd. 2736.

[13] See Table 1.

[14] Rhodesian sanctions and military withdrawal respectively.

[15] In addition, a 'rational' distribution must always take the actions of other donors into account, as well as the flow of private capital from Britain and other sources. For example Britain may wish to avoid giving aid to those countries which already receive large amounts from other sources.

[16] This applies equally to multilateral, e.g. World Bank, aid.

[17] Practices long favoured by some other donors, e.g. the US, France and the World Bank. The old Commonwealth Relations Office and the Foreign Office were firm opponents of such practices; they were considered to lead to political friction.
[18] See Clifford, op. cit.
[19] See Table 1.
[20] Cmnd. 2147, para. 31.
[21] The National Plan, 1965, pp. 17, 75.
[22] See Bryan Hopkin and associates, 'Aid and the balance of payments', *Economic Journal*, March 1970, pp. 1–23.
[23] Cmnd. 4234.

BIBLIOGRAPHY

By far the best picture of British aid can be built up from official and Parliamentary publications. They provide a good description of the thinking behind declared policies, and the latter, which are often highly critical of HMG, give useful summaries of the current position. The following are the more important ones; especially those marked with an asterisk :

1. *Statement of Policy on Colonial Development and Welfare, Cmd. 6175, 1940.
2. Grants in Aid of Administration of the Somaliland Protectorate, Cmd. 9666, 1955.
3. Aid White Papers : *Cmnd. 237, 1957; Cmnd. 2147, 1963; *Cmnd. 2736, 1965; Cmnd. 3180, 1967; *Cmnd. 4687, 1971.
4. *Select Committee on Estimates (Session 1959–60, 4th Report).
5. Reports of the Estimates Committee on Overseas Aid, House of Commons Paper No. 442 (Session 1967–8) and Select Committee on Overseas Aid, House of Commons Paper No. 299 (Session 1970–1) together with Evidence taken, published as *HCP Nos 285–290 (Session 1969–70).

There are no adequate up-to-date books on British aid, although sections on British aid can be found in general works on aid. Both economic and political aspects are fully covered in I. M. D. Little and J. M. Clifford, *International Aid* (Allen and Unwin, 1965). A more recent work, by Juliet Clifford and Gavin

Osmond, *World Development Handbook* (Charles Knight, 1971), should prove very useful to the non-economist.

The most comprehensive work on UK aid (covering the development of the programme from its origins to the establishment of ODM) is the series of five pamphlets entitled *British Aid*, published by the Overseas Development Institute. The series is updated in *ODI Review* (nos 1–5) the latest of which was published in 1972.

Statistics on British aid can be found in *British Aid Statistics*, published annually by ODM (now ODA), and *Development Assistance Review* published annually by OECD. The latter also contains detailed comments on the aid programmes and policies of all member countries.

9 Defence Policy and Foreign Policy

PETER NAILOR

THE POSSESSION of national armed forces was one of the earliest and is still one of the most distinctive attributes of sovereignty. Armed force represented the intention as well as the means of maintaining order internally and of ensuring compliance externally. There is a tendency, in Britain and the United States at least which have no dangerous land frontiers, to think of national defence organisations primarily in relation to their external role; but the domestic function of national forces has been historically important in all states and appears to be increasing in significance again. This has two implications of interest; the first is that the role of defence forces in supporting law, order and the established form of government has a useful, if indirect, effect in maintaining the reputation and credibility of the state so supported. The second is that the domestic tasks of the armed services, in their 'internal security' function, may call for a system of organisation and equipment which is different from that which ideally they would need in preparing to defend the state from an external threat.

We can point to this as an illustration of the type of dilemma with which defence policy planners have to try and deal: what is it that you want your defence forces to do, and how do you balance your efforts between different, and perhaps even incompatible, tasks?

The concept that defence forces have a 'role' which requires elucidation is inherently linked to their external employment, and entails the correlation of their function to a state's external relations. It is now more true than it was, even forty years ago, that this relatively sophisticated relationship entails a continuing domestic burden. It involves accepting the need for armed services that have a generally-based military competence that will allow them to be used in a range of possible situations; it involves the requirement to arm them periodically with improved equipment which bears some relationship to the opposition they might have to be matched against; it calls for a programme of professional education to enable the services to be developed, used and controlled effectively; and it points to a budgetary burden and a call on national resources which in recent times has proved to need a complicated and expensive management machine to keep it within bounds.

THE MINISTRY OF DEFENCE

The Ministry of Defence in its present form dates only from 1964. Between the end of the Second World War and 1963, a number of tentative steps were made towards reconciling an historical reluctance to concentrate such a crucial function as defence of the state into a single organisation at a level below the highest ministerial supervision, with a growing need to control and direct defence management as efficiently as possible. The need was emphasised by the growing cost of technical developments in the defence field as well as by the rapidly changing nature of the tasks that the services might need to meet. In an uneven series of moves, the departments of state which traditionally had managed the individual fighting services were brought together; the Statement on the 1970–71 Defence Estimates says of the culminating process 'In 1964, the Ministry was a comparatively loosely-knit federal organisation in which the single-Service Departments had been brought under the direct control of the Secretary of State for Defence, but retained their traditional structures and organisation more or less intact. Without weakening the management of the three Services, an organisation has evolved which reflects the essential unity of defence policy and operations, provides for clear political direction, ensures closer and more effective co-ordination between the Services and eliminates much duplication' [1]. The process of reorganisation is likely to continue sporadically, partly to take account of changing needs, as they are perceived, and partly in the search for economy and efficiency. There is no doubt however that, in a comparatively short period of time, the central elements of the Ministry of Defence have established a dominance within the organisation which has materially affected the mode of operation of the old departments, and the general style with which defence interests are presented. The speed, and the manner, of the changes was partly determined by a political turn of the wheel which gave to the newly federal organisation in 1964 a Secretary of State, Denis Healey, who was a dominant personality and, quite unprecedentedly, stayed in his post for more than five years [2].

The political direction of the Ministry of Defence is in the hands of a very small number of ministers. The chief is the Secretary of State for Defence, which is a Cabinet appointment, and goes therefore to a senior member of the party forming the government. He is assisted by a deputy, currently designated the Minister of Defence for the Armed Forces, a Minister of State for Defence Procurement and three junior ministers who at the present time have each a responsibility for managing (and accounting in Parliament for) one of the Services but who may well, in time, be given functional responsibilities covering all three Services (e.g. for manpower or administration). Below this elevated level, the organisation of the Ministry of Defence is staffed entirely by career officials of the uniformed or civil services, and there is no equivalent of the United States practice in which sub-ministerial appointments, at Assistant Secretary or even Deputy Assistant Secretary of Defense level, are made politically [3].

It is perhaps easiest to think of the general pattern of organisation in the Ministry of Defence as a rope, made up of three principal strands. These are the three separate but intertwining hierarchies of the military staffs, the scientific and engineering staffs (some of whom are military officers) and the civilian finance and general policy staffs. There is a fourth strand, which until recently had a separate ministerial and bureaucratic structure, concerned with the procurement of equipment – especially aerospace equipment. The best way in which to interpolate this responsibility into the general defence structure has for long been a matter for debate (in the United States as well as in the United Kingdom), but in 1971 it was decided to bring the major part of the task formally into the Ministry of Defence organisation [4]. It is difficult to describe the exact, or even the relative, importance of the main strands in the rope separately. The military staffs provide the indispensable professional guidance and direction without which the most important functions of the department could not be performed; the scientists and engineers provide the professional input without which research, development and the production of equipment could not be related to proven military needs; and the civilian policy staffs provide the basis for the financial and administrative management on which the department's affairs are based and presented to Parliament. If the efforts of these strands are efficiently organised and interrelated, the rope becomes a strong and effective mechanism (see the organisation diagram at the end of the chapter).

Although the three services still retain a good deal of managerial autonomy in day-to-day affairs, the changes which have taken place in the defence structure have created new and centrally-located appointments and organisations. One of the most important of these is the Chief of the Defence Staff; in the later 1950s he was merely the chairman of the Chiefs of Staff Committee, but his powers have been gradually developed so that he now directs the activities of the central military staffs which at present include the operations, planning, communications and intelligence staffs of all three services. The C.D.S., and his colleagues on the Chiefs of Staff Committee, are, for foreign policy purposes, one of the key defence mechanisms insofar as they supervise the exercise of military power and set the military limitations for plans for future developments and capabilities. Such plans of course are not only related to foreign policy objectives; the more salient – and even perhaps the more important – constraints are financial, technical and manpower limitations which arise directly from the feed-back which defence policy decisions create in domestic political affairs. All of these are overlaid by domestic political objectives which take into account that the defence budget is one of the largest expenditure programmes entirely under the direct control of the central governmental machine, and is therefore susceptible to manipulation for short-term budgetary purposes.

THE CONTACTS BETWEEN THE MINISTRY OF DEFENCE AND THE FCO

The formal machinery for inter-departmental policy co-ordination at the highest level is the Cabinet. Defence and foreign policy issues frequently come before the full Cabinet, because they are of major importance, and the discussion is usually focused on a memorandum which one or other minister has circulated before-hand. But it is normal practice for all defence and external policy problems first to be discussed by a Cabinet sub-committee, called at the present time the Defence and Overseas Policy Committee (DOPC). Defence, the FCO and the Treasury are the main departments represented; the Prime Minister is the Chairman. The DOPC was set up in July 1963, as a part of the fundamental reorganisation of the defence departments, but it follows in form the practice which has persisted since 1894 of having a specialist ministerial group in this area. Frequently issues can be disposed of by this Committee, without waiting for the complete Cabinet to be consulted. A feature of earlier Defence Committees had been a strong secretarial organisation, headed for more than twenty years by Sir Maurice Hankey (Lord Hankey), Father of the Modern Committee System. The DOPC however is serviced in the same way as all the other Cabinet committees which have grown up by the Cabinet Office secretariat, and supported by an official committee (OPD(O)) at Permanent Secretary/Chief of Staff level. The function of this official committee is to prepare the ministerial committee's business by preliminary discussion of the main issues and by eliminating, if it is possible, departmental disagreements on what is to be done. In the ordinary course of events, this type of machinery proves adequate; but in the general review of the United Kingdom's overseas responsibilities and commitments which was initiated by Mr Wilson's first adminis-tration in 1965, the scope of the investigation called for more detailed co-operation, at a level where the defence and overseas policy departments could jointly evaluate the questions which ministers had raised. This was the first occasion for many years on which departments were required to work out jointly what longer-term policy variations existed, rather than to cobble to-gether whatever could be represented as agreement from the sum of individual departments' preconceptions and appreciations. It was handled by an inter-departmental committee (at what might politely be called the Higher Working Level); this proved to be an effective and useful piece of machinery, and has been retained as a supplement to OPD(O), along with some more specialist groups handling specific issues, like disarmament and arms control policy.

The FCO normally sends a representative to attend the regular meetings of the Chiefs of Staff Committee. In matters relating to operational deployments, this may be the most convenient way to feed in, or exchange, up-to-date information; but in general the FCO representative will be expected to take a full part in the discussion on individual items, and fully to represent the views of the Foreign and Commonwealth Office.

Below this very senior level, the FCO is also represented on a number of important Ministry of Defence policy groups, including the committee structure which superintends the selection of material development projects, some of which may have export sales potentialities. The FCO also takes part regularly in the preparation of policy planning papers, in order to ensure that at this stage too the most up-to-date views and information are exchanged. Most frequently it is the FCO departments specifically charged with defence liaison that provide the information and the representatives (e.g. Defence Department or Defence Supplies Department). But on some detailed issues, like policy about over-flying rights, or whether a goodwill visit by the Royal Navy should be undertaken, consultation would take place between the officials most directly concerned. At this sort of level, and over this type of specific issue, formal consultation shades into informality, and the precise contribution of the individual organisation may be difficult to identify.

The nature of the FCO input obviously varies; but inherently it must be regarded as 'political', not so much concerned with facts, figures and tangibles, because these are usually available from other sources, including the Ministry of Defence itself, as with the elucidation of policy choices. Nevertheless the 'political' role of officials has considerable limitations. The prime responsibility which officials have, even at Chief of Staff level, is to present a case for politically appointed ministers to rule on. This is both gospel and practice, although there is obviously a very

large number of issues or cases which a minister does not see and
which are settled in the belief that a particular decision will be
in accordance with the government's general aims. In an article
published in the summer of 1970, a businessman who had been
brought into the government machine wrote this about his
impressions :

> . . . I also learned about some of the constraints within which
> officials have to work :
> - of the difficulties of real delegation of responsibility and
>   authority, while ministers remain answerable to the House
>   (*of Commons*), since ministers today inevitably want to take
>   the decisions for which they must answer
> - of the inevitable involvement of each department in sup-
>   porting the political power struggle of its minister with his
>   Cabinet colleagues
> - of the need to treat all citizens equally and fairly, not only
>   now but in the light of previously established precedent :
>   and the extent to which this is imbued in the thoughts and
>   actions of officials . . .
>
> In the Departments of State we provide a hierarchy of officials
> well skilled at analysing every problem and presenting to the
> Minister a well-balanced brief about the decision he has got to
> take. But the Minister whom we put into the decision-making
> chair we draw from the field of politics, where as often as not
> he has received no training at all in decision-making, either
> before entering politics, or as a back-bencher [5].

Mr. de Paula also makes the point that, as far as the officials
are concerned, many do not get involved in the sort of decision-
making that in commerce is needed to get things done from day
to day, and perhaps get more job-satisfaction from the preparation of a well-balanced policy paper than from the taking of
decisions which get things done.

These observations offer a useful insight from a viewpoint
which is not often made available. But as far as getting things
done is concerned, the Ministry of Defence has a huge managerial
role of its own, covering, even now, more than 10 per cent of the
public budget and nearly a quarter of the entire civil service. It
administers or awards contracts relating to research, development
and production in a wide range of industries, including many in

the advanced technology field which seems to have strong political sex-appeal as well as genuine industrial importance; it procures the daily requirements for what are still very substantial and well-equipped military forces. All in all, the Ministry of Defence has a requirement for managerial competence which is in no way less pressing than that necessary in any large and complex industrial organisation. The FCO too is concerned with a wide range of activities which – in an age where improved communications create a pressure for response which has only to be experienced to be deplored – requires sound management and a substantial degree of flexibility for the office machine to function at all.

The arrangements for day-to-day consultation and co-ordination work reasonably well between the FCO and the Ministry of Defence, and it could be argued that the amalgamation of the three Overseas Departments (Colonial, Commonwealth and Foreign Offices) into one during the 1960s has, as a matter of practice, made the achievement of good working relations easier. This argument does however involve the assumption that unified advice can be procured from the amalgam; and although this may be an increasingly reasonable assumption to make as the effectiveness of the unified FCO is developed, it was not always the case in the middle and later 1960s while the reorganisations in 1966–68 were being prepared and then implemented.

In this respect, the emergence of a more orderly 'defence' view from the new Ministry of Defence ran two years or so ahead of the coordination of external policy objectives in the reorganised FCO. Nevertheless, it is generally true that in any inter-departmental arguments about the priority to be given to any particular issue, or about the balance between the external and the domestic pressures affecting a major decision, the FCO and the Ministry of Defence are more likely than not to see their separate interests as compatible; and they are highly likely to support each other against traditional enemies such as the Chancellor of the Exchequer and the Treasury.

Collaboration between the Ministry of Defence and FCO is of course of long standing; it extends beyond Whitehall to overseas embassies and consulates, where visiting ships or other forces naturally turn to HBM's local representative for assistance in arranging their programmes and meeting their needs, and in the

majority of capitals it has up till now included the accreditation
of service attachés. The number of attaché posts has declined in
recent years, and in the shadow of the Duncan Report will reduce
even further. A number of areas remain important enough for
sizeable military missions to be retained, as attachés are, on
Ambassadors' staffs; the most notable are in Washington, Can-
berra and Ottawa, where not merely the normal liaison and
information-exchange duties are to be performed but where staffs
are needed to deal with the consequences of buying and selling
equipment. For example, when the United Kingdom decided to
purchase Polaris weapon system equipment and McDonnell-
Douglas F-4 Phantoms from the United States, specialist staffs
were established in Washington and elsewhere to handle the
resultant business.

The other, more recent, development which calls for the
combination of FCO and Defence personnel is the growth of
regional security organisations, of which the largest and most
important to the United Kingdom is NATO. First in Paris and
Washington, and then in Brussels, the British NATO delegation
has been made up jointly from the FCO and MOD, and from
civilian and military personnel; the permanent head of the
delegation is a senior Ambassador, and both he and the UK
National Military Representative at SACEUR's headquarters are
important links in the chain of communication between the UK's
national interests and the common interest of the Alliance as a
whole. CENTO and SEATO also have British national representatives accredited to them; but the size of the staffs is very
much smaller, and neither alliance has ever been considered
important enough to merit the attention which has been given to
the NATO connection.

THE RELATIONSHIP BETWEEN DEFENCE
AND FOREIGN POLICY

The maintenance of armed forces as a signification of sovereignty
is an attribute which even small states seek to possess; sometimes
it is manifested in purely symbolic terms, as in San Marino. The
processes by which mere possession is turned into advantage in
external relationships are however becoming more costly and

complex; and even relatively wealthy states now have to choose
carefully what range of military power they both wish and can
afford to retain under their national control. It used to be the
case, especially where homeland defence was a pre-occupation,
that the forces which had military and diplomatic utility in
deterring war were also essentially the same sort of forces that
it was necessary to have in order to prosecute and win wars. The
level of forces in being was not so important as the mobilisation
base, from which continuing war-fighting strength could be
drawn; and no one state was so inordinately powerful in relation
to its neighbours that an alliance of the traditional 'declaratory'
type might not restrain or, if the worst came to the worst,
successfully dispute its ambitions.

The consequences of the Second World War and the advent
of nuclear weapons have changed these assumptions. The growth
in the size of the international community, the decline in the
relative power of the European countries (though not of their
intrinsic importance as a major centre of industrial potential and
culture), and the emergence of the Super-Power states, have all
created new difficulties for all states in defining their policy
objectives, and then in achieving them. The United Kingdom has
had a particular problem in reconciling ends and means – of
finding a policy base by which, as one unkind critic said, she
might *'reculer pour mieux reculer'*.

Military force as an instrument of policy has not however lost
its utility; the British armed services have been involved in over
one hundred operations of various sorts since the end of 1945.
But force has come increasingly to be questioned as an essential
component of *major* policy making, and in particular as an
instrument to ensure acquiescence in disputes between 'Imperial'
Powers and less advanced countries. The Suez operation was an
aberrant and anachronistic use of force with these objectives, and
contrasts with other operations, such as the 'Confrontation' in
Borneo from 1962–66, where a minimum of force was used, in
conjunction with positive and reasonable political aims, to achieve
a political settlement [6]. In a somewhat similar way, the process
of Empire-breaking was marked by a number of occasions when
force was used in order to create or maintain a *status quo* whereby political considerations could be debated or conceded in an
atmosphere of less than total anarchy. The recipe did not always

produce the desired result, for example in Aden; but it worked surprisingly often, and was a major determinant in giving active professional employment to the British Army for a quarter of a century. It seems that the situation noted by Michael Howard in 1964 still persists : that in the post-nuclear world, the function of conventional military force may be related to the role of gold in the post-Keynesian economic world. Gold and conventional force are still indispensable, though nobody is really sure why this should be [7]. The consequence however is that military forces still have to be militarily efficient in order to be useful; a mere elegance on parade is not enough either to sustain internal force morale or to persuade friends (who take more persuading than enemies) that a state's military potential is a worthwhile asset.

Military force also retains its utility in diplomatic power-play. The British forces in Germany – though not as large or important to the NATO alliance as the United States contingents – have a worth beyond their innate military competence. Whether it is as an earnest of full commitment, or as a hostage to involvement, depends rather upon the view that one takes of treaty obligations in the nuclear age, and of the possibility of East-West war breaking out in Central Europe. It is nevertheless clear that the withdrawal of either British or United States forces from Germany without the most careful diplomatic preparation would have a major political effect upon the alliance, and it would be an effect not specifically related to those forces' abilities to perform their allotted military function. The British obligation to maintain a defined level of army and air force units in Germany was made in 1954; it might now perhaps be arguable that a different level of force or a different contribution altogether to the alliance might be more appropriate. But because a treaty obligation exists – and because British attempts to vary the commitment have almost always been intended to reduce the strength of the units – it is clear that no major variation of this particular obligation can be envisaged without calling much wider diplomatic issues into review. Nevertheless, we might call this type of politico-military interplay 'traditional'; soldiers, guns and ships embody values which, though they may be erroneous, have familiarity in an international vocabulary which is really rather limited. To move a division or to send a gunboat is a procedure that all Foreign Offices know about and can react to.

It is worth mentioning briefly in this connection the question of arms sales and military support to foreign and Commonwealth countries. These activities are seen, in general political terms, as being in support of the United Kingdom's general overseas interests, and they are undoubtedly used both generally and in specific circumstances (for example in Nigeria in 1968–70) to support policies and regimes for which the United Kingdom has a concern. Although this is a perfectly legitimate, and very common, activity, it does have political dangers, such as when the policy supported is unsuccessful, or when the regime is so weak as, paradoxically, to be able to dominate the relationship. Economically, the figures that are available appear to support a contention that the traffic is profitable [8]. Sales of defence equipment by British private industry in 1971–72 were estimated at about £212 million, and by Government at £58 million. These have to be offset by arms purchases from abroad, of about £96 million, and by the secondary costs of providing training and support for overseas personnel. Over 3000 men, from 40 countries, were involved in service training in the same period; and although charges are levied to cover at least some of the costs the men create, it is questionable whether full costs are recovered (or indeed ought to be charged, if it is politically desirable for such training to be proffered). More generally the case can be argued that the general capacity of industry to produce a wide range of conventional military equipment is enhanced by overseas sales, which pad out a domestic demand that in the United Kingdom is relatively small and therefore tends to impose an economic consequential in high unit costs for individual weapons or systems. This is especially true of systems using advanced technologies and expensive research and development resources, and is one of the factors which enhances the attractiveness not merely of selling military equipment abroad but also of sharing costs by collaborative schemes of procurement. But collaboration, whether in buying equipment or in developing new systems, presupposes that industrial policies, as well as security objectives, are sufficiently stable and closely aligned for the fruits of the co-operation to be nurtured over a long period of years; it takes anything up to ten years for a complex system to be developed and put into production, and a number of joint projects, like for example the development of an Anglo-French variable geometry aircraft, have had to be abandoned, either because costs have got out of hand or because national priorities have had to be changed.

The acquisition, or renunciation by a state, of a nuclear capability is not so familiar an international phenomenon as the deployment of conventional military power, and by this fact alone is more awesome. The military power of nuclear weapons is without parallel; but we have reached a position where we believe – or, to be more accurate, we in the West *assume* – that the military utility of nuclear weapons relates principally to their non-use and, so far as the minor national deterrents are concerned, may be more advantageous in influencing friends than in frightening enemies. Their precise value and the distinction to be drawn between their military and their diplomatic usefulness remain unclear; because there is no relevant experience on which we can draw, there is no special military 'expertise' about nuclear weapons and the field is open to assertion, deduction and also to denunciation about their relevance. Mr Attlee in 1955 was quite clear that the British atomic programme had given him some additional, if undefined, status as the spokesman for Britain abroad [9]; his successors, though periodically less certain, have not been able to discount his assertions enough to denude themselves of a military capability which is still shared by only a very small number of states which, *ipso facto*, are technically pre-eminent in this particular part of the military field.

None of the operations in which the services have been engaged since 1953 has entailed the use, or the threat of use, of the British nuclear capability. Very few of them would have warranted its involvement, either on military or political grounds, by any standard of judgement, and one is left with the presumption that, in spite of some carefully loose wording about the inalienably sovereign nature of any decision to commit nuclear forces owned by the State, the British nuclear forces are inherently related to homeland defence, and to the alliance on which successive governments have seen national security ineluctably dependent.

But how can possession of any or all of these forces be turned to advantage? The perspectives of the foreign policy planner and the defence planner touch but they do not coalesce. Denis Healey, who was Secretary of State for Defence from 1964 to 1970, averred that 'defence is the hand-maiden of foreign policy'; but the truth is that the relationship is too complex to be encapsulated in an aphorism. In short-term issues, when foreign policy may need to use what defence forces exist, the relationship is relatively straightforward, and the armed services have a good record in doing what is asked of them. Perhaps indeed they are too ready to respond to calls, and are not sufficiently prepared to question whether a particular situation can only be handled by the interposition of military force. They are however recruited, trained and taught to respond, with loyalty and courage, to the requirements of the State, and the one or two incidents where responses have been qualified are attributable more to intersocietal struggles than external threats : the 'Curragh Mutiny' in 1914 was a case in point.

Even in the short term, some of the discrepancies which exist between defence and foreign policy parameters become apparent. 'Defence' consists of men and material : and costs a great deal of money. 'Foreign policy' may be no more than a verbal exchange, and has no dominating logistic tail. The military planner will press for explicit details, for time-scales, for a clear definition of the task that he is being asked to handle, and for as much warning and preparation time as possible. But once the force he has planned is committed, a part of the freedom to manoeuvre that the diplomat needs to retain has been cut away; *he* will not want to commit himself until the last possible moment, and will then need to move swiftly and effectively. Precision and clearly defined alternatives may be inimical to his purpose of achieving compromise and settlement : of living to negotiate, and only perhaps to fight, another day.

This type of divergence is no less acute in 'peace-keeping' interventions than in 'war-fighting' interventions. Britain has a number of defence agreements with former dependencies, and most of them provide for assistance to be offered in the event that the former dependency asks for help. From the political point of view, such agreements exemplify a friendly relationship and a willingness to bolster the stability of newly independent governments from external threats. Hopefully it is an offer of protection that need not be activated, and is altogether a better political arrangement than trying perhaps to keep a resident protective garrison in a state which almost by definition is going to be sensitive about the outward and visible signs of the inward and spiritual achievement of freedom. It does however put additional burdens upon the defence planner, who will still have to earmark forces than can be deployed to the country in question, to maintain those discreet staff papers known as 'contingency plans', and to provide the facilities – like transport aircraft, or yellow fever vaccines – that will enable any force to arrive expeditiously and with some semblance of immediate military utility. There is an inevitable military tendency in these circumstances to presume that larger, rather than smaller, forces will be required, and a rather fearful (but wholly understandable) concern about back-up arrangements for supplies and reinforcement. The obsession of the military is that they will be called in too late to deal with a situation that is already beyond repair : that they will arrive with too few forces to be able to do either a successful or creditable job; and that they will be left to try and contain circumstances which their intervention has made less malleable, and which grumble on while stalemate is left to develop the attribute of a positive political virtue.

The virtual withdrawal of British forces from bases overseas – with the exception of a few remaining colonial outposts, like Hong Kong – provides a new complication for defence planners who may still be asked to produce forces to honour obligations undertaken before Imperial retrenchment was so complete. The mechanism of a 'strategic air-lift' is an effective, but expensive, tool which can help to bridge time and mileage gaps that might otherwise make military assistance pointless [10]. But even here, over-flying barriers, and the countervailing influences of the mass media in disseminating information quickly, may make long-range interventions a chancy business, insofar as even the most efficient airlift mounted from a 'standing start' may take several, perhaps crucial, days to reach its objective.

It was exactly this kind of calculation that led the British government in 1966 to declare, in maintaining a capability for deployment outside Europe,

first, that Britain would not undertake major operations of war except in co-operation with allies;
secondly, that Britain would not accept an obligation to provide another country with military assistance unless it was

prepared to provide the facilities that were needed to make such assistance effective in time; and

thirdly, that Britain would not attempt to maintain defence facilities in an independent country against its wish [11].

As principles, these considerations seem unexceptionable; but to the defence planner they can give no guarantee that he will not be asked at some future time to prepare an operation that cuts across any or all of them.

This is particularly true in the longer term – that future time when current equipments will have passed out of service and when new weapons and new forms of organisation may be needed to deal with different, and largely unknown, sets of circumstances. It is in this time scale that the needs of defence and foreign policy planners are less compatible. Neither technological nor political forecasting over a ten-year time-frame is likely to be of lasting validity; most of the predictions made in the past read very oddly now and, particularly on the political side, the value of apparently sophisticated predictions is related less to the techniques that are now available for use than to the quality of the largely unprovable assumptions on which they are based. Yet for the defence planner at least, the attempt to predict has to be made, if only to make explicit assumptions which can be examined against the background of his obligation to commit large sums of money to procurement programmes, covering a long period of time [12].

One of the most obvious difficulties is the inherent unreliability and uncertainty of forecasting trends in an environment where so many of the contributing elements are not susceptible to individual national influence or control. But even if some uncertainties are removed by skill, or luck, it is probable that longer-term predictions will only be of limited relevance to short-term political and financial constraints. If for example we could now foresee that in ten years time NATO would disappear in the worst possible circumstances; that Western European strength would be dissipated by a wide variety of conflicting national outlooks, and that the United States would no longer believe that the security of the Continent was important to her own safety and prosperity, it is at least unlikely that these disastrous possibilities would be able to be used as a justification for a radically new – and presumably very much more expensive – defence programme, against all the other immediate competing claims on the country's resources. Political forecasting is of a different order of complexity, and even of relevance, to the defence planner from the technical forecasting on which most of his detailed equipment planning is based.

Here he can make extrapolations from trends which are a little better able to be quantified and measured; and he is on slightly thicker ice in seeking to determine whether combat aircraft should fly high or low in ten years' time, or in hoping that lasers or infra-red beams can by then confer that good night-vision on the soldier that carrots never can. Even here there are pitfalls. The time scale in which invention can be turned to reliable operational use is very uncertain – occasionally there are break-throughs which are surprisingly quick (for example the miniaturisation of H-bomb warheads, or the development of stable large solid-fuel rocket motors), but more often there are considerable delays between the first practical application of a new principle and its appearance in front-line equipment (for example air-cushion vehicles, V/STOL aircraft).

In the meantime, both defence and foreign policy planners develop their longer-range thoughts against such general assumptions as can bridge the gap between utility and uncertainty. These necessarily tend to be of a high level of generality, and may indeed become so elevated as to be able to be used in public policy pronouncements. But they do serve the purpose of being, at least, explicit assumptions, and in the absence of an all-embracing ideology, this is perhaps the most that a democratically based government can expect to achieve. The British government has in this vein therefore, on a number of recent occasions, determined its defence priorities to be, first of all the maintenance, in strength and vivacity, of the North Atlantic Alliance : second, the maintenance of Britain's obligations to protect British territories overseas, and to render assistance to those 'to whom she owes a special duty by treaty or otherwise', and thirdly, to support the efforts of the United Nations in peacekeeping and in working to eliminate the sources of conflict between nations [13].

The NATO alliance is not the first combination of states in which Britain has endeavoured to assimilate her national interests into a wider pattern of objectives; but it is the first peace-time combination for a great many years in which she has not been preponderant. It is nevertheless a combination upon which the national security of the United Kingdom depends, and in particular it is the vehicle by which United States support is harnessed to the whole of Western Europe. The correlation of alliance aims – in both diplomatic and military terms – with national objectives has therefore been an additional complication affecting both the FCO and the Ministry of Defence. The divergence that may arise between national and alliance perceptions is displayed in its most interesting form in analyses relating to medium- and long-term planning. There are not many national organisations within the alliance capable of providing alternative postulations to those developed by the very large, and now very skilful, staffs in Washington; the British, French and latterly the West German, diplomatic and defence organisms are the major counterweights. But they have all had different pre-occupations and different perceptions of risk-taking, and have only rarely been able to attain agreement among themselves or to stimulate discussion about alliance objectives at levels which have had some relevance to the problems of individual governments within the alliance. The NATO stance – military as well as diplomatic – is composed of the individual contributions of the membership; and for individual national military staffs this stance resolves itself into a series of dilemmas about how, when and in what form existing forces should be varied, replaced and improved. Because NATO has remained essentially inter-governmental rather than supranational, the replacement of forces as well as the provision of existing forces has also remained a problem for balancing national needs and perceptions against alliance requirements: a problem in which existing national patterns and capabilities ally themselves with geography, history and industrial pressure groups, to weigh in the balance against strategic, economic and analytical logic.

REFERENCES AND NOTES

[1] Cmnd. 4290, February 1970: ch. 1, para. 48.
[2] For a comprehensive account of the development of the Ministry of Defence since the Second World War, see M. E. Howard, *The Central Organisation of Defence* (Royal United Service Institution, London, 1970).

[3] For an explanation of the United States' system, see *The Civil Services of North America: a report by the Civil Service Department*, HMSO (London, 1969).

[4] A separate procurement organisation was first set up in 1939, as the Ministry of Supply. It went through a number of name-changes and reorganisations over the next thirty years, but remained the principal procurement agency for the Royal Air Force and the Fleet Air Arm. It also provided, for a lengthy part of the period, a part of the Army's material needs. The Royal Navy retained control of the Dockyards and its own research establishments throughout. In April 1971, it was announced that military procurement and development would be brought into the Ministry of Defence, and civil aerospace affairs would be hived off to the Department of Trade and Industry (*Government Organisation for Defence Procurement*, Cmnd. 4641). Although the reorganisation is likely to produce improvements in production control procedures, it is at the present time difficult to forecast whether the highly complex issues of judgement (and luck) that arise in the research and development field will be susceptible to better control in the new set-up; the reorganisation took effect in 1972.

[5] Clive de Paula, 'A businessman in Whitehall', *The Times*, August 4, 1970 (page 19).

[6] See D. Acheson, *Present at the Creation*, Hamish Hamilton, 1970, ch. 52, for a brief account from the United States viewpoint of the Iranian crisis in 1950–51, where it seems that the use of force to ensure compliance might have been considered by the Attlee government.

[7] M. E. Howard, 'Military Power and International Order' in *International Affairs* Vol. XL. 3 (July 1964).

[8] See 'Unwritten rules of the arms business' by Henry Stanhope in *The Times*, March 31, 1971, for a brief summary of the international position, and of the British official organisation.

[9] 537 House of Commons Debates, 2 March 1955, Col. 2175.

[10] The cost of 'air mobility' forces in 1971/72 was assessed as £112 million, of which £67 million was attributable to medium and longer range aircraft. 16,700 military and 3,600 civil personnel were implicated in the 'air-mobility'

DIAGRAM. THE STRANDS OF LEADERSHIP IN THE MINISTRY OF DEFENCE

Political	*Military*	*Scientific*	*Civilian*
The Secretary of State For Defence	*The Chiefs of Staff Committee*		
The Minister of Defence for the Armed Forces	The Chief of the Defence Staff	The Chief Adviser (Projects and Research)	The Permanent Under Secretary
The Minister of State for Defence Procurement	The Deputy and Vice Chiefs of the Defence Staff: The Chief of Personnel and Logistics	The Deputy Chief Advisers (Research and Studies: Projects and Nuclear)	Deputy Under Secretaries: Administration Civilian management Equipment Finance Personnel and logistics Policy and programmes
The Under Secretary of State for the Royal Navy	The Chief of the Naval Staff The Chief of Naval Personnel The Controller of the Navy The Chief of Fleet Support The Vice-Chief of Naval Staff	The Chief Scientist (Royal Navy)	Deputy under Secretary (Royal Navy)
The Under Secretary of State for the Army	The Chief of the General Staff The Adjutant-General The Quartermaster-General The Master General of the Ordance The Vice-Chief of the General Staff	The Chief Scientist (Army)	Deputy Under Secretary (Army)
The Under Secretary of State for the Royal Air Force	The Chief of the Air Staff The Air Member for Personnel The Air Member for Supply and Organisation The Vice Chief of Air Staff	The Chief Scientist (Royal Air Force)	Deputy Under Secretary (Royal Air Force)

Note: The interposition of the Defence Procurement Executive (Cmnd. 4641) will introduce new patterns of relationships between all the strands.

function (see Annexes A and B in Statistical Annexes in *Statement on the Defence Estimates 1971*, Cmnd. 4592).

[11] See *Statement on the Defence Estimates, 1966 (Part I)* (Cmnd. 2901), Section II, para. 19.

[12] See *Statement on the Defence Estimates, 1966* (Part I) (Cmnd. 2901), Section II, for a general statement of these considerations.

[13] See, for example, *Statement on the Defence Estimates, 1970* (Cmnd. 4290), published by the Labour government, and *Supplementary Statement on Defence Policy 1970* (Cmnd. 4521), published in October 1970 by the new Conservative government.

BIBLIOGRAPHY

Buchan, A. (ed.): *Problems of Modern Strategy* (Chatto and Windus, 1970).

Knorr, K.: *On the uses of military power in the nuclear age* (Princeton, 1966).

Martin, L. W.: 'The changed role of military power' in *International Affairs*, Nov. 1970; *British Defence Policy: The Long Recessional*, Institute for Strategic Studies, 1969.

Pierre, A. J.: *Nuclear Politics* (Oxford University Press, 1972).

Snyder, W. P.: *The Politics of British Defence Policy* (Benn, 1964).

Wallace, W.: 'World Status Without Tears' in *The Age of Affluence*, ed. Bogdanor and Skidelsky (Macmillan (MSE 274), 1970).

C The Foreign and Commonwealth Office and the Social and Political Environment

10 Parliament and the Parties

PETER G. RICHARDS

CABINET CONTROL OF PARLIAMENT

THE BRITISH system of government rests on the theory of parliamentary supremacy. Ultimate authority for all acts of state is the assent of the Queen-in-Parliament. Legislation must be accepted by Parliament and then receive the Royal Assent before it becomes effective. Of course, the agreement of the monarch, *La reine le veult*, is a formality and the powers of the House of Lords have been restricted by the Parliament Acts of 1911 and 1949. So parliamentary control over legislation is now firmly in the hands of the House of Commons. Foreign affairs however are not for the most part a matter for legislation. Negotiations with foreign governments are conducted under the authority of the Royal Prerogative – 'the residue of discretionary or arbitrary authority which at any time is legally left in the hands of the Crown'. Powers of the Royal Prerogative are exercised, not by the monarch but by Ministers; the Ministers hold office because they have the confidence of the majority of Members of the Commons. Again there is a direct link between the balance of opinion in the House of Commons and the way in which the power of the state is used.

This formal, legal picture could lead to the conclusion that the Commons do have substantial control over British foreign policy. Such a view would be over-simple and misleading. In all normal circumstances the Commons do not command Ministers; on the contrary, Ministers command a parliamentary majority through the operation of party discipline. Ministers can take crucial decisions on foreign policy secure in the knowledge that if and when the Commons debate the decisions, party loyalty will be strong enough to sustain the authority of the Cabinet. No Cabinet with a clear majority in the Commons has been dismissed from office by Parliament during this century. Government backbenchers even when deeply disturbed by the actions of their leaders almost always vote to support them in moments of crisis. An individual rebel faces the prospect of rejection by his party and the end of his political career. A major collective rebellion could force the resignation of the Government, an early general election and the probability that the Opposition would succeed to office. 'United we stand, divided we fall' is a basic maxim of party conflict. Politicians heed the warning and Cabinets retain their majority in the House of Commons.

Yet to have an assessment of the Cabinet-Commons relationship solely on the realities of party discipline would also be over-simple. Ministers must take some account of public and parliamentary opinion if only because they wish to win the next election. When a Cabinet seriously offends its supporters in Parliament, it also offends a proportion of its loyal party workers in the constituencies and loses popularity in the country as a whole. Ministers want to be successful; in politics, being loved is a large part of being successful. So Ministers do not behave in an autocratic manner and ignore opinion. Where possible they try to avoid giving offence. Even major policies may be changed in deference to public or parliamentary outcry. In 1969 the Wilson Labour Government modified its policy on industrial relations because of stern opposition from its trade union supporters inside and outside the Commons. It also withdrew proposals to reform the constitution of the House of Lords due to the resistance of backbench Members in both major parties. Both these examples refer to domestic politics, not to foreign affairs, and it is difficult to produce equally clear-cut examples of parliamentary influence on the international scene. In 1956 the Eden Conservative Government reversed its Suez policy, but the change of mind was due more to international pressure than to the furore in the Commons. In 1935 the Conservative Foreign Secretary, Sir Samuel Hoare, resigned after widespread protest against his idea that the Italian–Abyssinian dispute could be settled by the partition of Abyssinia.

There are a number of reasons why it is more difficult for

Parliament to influence foreign affairs as contrasted with domestic policies. The essence of foreign policy is negotiation which may or may not lead to a need for legislation to be placed before Parliament : any important change in internal policy will certainly require legislation. It is on the detailed debates on the clauses of proposed legislation that parliamentary resistance to the will of Ministers can be most effective. An international treaty may be presented to Parliament for ratification, but this is a simpler process than the detailed scrutiny of legislation and the Government's parliamentary majority can more easily be deployed. Next, quite obviously, international affairs are not under the full control of the British Government. Ministers may be forced to acquiesce in situations which they find deeply disturbing because of the attitudes of other states. In recent years this has been a common experience. The world role which Britain played at the start of this century has receded steadily with the relative decline of British military power. The United Nations has also had a limiting effect. So the foreign policy that Ministers present to Parliament is not always the foreign policy the Cabinet would wish to have : it may simply represent the best arrangement that can be made to protect British interests in a particular situation : a leading example is the trading relationship with Europe. If Ministers are not in full command at an international negotiation then *a fortiori* Parliament is in a weak position if it wishes to influence the outcome of events. Faced with complaint about the details of some international agreement, treaty or convention, Ministers will argue that the terms are the best that could be obtained, that the alternative was not a better agreement but no agreement. Thus Parliament may be presented with what is tantamount to a *fait accompli.* At the earlier stage, when negotiations are under way, the diplomatic bargaining may be shrouded in secrecy. Even when it is not, the Government will seek to avoid debate on unfinished negotiations. Ministers do not have full control over the parliamentary timetable as the Opposition has the right to decide the subject for debate on twenty-nine days each session. Nevertheless, when the leaders of the Government and the Opposition are in broad agreement (and this is often the case with foreign affairs) an embarrassing discussion can always be avoided.

There is one more serious impediment to parliamentary

influence in foreign affairs – lack of information. Inevitably, M.P.s know less about events abroad than events at home. In part this is a function of distance; sometimes it is a matter of language difficulty; above all, it reflects lack of interest caused by lack of time. No Member can keep abreast of all aspects of public business that come before Parliament. Members must specialise. They concentrate on two or three main topics. The choice of topics depends on both the inclination and experience of a Member and the interests of his constituency. These factors tend to produce a heavy emphasis on domestic issues : voters are concerned with local economic prospects, with prices and taxes, with the quality of the social services. Save at moments of international crisis, it is rare for a Member to receive local complaints about foreign policy [1]. So the group of Members in both main parties who specialise in foreign affairs is relatively small. They tend to be drawn to this field either for ideological reasons or because they have travelled extensively and have interests abroad. They dominate the formal debates in the Chamber on foreign affairs. Certainly, it is an advantage that parliamentary debates are conducted by the Members best informed on each subject. It is also the case that the course of the general foreign affairs debate tends to be predictable; this is not so true of more limited debates on particular problems.

Thus in normal circumstances Parliament stands apart from the task of making decisions which shape the nation's commitments abroad. Parliament does not shape foreign policy any more than it drafts legislation. What Parliament does is to discuss and scrutinise. Ministers must explain and answer for their actions to the legislature. The traditional term to use in this context is 'ministerial responsibility'; this phrase can be misleading for, in common parlance, if A is responsible to B then B can dismiss A or make him change his ways. As noted already, in the modern British Parliament such sanctions are never invoked, because of the strength of party loyalties. Were party discipline ever to break, or if the electors failed to return a party with a clear majority in the Commons – then the control of Ministers over foreign policy could be undermined.

THE TREATMENT OF FOREIGN AFFAIRS
IN PARLIAMENT

Formal parliamentary attention to international affairs in the Chamber – as opposed to informal activities in committee rooms and elsewhere – has four main types of procedural base. They are legislation, questions, statements and debates on motions. The motions have many forms; they can be moved by the Government, the Opposition or a backbencher; they can form the basis of a major two-day debate, a three-hour emergency debate or a half-hour adjournment debate. Parliamentary procedure is not lacking in variety [2].

On domestic matters, legislation is the central feature of the proceedings at Westminster. On foreign affairs, legislation is intermittent and sometimes formal and unimportant. It is possible for a whole session to pass without a measure being brought forward by the Foreign Office. Equally, legislation resulting from an international treaty or agreement could be extremely controversial and important. The legal consequences of entry into the Common Market will be both extensive and complex and will surely consume much parliamentary time.

Questions are numerous. At a rough estimate rather less than 1,000 per session refer to foreign policy. But this is still only of the order of 5% of the total of parliamentary questions. Most of these are addressed to the Foreign Secretary; a few, which raise matters of major importance, are addressed to the Prime Minister. However, due to the shortage of parliamentary time the majority of questions are not dealt with by verbal exchanges on the floor of the House but by a written reply in *Hansard* which provides no opportunity for further interrogation of Ministers through supplementary questions. Further, the opportunity to put questions to Foreign Office Ministers is relatively infrequent. When Parliament is sitting there is a question hour each day from Monday to Thursday but priority of questions as between Government Departments is determined by a rota. Only when a Department is at the top of the daily list is it certain that some of its questions may be reached. The interval between such days can be as long as five weeks. Questions to the Prime Minister are allocated a quarter of an hour each Tuesday and Thursday, but these cover all aspects of government policy and foreign affairs may be squeezed out.

Backbenchers are at a considerable disadvantage if they challenge Ministers through this interrogatory procedure. Usually their questions are framed to provide the opportunity for a searching supplementary which it is hoped will attract publicity to a grievance or catch a Minister unawares. Official answers are drafted with the assistance of senior civil servants and are prepared in such a way as to minimise the possibility of embarrassment for the Minister. The result is an intriguing parliamentary game, but one that does not necessarily provide much additional information about foreign policy. Of course, there are exceptions: a Minister may arrange for a question to be asked as a means of attracting publicity for some development.

Rather more information may be obtained from a ministerial statement at the end of question time. This will refer to a topical matter of some gravity. It is followed by an opportunity for questions – rather more opportunity than would be allowed at question time. Even so, a statement cannot lead to a debate. Any major, searching examination of public policy demands a debate.

Parliamentary debates on foreign affairs can be divided into two broad categories. Some are wide-ranging reviews of many international problems : others are restricted to particular issues, e.g. Vietnam or British entry to the Common Market. By tradition, the opening debate in each session of Parliament is the Address in reply to the Queen's Speech; one day of this debate is devoted to a broad or unstructured discussion of the international scene. Normally there is at least one other such general discussion, commonly lasting two days, each session. The frequency of the specific type of debate is far more variable : it depends wholly on the pressure of events. Certainly, the debates with a precise focus are more impressive as the limited subject-matter permits fuller explanation by Ministers and more detailed and searching criticisms by their opponents.

The use made of parliamentary time is arranged through negotiation between Government and Opposition. Each Thursday a Government statement is made which announces the business for the following week. Thus the pattern of debates is fixed well in advance to enable Members to prepare for them and the agenda could be too inflexible to allow Members to

debate unexpected events abroad which may have serious consequences for British interests. There is an obvious need for
emergency procedure which can be used in emergency situations.
The House of Commons does have such an arrangement known
as Standing Order 9. This allows the motion for the adjournment
of the House to be used to discuss an urgent and specific matter
of great importance. A Member may request such an emergency
debate at the end of question time and is expected to give Mr
Speaker advance notice of his intention. The Speaker has to
decide whether the request falls within the terms of the Standing
Order. If he assents and if the request is supported by 40
Members – which it always is – then the emergency debate will
take place for three hours after questions on the next day the
House is sitting, or on Monday if the request is made on a
Thursday. This delay does give greater time to prepare for the
emergency debate and should increase its value. Before 1967
Standing Order 9 was so rarely used that one feared that the
procedure might disappear altogether through decay. The rulings
from the Chair about its use had become increasingly restrictive.
Any decision on whether a matter is of sufficient gravity to justify
disturbance of the agreed parliamentary timetable must be subjective; the tendency had been for the Speaker to rule that topics
raised were not of sufficient gravity. There were two other
restrictions. The adjournment was not to be granted if there was
any other opportunity of raising the matter in the House in the
near future; nor was it to be granted if the issue raised fell outside
the responsibility of Ministers. The latter restriction was of
particular significance to foreign affairs for the action of a foreign
government does fall 'outside the responsibility of Ministers'
although it may be detrimental to British subjects. In 1967 the
severity of the restriction was limited : the Standing Order now
decrees that when Mr Speaker has to decide whether to agree to
an emergency debate he 'shall have regard to the extent to which
(the subject) concerns the administrative responsibility of Ministers
or could come within the sphere of Ministerial action'.

There have been four emergency debates in each of the
sessions, 1967–68, 1968–69, 1969–70. The subjects are listed in
the table below and it will be noted that all, save one, have
international implications. It is quite certain that revision of the
emergency Standing Order has added an element of surprise

together with vigour and immediacy to the Commons' discussions on foreign affairs. The break in normal parliamentary routine also has news value for the mass media and ensures wide publicity for the main speeches.

TABLE 1. EMERGENCY ADJOURNMENT DEBATES
Sessions 1967–68, 1968–69, 1969–70

Date	Subject
5 Dec. 1967	Letter of intent to the International Monetary Fund
19 Dec. 1967	Supply of arms to South Africa
7 May 1968	Gibraltar: closure of frontier
12 June 1968	Supply of arms to Nigeria
30 Jan. 1969	Postal service
25 Feb. 1969	Anglo-French relations
22 April 1969	Events in Northern Ireland
17 June 1969	Tanks for Libya
26 Jan. 1970	Relief for Nigeria
7 April 1970	Situation in Northern Ireland
5 May 1970	Extension of war in Indo-China
14 May 1970	South African cricket tour

The pattern of business in the Lords is similar but not identical to that of the Commons. Questions are much fewer; half a dozen on one day is a large number. Their Lordships spend less time on economic affairs so a higher proportion of their time can be devoted to foreign affairs. This does not mean that the Lords devote more debating time to foreign affairs than the Commons because their sittings are fewer and shorter. Since the Upper House has a permanent Conservative majority, any non-Conservative Government is liable to be defeated at any time. When the Lords pass a motion displeasing to the Government, the defeat can be ignored with impunity. Rejection of an item of legislation however is very serious. In June 1969, the Order continuing sanctions against Rhodesia was turned down by their Lordships. The margin was narrow – 193 votes to 184. Nevertheless, the decision was a major challenge to the Wilson Labour Government. A Bill rejected by the Upper House can still become law after a delay of twelve months if it is passed by the Commons a second time, but this technique for overcoming the Lords' veto does not apply to Orders issued under the authority of Acts of Parliament. In any case, a delay of twelve months on a matter of this kind would have been wholly unacceptable to the Government. After a short interval the Lords allowed a second Order authorising sanctions to pass : the alternative would have been a major constitutional crisis.

So far this section has been concerned with the formal proceedings of both Houses. But M.P.s have other means of expressing views. Both Conservative and Labour Members have formed unofficial committees (known as groups) of backbenchers to pay particular attention to a field of public policy. So there is a backbench Labour group on foreign affairs and a similar Conservative one. Not unnaturally, these bodies are dominated by Members who have the most active interest in foreign affairs. How a group works depends partly on whether it is formed of Government or Opposition supporters. An Opposition group is little more than a debating society that may have interesting outside speakers. The Government backbench group will be in constant touch with the Foreign Secretary through the latter's parliamentary private secretary – this is a Member who acts as an unpaid liaison officer between a Minister and backbenchers. From time to time a Foreign Office Minister will be asked to speak to his Party's group. In these conditions a group may be quietly influential. Particularly with the Conservatives, these discussions are conducted privately and confidentially so that the extent of backbench influence on a Conservative Government is impossible to assess. The Labour Foreign Affairs group has been more contentious. Membership of these party groups is open to any Member in receipt of the Party Whip; thus a group need not be representative of opinion within the Party. Left-wingers have played a prominent role in the Labour Foreign Affairs group and this has led to tension between the group and Labour Ministers, in particular Ernest Bevin, Foreign Secretary in the Attlee Government, and Michael Stewart, Foreign Secretary in the Wilson Government. But this left-wing pressure has had little effect on policy except when Ministers themselves held divided opinions, as over the supply of arms to South Africa.

Other informal groups of M.P.s are organised on a non-party basis. Some exist to promote friendly relations with a particular foreign government and the extent and significance of their activities will depend upon the country forming the link : a group connected with Israel or an Arab state will be more controversial than one connected with a NATO country. An informal coterie of M.P.s and peers may gather to campaign for a particular cause : non-party meetings can be very useful for they serve to emphasise that parliamentary opinion is not split strictly on party lines. One example is the United Nations Parliamentary Group. Another is the group associated with the Common Market Safeguards Campaign which is critical of the proposal to join the European Economic Community.

There are, of course, links between pressure groups formed outside Parliament and these informal gatherings of M.P.s. A few such pressure groups have been large, prestigious and influential, notably the Campaign for Nuclear Disarmament and the various bodies formed to fight the Common Market issue. Yet foreign affairs do not produce the same wealth of political activity as domestic politics because the general level of public concern with international questions is low. This is illustrated by the lack of parliamentary interest even in international topics which do have social and economic implications : the work of the specialised agencies of the United Nations attracts little attention in the Commons. Again, apart from the Common Market controversy, tariffs do not arouse as much interest as in the earlier years of the twentieth century. Individual Members are sensitive to movements in trade which affect their own constituencies but the number of Members aroused by any particular change in trading patterns – higher imports of cauliflowers or tomatoes – will be small.

There is a widespread feeling both among M.P.s and among commentators outside Parliament that discussion at Westminster is most valuable, constructive and possibly influential, when conducted among small numbers of Members who specialise in the subject under consideration. It is argued that the Commons would serve a more useful purpose if M.P.s formed a range of Select Committees specialising in particular subjects [3]. Select Committees do not hold debates of the style used in the Chamber of the House. Instead they receive evidence, examine witnesses and produce a report containing recommendations. The tradition is that Select Committees work in a non-party atmosphere and are free from control by the Whips. A few specialised Select

Committees were established in the 1966–70 Parliament. Barker and Rush found that 80% of Labour Members and 56% of Conservative Members favoured extension of this form of parliamentary activity [4]. In spite of this impressive amount of support for specialised committees one suspects that there is still confusion and hidden disagreement over what functions they can usefully perform. At least three alternative models are possible. A Select Committee could be a highly political body used by Members to press their own political attitudes; it could be an objective, fact-finding body; if the subject-matter were sufficiently non-controversial, it could become a public relations *aide* to Ministers. Advocates of Select Committees will claim that these models are not mutually exclusive and that the prime task of these bodies is to collect information and frame recommendations which will assist the House of Commons as a whole to maintain more effective scrutiny over executive actions.

No Select Committee has yet been established to review foreign affairs. Such a Committee would encounter special difficulties. Some of the information which has a vital influence on foreign policy is strictly confidential, at least in the short term : there are obvious objections to increasing the availability of such information. Foreign policy is also either acutely controversial or it arouses little interest. A Foreign Affairs Committee might be tempted to act on the political model described above. If it did so, the Committee would then lose its non-party character and the Government would invoke party loyalty and party discipline to prevent any serious challenge arising from its deliberations. International relations do not fall within the category of fairly limited or technical topics that are most obviously suitable for Select Committee treatment. Nevertheless, I have argued elsewhere that the experiment of a Commons' Foreign Affairs Committee should be tried [5].

PARTY ATTITUDES TO FOREIGN POLICY

In the past the leadership of the major political parties have normally been in broad agreement over their basic approach to foreign policy. Of necessity, this has blurred the impact that Parliament might have made on international issues. The consensus has been based on a shared appreciation of the nature of British interests. Britain is a 'satisfied' power. Its concern has been to maintain the *status quo*; to insist on respect for existing international agreements; to prevent any state or combination of states from exercising unchallenged sway over Europe. A balance of power in Europe, combined with the security obtained from her insular situation, provided a foundation for British independence. Domestic support for the balance of power policy has been facilitated because the states which have challenged the balance in the last forty years, Nazi Germany and subsequently the Soviet Union, have been authoritarian regimes. Thus British policy in Europe has been represented, and correctly represented, as support for democracy; but it also constitutes support for the balance of power.

British policy is also to favour peace rather than war. All political parties accept this principle. But the reasons for desiring peace have changed over time. An Imperial power, a satisfied power, with colonial possessions in every continent, will wish for peace; war or other limited disturbances are a threat to its established authority. With the growth of nonconformist influence in public affairs, the moral desirability of peace began to be stressed. Now, in the nuclear age, the consequences of total war between the major powers are so horrifying that the need for peace requires no emphasis. So British statesmen of all parties have tried to cool the tensions between East and West while keeping Britain firmly within the NATO alliance. Churchill in his declining years as Prime Minister tried to arrange a 'summit' meeting with the Russian leaders. Macmillan worked hard to bring about the abortive summit conference of 1960. When the Russian Prime Minister Kosygin visited London in 1967, the British Prime Minister, Harold Wilson, tried unsuccessfully to use the visit as a means to promote peace in Vietnam. Linked with the desire to reduce world tension is also the desire that Britain should be present at all major international negotiations. Wilson and his Labour Cabinet, 1964–70, had this urge at least as strongly as Conservative Ministers. The status of Britain as a world power has declined substantially since 1945 : perhaps the desire for a seat at the 'top table' is partly due to sensitivity about this fall in Britain's international status, but there is also a fear that the super-powers, United States and Soviet Russia, meeting without the presence of a British representative could come to arrangements that would be detrimental to British interests.

The basic agreement on these fundamental considerations between the Conservative, Labour and Liberal Parties sometimes tends to conceal disagreement on foreign policy within the main parties. This is particularly true of the Conservatives. The Tory right wing regrets the loss of Britain's dominant role in world politics and has been unenthusiastic about the grant of independence to colonial territories. Those who share this view urge the need for higher levels of expenditure on defence to strengthen the British presence overseas; in particular, the need to ensure the freedom of maritime routes is stressed. Such a scale of values helps to explain why the Eden Government undertook the ill-fated Suez expedition in 1956 and why in 1970 there was a Conservative policy to resume arms sales to South Africa. On occasion right-wing Tories have clashed openly with a Conservative Government, notably in 1935 over the degree of independence granted to India and in 1954 over the agreement with Egypt to withdraw the British base from the Canal Zone.

Disagreement between Labour left-wingers and the Labour leadership has been rather more persistent and obvious. There is a difference in style between the two parties. Conservatives tend to argue quietly and privately : Labour supporters argue openly at meetings. Labour has a tradition of deciding policy by taking votes. This is open and democratic, but not always effective. At the 1966 Labour Party Conference two resolutions on foreign policy were passed contrary to the wishes of the party leadership : one resolution called for a reduction in military expenditure east of Suez while the other called on the Labour Cabinet to bring pressure to bear on the United States to stop the Vietnam war. The Prime Minister, Harold Wilson, commented 'While we are always keen to know the views of Conference, the Government is, of course, responsible to Parliament. It would not be possible to run a coherent foreign policy or defence policy if you could be forced to change direction, perhaps even to break treaties or alliances, on the basis of a single vote'. In fact, the Labour Government did subsequently decide to cut military commitments east of Suez, but only after the devaluation crisis in the autumn of 1967. The Conference resolution on Vietnam had no noticeable effect on Government policy.

Left-wing sentiment in the Labour Party is deeply hostile to *laissez-faire* capitalism which is characteristic of the United States. It is also hostile to militarism as being an immoral and irrational means of settling international disputes. Radical attitudes favour equality, individuality and oppose authoritarianism. Labour left-wingers tend to a neutralist approach to the East-West struggle, but they are not a clearly defined or separate political force and their policies vary with changing circumstances. Sympathy for the Soviet Union declined sharply after the invasion of Hungary in 1956 and again after the invasion of Czechoslovakia in 1968. The most notable triumph achieved by the left-wing was the vote at the 1960 Labour Party Conference in favour of nuclear disarmament. Hugh Gaitskell, then Leader of the Party, refused to adjust his policy to meet the resolution and the vote was reversed at the 1961 Party Conference. Among Labour M.P.s the left-wingers have always been in a minority. Their strength varies from time to time, from issue to issue. As a rough estimate one may say that up to a quarter of Labour M.P.s may favour left-wing or neutralist policies: seventy Members voted for Aneurin Bevan in the leadership election of 1955 and sixty-seven Members voted for Michael Foot in the contest for deputy leader in 1970.

The recent lowering of tension between the Soviet Union and the Western democracies has been associated with the emergence or re-emergence of other international issues. The latter have disturbed quite substantially the traditional consensus on foreign policy supported by the main political parties. On some questions, opinion is now divided on party lines; elsewhere both parties are divided and the cleavage of opinion cuts across normal political allegiance. An example in the second category is provided by the Arab-Israel conflict, for it is possible to find both Jewish and Arab sympathisers in the Conservative Party and the Labour Party. Even more striking is the confusion of views over the prospect of British entry to the Common Market. Here the dominant feeling is one of anxiety verging on fear. Some are worried that if Britain does not face the challenge and grasp the opportunities provided by admission to the Economic Community, then the rate of advance in the standard of living will fall behind that of other European states. Others fear the consequences for price levels or for particular sections of the community, for example, farmers and industrial workers faced with European competition; alternatively, there is concern about the loss of sovereignty or about damage to the relationship with the Commonwealth. Some left-wing opinion sees the Common Market as another buttress to the anti-Communist coalition of states which would make it more difficult to follow an independent neutralist-style foreign policy. Inevitably, the result of this anxiety complex is political confusion. An organisation known as The Conservative Group for Europe was formed in 1970 under the presidency of the Prime Minister, Edward Heath, to express support for the application to join EEC. The Labour pro-Market pressure group is The Labour Committee for Europe whose chairman in 1970 was Sir Geoffrey de Freitas. The Anti-Marketeers were organised on an all-party basis and in 1970 a Common Market Safeguards Campaign was launched which co-ordinated the efforts of earlier anti-Market organisations. The officers of this Campaign included three M.P.s, and a further 46 M.P.s, some Labour and some Conservative, agreed to be 'patrons' of the Campaign.

Where the pattern of opinion runs parallel with the normal lines of party allegiance, public and parliamentary debate is more frequent and less inhibited. In 1970 the Conservative and Labour Parties disagreed over the need to maintain a British military presence east of Suez. This is a foreign policy and defence issue; it is also an economic issue since it affects the size and nature of Government expenditure. At the same time another and even more important issue divided the parties – the sale of arms to South Africa. The policy of Sir Alec Douglas-Home, the Foreign Secretary, was to sell such armaments as would help to ensure the security of the sea routes round the Cape but which could not be used for internal oppression of the native African population. The Labour case was that no such distinction between categories of armaments was possible in practice, that any military assistance rendered to South Africa would be interpreted throughout the world – and especially in the British Commonwealth – as support for the apartheid policies of the South African government. Here was a foreign policy issue with profound moral implications which aroused not only political but also religious opinion.

The dispute over arms for South Africa was the most contentious issue during the debate on the Queen's Speech when the new Parliament assembled after the 1970 General Election. The consensus on foreign policy was broken, and with it the rather paternalistic attitude that leading politicians of all parties sometimes adopt towards public discussion of foreign affairs. A former Minister of State at the Foreign Office in the Attlee Labour Government has written :

> In the absence of devastating party strife, it should, I believe, be possible for a government in this country to secure acceptance of its basic foreign objectives, by means of adequate exposition by the Prime Minister and the Foreign Secretary in Parliament and to a less extent through the public relations machinery of the Foreign Office. . . . It is no reflection upon the intelligence of the public to say that in foreign matters they stand particularly in need of clear and honest leadership [6].

In my view a democracy must reject the theory that foreign affairs are a matter for the executive branch of government, that Ministers lead, Ministers explain, and then most people follow. The more foreign affairs raise issues which affect the domestic economy or impinge on moral principles, the more vigorously will foreign policy be debated in Parliament and elsewhere. Surely the prospect for the future is that international questions cannot be kept in a separate watertight compartment.

REFERENCES AND NOTES

[1] The question of entry into the Common Market is an exception because these international relationships could have a major impact on the internal economic situation.
[2] For a full account see Peter G. Richards, *Parliament and Foreign Affairs* (Allen & Unwin, 1970), Ch. V.
[3] Bernard Crick, *The Reform of Parliament* (Weidenfeld & Nicolson, 1964) puts the case with great vigour and clarity.
[4] *The Member of Parliament and his Information* (Allen & Unwin, 1970), p. 151.
[5] *Parliament and Foreign Affairs*, Chap. VIII.
[6] Kenneth Younger, 'Public Opinion and Foreign Policy', *The British Journal of Sociology* (1955), Vol. 6, p. 175.

BIBLIOGRAPHY

Epstein, Leon D., *British Politics in the Suez Crisis* (Pall Mall, 1964).
Northedge, F. S., *The Foreign Policies of the Powers* (Faber, 1968).
Richards, Peter G., *Parliament and Foreign Affairs* (Allen & Unwin, 1967).
Waltz, Kenneth N., *Foreign Policy and Democratic Politics* (Longmans, 1968).
Younger, Kenneth, 'Public Opinion and Foreign Policy', *The British Journal of Sociology*, 1955, Vol. 6, pp. 169–75.

11 The Role of Interest Groups

WILLIAM WALLACE

IT IS a commonplace of academic writing that foreign policy-making is an area both separate and distinct from the process of domestic politics. The argument is made partly from the nature of the values with which foreign policy is concerned, partly from the particular conditions under which foreign – as opposed to domestic – policy-makers operate, and partly from observation.

Certainly the values at stake in foreign policy are intimately linked with the idea of the nation state: with nationhood, nationalism, a country's 'place in the world', with all the implications such terms carry for a nation's image of itself and for its feelings about national standing. The defence of the realm, the safeguarding of national security and the protection of citizens abroad, were historically among the first duties of national governments. The responsibility of governments for promoting and protecting foreign trade has grown, with the development of an interdependent international economy and the expansion of governmental control of the domestic economy, into a further foreign policy concern of fundamental importance to the state: the preservation and promotion of national prosperity. It is hardly surprising therefore that an area so vital to the survival and security of the state should be regarded as 'outside' the arena of domestic politics. Over education or incomes policy, over social security benefits or tax reform, the state may safely act as arbiter among the clash of sectional interests and the lobbying of affected groups. But 'politics' should be kept out of foreign policy. Where the national interest as such is at stake, politicians (it is argued, and widely accepted) should prefer their country to their party, and pressure groups their country to their own interest.

Foreign policy is also distinguished from domestic politics, it is argued, by the different circumstances under which policy-makers are forced to operate. In its external relations a government is not simply involved in a domestic political process, over which it retains the ultimate authority. On the international level it is only one actor among many, without the authority or power to execute its decisions, with only limited means available to implement its preferences [1]. The most important participants in the process of international politics are beyond the government's authority : the foreign governments with which it must deal. The pressures they exert must often outweigh domestic pressures; the balance of international forces necessarily limits its freedom to manoeuvre in response to domestic demands. Moreover the intricacy and the insecurity of international diplomacy require a level of secrecy about government intentions which severely limits the possibility of domestic debate.

This picture of external affairs as outside and above domestic politics has never been entirely accurate. Even in the nineteenth century heyday of the nation state, governments were unable to exert complete control over political relations across state boundaries, or entirely to exclude such 'matters of state' from the rough-and-tumble of domestic politics. In the increasingly inter-dependent international society of the contemporary developed world the line between domestic and international considerations, political, economic or social, is becoming less and less distinct. The traditional image of foreign policy as 'high politics', as primarily diplomacy and defence, does not extend to the range of interconnected questions of commercial, financial, or cultural relations with which foreign policy-makers in their daily work are as immediately concerned. At these lower levels of external relations the national interest is not so clear, and the possibilities for influence and for domestic dispute are wider.

Yet in most areas of external policy the executive branch is still uninhibited by many of the limitations on its freedom of action which affect the policy-making process in domestic policy. There is relatively little legislation in the foreign policy area, and this deprives interested groups of a convenient focus for activity, of the conventional pattern of consultation and lobbying which characterises the legislative process [2]. With the enormous and crucial exception of the defence budget, foreign policy in general is a relatively minor consumer of government resources. A politician may gain a little short-term publicity by attacking the size of the aid budget, or the distribution of British Council expenditure, or the style of living at Embassies abroad; but it will not release any sizeable funds for other programmes if he is successful in reducing them. The flow of foreign policy is not one of annual reviews and regular decisions, but of shifting and flexible positions the pattern of which it is often difficult for the outsider to trace. In the foreign policy area then, the targets for group pressure are more elusive, more difficult to grasp.

The issues of foreign policy are mostly remote from the daily concerns of the population. In spite of the emphasis which both press and television give to foreign affairs the level of popular attention to foreign policy remains in general low. A crisis may bring a sudden upsurge of public interest, an apparent foreign disaster create a sense of involvement for the normally uninvolved; the Suez invasion brought crowds out into the streets, the Biafran tragedy aroused a great many. But after each crisis the interest of the mass public subsides back to a position of relative unconcern. The attentive public for foreign policy is only a small proportion even of the politically interested – those with a particular commitment to external concerns (and probably a particular view of the world), those with a personal link to a particular foreign country or region, and those whose professional interests involve them in external affairs. This lack of mass interest severely limits the possibilities for group recruitment, for putting pressure on the Government on the basis of a public campaign. It offers however some compensating advantages. Where the number of those who are both interested and informed is small and concentrated, the opportunities for the exercise of influence through informal élite channels are greater [3].

The corollary of the lack of domestic interest is that there are in Britain few domestic interests (in the narrow sense of that term) at stake in foreign policy. Unless one considers the armed services as an interest, the only domestic groups whose active co-operation the government must have in order to implement its foreign policy are trading companies, banks and industrial firms in the field of external commercial and monetary policy. Jews,

Pakistanis, East European refugees and other ethnic groups represent a foreign policy interest of a different order; churches and trade unions retain a rather weaker sense of interest in their fellow-believers and fellow-workers overseas. But none of these have any sanction over the execution of government policy more direct than the ballot box, or faintly comparable with those which the medical profession can exert over the Health Service or teachers over educational policy [4]. The network of consultative committees through which the British Government involves affected interests in the formulation, and occasionally the execution, of domestic policy exists in the foreign field only in commercial matters. A survey of advisory committees in 1960 found that the Foreign Office sponsored none, the Commonwealth Relations Office only five [5].

THE RANGE OF GROUPS

It might seem reasonable to conclude from this that the activities and influence of non-official groups in the British foreign policy process are weak and intermittent. Yet organisations, 'campaigns' and societies exist and operate in bewildering profusion over the whole field of foreign policy. There are few safe generalisations that can be made about their purposes of activities : groups with similar titles often pursue radically different purposes, and the aims (and strength) of many groups change considerably over a period of time. A brief attempt at classification may nevertheless help to introduce the reader to the field [6].

Probably the largest number of organisations – though not necessarily the majority of the most influential – can be classified as 'promotional' : groups which exist to further a cause which is not primarily their own self-interest. There is nothing very new about promotional activity in external affairs. Anti-Slavery groups existed in the late eighteenth century, and conducted a long and eventually successful campaign to alter the direction of government policy. Zionist organisations – which may best be considered as partly promotional and partly based on sectional interest – were intimately involved in the events which led up to the Balfour Declaration, and in the evolution of British policy towards the 'Jewish National Home' in Palestine. The League of Nations

Union in its heyday had half a million members, and the 'Peace Ballot' made a deep impression on the debate over collective security and disarmament. A number of organisations whose main activities are in other areas concern themselves, amongst other things, with foreign policy. Women's organisations, social groups, and churches often pass resolutions on external questions – though few except the churches take their concern much beyond communicating their opinions to their local newspaper or M.P. More exclusively foreign policy promotional groups range from the respectable and all-party United Nations Association to the predominantly left-wing Movement for Colonial Freedom, and the extra-parliamentary Vietnam Solidarity Campaign.

Almost as many organisations as there are sovereign states exist 'to promote the closest possible understanding between the peoples of Germany [or Turkey or Thailand] and the United Kingdom in all appropriate fields of activity and relationship' [7]. The oldest of those now active were set up in the wake of the First or the Second World War, growing out of committees which had raised money for refugees, helped exiles, or worked to encourage the re-establishment of democracy, or out of attempts to retain British interest in areas where wartime exigencies or the reduction of British investments had weakened previous ties. In membership they range from the Anglo-Austrian, with 3,000 members, to the Anglo-Mongolian, with 35. Most societies include companies as corporate members, businessmen with related interests, scholars, returned tourists, Embassy representatives, and a sprinkling of notables – M.P.s, peers, retired diplomats. Many have charitable status, and would consider their activities entirely outside politics. But it is hard for the Anglo-Hellenic League, or the Society for Anglo-Chinese Understanding, to be completely above politics in promoting closer relations between their respective peoples and governments. The chairman of the Anglo-Cameroons Society felt moved in 1969 to make a public protest over an airport incident involving the Cameroons Prime Minister's son; the Anglo-Zanzibar Society sent a deputation to the Foreign Office in 1970 to urge the Government to make representations over forced marriages on the island [8]. The Anglo-Rhodesian Society might better be described as promoting a cause than as a primarily cultural and social organisation.

The organisation of interests concerned with the protection and promotion of foreign trade and investment is as old as promotional activity in external affairs. 'From the early 18th century the West Indian sugar interests were a continuous and powerful force'; in 1785 Josiah Wedgwood's General Chamber of Manufacturers 'helped to wreck Pitt's proposals for Anglo-Irish free trade' [9]. The Association of British Chambers of Commerce was established in 1860, and immediately began sending deputations to the Foreign Office on the subject of foreign tariffs, and complaining about the Office's dilatory attitude to trade; the Corporation of Foreign Bondholders was incorporated in 1873, to protect its members' interests and to make representations when necessary to the Government. In this area again organisations with more general interests, the CBI, the Chemical Industries Association, the British Trawlers' Federation, are paralleled by groups whose exclusive concern is with external questions – the West Africa Committee, the United Kingdom-South Africa Trade Association, the Canadian Chamber of Commerce in Great Britain. Their close relationship with government, through regular informal contacts and through a network of advisory committees, was probably at its most intimate in the 1930s, when through the Import Duties Advisory Committee the Federation of British Industries and the larger trade associations attained a 'strategic position' over tariff policy and administration [10]. The growing preoccupation of British governments with the promotion of exports as the first objective of external policy has added to these a further network of semi-official committees, grouped (until its abolition in May 1971) under the British National Export Council, to complete a pattern of bewildering complexity and considerable duplication.

It is arguable that one should include foreign governments as a fourth category of groups involved in the British foreign policy process. Foreign governments and their embassies perform many of the activities which are familiar to non-official groups, with many of the same aims : advertising extensively in the quality press, sending publicity material to selected groups, writing letters to newspapers, entertaining the influential and inviting them to make sponsored visits to their own countries [11]. Their cultural institutes in Britain are intended to widen interest in and understanding of their countries. Their trade missions spend often considerable sums on promoting their trade – and some, like the East German trade mission, serve other purposes as well. Indirectly their activities are wider : they provide financial and organisational support for Anglo-Ruritanian societies, they finance scholarships, they employ public relations agencies to promote their image or purvey their press reports – usually without arousing political controversy, though Voice and Vision's efforts to promote the Central African Federation and Markpress's publicity for the Biafran cause aroused considerable comment. The representatives of international organisations may perform a similar if much more discreet, role. The United Nations Information Office in London provides advice, information and encouragement to the various groups promoting UN concerns, and for a short period until 1962 the European Communities Information Office supplied enthusiastic supporters of the Common Market as speakers to interested groups [12].

An alternative classification might focus on the different types of aims which groups involved in external policy pursue. Clearly a great many are primarily concerned to influence the British Government – though their sights may be set at very different levels. The CBI in a particular instance may simply be concerned to prevent damage to its members' external interests, the 'Sugar lobby' to protect West Indian trade. The various organisations of the Aid lobby have been immediately concerned, in recent campaigns, to prevent further cuts in the Government's aid budget, and to raise its projections for aid in the next five years : both tangible and attainable targets, which already had some support inside Whitehall [13]. The organisations of what is often called the Peace Movement, in contrast, are working for a revolution in British foreign policy which commands little sympathy in Whitehall or in Parliament. Some groups have been less concerned with converting the Government than with committing one of the major Parties to a particular line of policy, to be implemented when office was regained. The main target for CND was the Labour Party; for the South African lobby it has been the Conservatives. Other groups are concerned above all to present their side of the case in what they see as an unfavourable climate of public debate and biased communications – as the Council for the Advancement of Arab-British Understanding attempts to do in the propaganda 'war' on the Middle East in London. Still others – such as Amnesty, or Anti-Apartheid, or

the Anti-Slavery Society – are primarily concerned with influencing not the British but foreign governments, and attempt to
influence the British Government (if at all) only as a means of
increasing the pressure on them. A great many other organisations
are not immediately concerned to affect the course of government
policy, but rather to mould and educate public opinion – a less
directly political activity, but one which is nevertheless intended
to have political effects in the long run.

Any such classification must over-simplify enormously the
proliferation and variety of function which characterise the field.
Groups with a wide area of concern, such as the United Nations
Association, the British Council of Churches, the CBI, or the
London Chamber of Commerce, not only associate many single-
purpose organisations with their activities but sponsor new groups
either as *ad hoc* bodies or as more permanent committees or
organisations, as new needs or causes emerge. The duplication of
effort in the commercial field between trade associations, Chambers of Commerce, the major federations and the new semi-
governmental bodies is paralleled by a similar duplication in the
promotional field, where in the Aid lobby, the Peace Movement,
or the anti-South African lobby each new generation has set up
its own organisations, presenting a confusing picture of overlapping bodies of varying age, strength, and respectability or
radicalism [14]. Some organisations set up affiliates to broaden
their appeal to particular groups. The European Movement
sponsors some twenty such bodies, from the Labour Committee
for Europe to the Young European Management Association :
the British Peace Committee in the early fifties sponsored, among
others, Artists for Peace and the Medical Association for the
Prevention of War. A complicated network of co-ordinating
committees, overlapping memberships and cross-affiliations, complicated by differences on tactics or policy and clashes between
the strong personalities which dominate so many groups, holds
the field together. The M.P. who is interested in external affairs is
likely to appear on the letterhead of several dozen organisations;
a company with extensive overseas interests, or a merchant bank,
may pay subscriptions to over a hundred bodies promoting trade
or cultural relations. A more fundamental difficulty is that
some of the most influential 'groups' are not, strictly speaking,
organised. The 'lobby' which changed the Labour Government's

mind over arms sales to South Africa in December 1967, the similar 'group' which watched any sign of concessions over Rhodesia, were not recognisable organisations but groups of people centred on the Labour Party inside and outside Parliament.

The boundary between political and non-political activity is hard to define. The aid organisation with charitable status whose primarily money-raising function has expanded into 'educational activities' and close contacts with the Government, shades into the primarily promotional body, with an associated charitable trust to finance its educational activities. The Society of Friends is a religious body, not a political organisation; but the work of the Friends Peace and International Relations Committee, in spelling out the Quaker concern for peace in the world, nevertheless involves it in activity intended to influence our own and other governments. Many 'non-political' organisations could more correctly be described as non-partisan but political in function. Motives and interests are often mixed as well. Promotional groups of British sympathisers for a foreign cause shade into exile groups hoping, or plotting, for their eventual return. Businessmen with interests in black Africa are associated with groups concerned to bring pressure to bear on southern Africa; the Aid lobby overlaps the Sugar lobby in concerns and membership, and both share members and interests with bodies concerned to promote attachment to the Commonwealth.

The boundary between official and non-official, between governmental and non-governmental, is equally difficult to trace. The British National Export Council was 'an independent organisation run by businessmen whose contribution in time and expertise is matched by the government which provides the funds for its day to day operations' [15]. The United Kingdom National Committees for UNESCO and FAO are serviced by the Overseas Development Administration, and their chairman is the Minister for Overseas Development – though the UK Committees for UNICEF and the WHO have a rather more independent status; the Foreign and Commonwealth Office gives financial and other assistance to a limited number of promotional groups. The Committee of the British Council of Churches, the report from which in 1966 contained the first public declaration by an influential body of the need for aid organisations to take political action as well as to raise money, included observers from the ODM, the

Board of Trade and the Ministry of Agriculture, as well as the distinguished exile, Dr K. A. Busia, who later became Prime Minister of an aid-receiving country. The Anglo-Brazilian Society, which receives a grant from the Brazilian Government, has representatives of the BBC, the British Council and the Brazilian Embassy on its executive council, and in its turn nominates representatives to the official 'House of Brazil'. The Anglo-Jordan Alliance received £100,000 in 1968–69 for its activities from the Shaikh of Abu Dhabi [16].

THE PROBLEM OF ACCESS

The nature of the foreign policy process makes the problem of access peculiarly difficult for interest groups. In the past their difficulties were made more acute by 'the persistence of an aloof attitude' in the Foreign Office [17] – though there are many indications that this traditional aloofness has lessened considerably in the past decade. Those groups whose aims are more or less in harmony with official policy, whose respectability is accepted by ministers and civil servants, may develop a close relationship with the Foreign and Commonwealth Office; the United Nations Association for example has a close formal and informal relationship with the two UN departments in the Office. Responsibility for liaison with non-official organisations within the Foreign Office rests primarily at the departmental level. Many see it as their duty to offer advice and encouragement to 'their' groups, and most accept as one of their functions the need to keep in touch with informed and organised opinion – though some, such as the Near Eastern Department, have little need to encourage outside pressure. Correspondence from 'respected' groups receives a degree of consideration second only to that given to letters from M.P.s; deputations will be received by a minister. For commercial and business organisations of course the relationship is far closer; they after all represent major British external interests in themselves. The more important groups are in constant touch with the ministries concerned, exchanging information and advice through a variety of formal and informal channels.

Since 1964 there has been some limited experimentation with advisory committees in external policy outside the traditional

Board of Trade field. The UK Committees for UN organisations already acted in effect as advisory committees to their respective ministries. Co-operation on publicity for the United Nations and on the celebration of UN Day had taken the form of a liaison committee between the Foreign Office and interested organisations – which was extended for the celebration of the UN's 25th anniversary into a special committee with a retired ambassador as Chairman, a staff member of the United Nations Association as secretary, close contact with the UN Information Centre, and considerable assistance from the Central Office of Information. The Labour Government introduced two 'Advisory Panels', on the United Nations and on Disarmament, shortly after taking office – closely associated with the Labour pledge to increase the attention given to these areas, with the naming of ministers responsible for them, and with the establishment of a new Disarmament Unit within the Foreign Office. The intention was to provide the Office with outside advice on a more formal basis, and also to keep informed opinion in closer touch with government thinking. Both tended to operate in practice rather more as sounding boards for government policy than as sources of outside initiative – though outside advice was valued on occasion, and sub-committees of the Disarmament Panel at one point provided papers. The composition of these panels reflected the mixed motives behind their establishment, ranging from M.P.s to academics, with a number of notables included as much for their eminence as their expertise; both included lawyers, and the Disarmament Panel scientists as well. Although not officially representative in membership, members of the panels had links with most of the respected groups. The Conservative Government on their return to office considered the experiment sufficiently successful for it to be continued; particular attention was given in reconstituting the Disarmament Panel to recognising the churches' interest.

Attempts under the Labour Government to institutionalise consultation with interests over other areas of foreign policy were less successful. An Industrial Consultative Committee on the Approach to Europe was constituted in December 1966, under the sponsorship of the DEA; its non-official members were drawn at top level from the CBI, the TUC, and the City, with representatives also from the Co-operative Movement, the NFU, and the London Chamber of Commerce. All sides found it unsatisfactory, and after four meetings it lapsed [18]. An Export Promotion Advisory Panel was attached to the Foreign Office Export Promotion Department in 1968–69, but this lapsed after six meetings. Less formal confrontations through well-established channels, usually at lower level, appear to be more effective means of consultation between government and industrial interests on external affairs.

The weakness of Parliament in the foreign policy field might be thought to reduce the appeal of Parliamentary connections as a means of access. Yet M.P.s and peers are valued contacts, and sought-after honorary officers, for groups in this field; and many groups attach importance to creating or supporting an associated Parliamentary Group. Partly because foreign policy is such an intangible process, because policy is so hard to pin down, any means of coming to grips with the Government is valuable; partly, too, Members of Parliament form an important section of that informed opinion to which policy-makers are attentive. A well-placed parliamentary question – drafted perhaps by an interested organisation – may provoke the government into framing and publicly announcing policy on an issue. An early day motion with a three-figure list of signatories will be treated by both the British and foreign governments as a storm warning of possible trouble ahead. Over and above these advantages, parliamentary associations bring valued prestige to foreign policy groups. To include an M.P. or two on a deputation to the Foreign Office is to increase one's chances of seeing the Foreign Secretary rather than a junior minister. Links with M.P.s make it possible to use the Houses of Parliament for meetings, receptions and dinners, which in its turn helps to attract more influential people to them. At the lowest level, it impresses foreign visitors to meet parliamentarians, or to be shown round the Palace of Westminster by a Member; for foreign governments without much knowledge of the British political process an association with a backbencher, perhaps with a fee to seal his attachment, may offer at least the illusion of influence [19].

Indirect access may be gained through participation in the semi-private debate which makes up the 'climate of opinion' on foreign policy issues. There are a number of convenient forums where members of the Diplomatic Service, M.P.s, journalists, academics, businessmen and members of respected non-official organisations may meet on neutral ground. Institutes such as Chatham House and the International Institute for Strategic Studies, bodies such as Canning House or the Middle East Association, organisations like the Federal Trust, provide such meetings grounds [20]. Many of these include a number of banks and companies as corporate members. Groups themselves sponsor conferences which representatives from the Foreign Office and interested M.P.s attend, and their discussions may later develop into policy initiatives. Embassies and embassy receptions offer further opportunities for discreet and informal discussion. It is more difficult for groups to use embassies to take up questions on their behalf; the High Commissions of some new Commonwealth countries have a peculiar relationship with government departments and immigrant groups, but that lies on the border line between international and domestic politics.

A remarkably high proportion of interest groups in the foreign policy field have among their aims the creation of an informed public opinion, 'to encourage British understanding of French political, artistic, scientific, social and economic developments', 'to advance the education of the people of Great Britain about Chile' [21] : to educate, inform and where possible arouse active interest. The amount of effort put into public education by primarily cultural, promotional or commercial organisations may suggest that all find direct channels of influence so unpromising that the long and difficult road of converting the public, of working outside the governmental structure, is the only alternative left to them. For some groups – particular for those whose aims, like the Peace Movement, are far from those accepted within élite circles – this is the case. But for others, such as UNA and its associated Council for Education in World Citizenship, for aid organisations like Oxfam, and for the many Anglo-Ruritanian societies, there are also more positive and compelling reasons. So long as there are little or no votes to be gained by politicians' committing themselves to a larger aid programme or campaigning for greater international co-operation, so long will governments be tempted to cut the aid budget before the road budget, to prefer domestic advantage to international collaboration, however active small groups of the committed may be. In the long run therefore the furtherance of a group's foreign policy aims depends upon the creation of a favourable climate of opinion, not only among the informed élite, but among the public at large. How long-run their thinking may be can be gauged by the attention these and other organisations give to education in the schools. For groups interested in promoting relations with particular countries the maintenance of libraries, the sponsoring of scholarships and travel grants, the promotion of university studies, have rather more mixed, though similarly long-term, aims. To raise the level of Spanish teaching and Latin-American studies in schools and universities is to make it more likely that future politicians will pay more attention to that continent, and that future businessmen's minds will turn there more naturally when thinking of trade. 'Culture', the secretary of one group remarked, 'is the soft underbelly of business.'

The range of publicity- and influence-seeking activities by groups in the foreign policy field otherwise differs little from those of groups in other areas. For the radical the public rally retains its appeal, though the effectiveness even of such massive demonstrations as the 1968 'Grosvenor Square' Vietnam march may be doubted. Conferences, summer schools, meetings, some 'baited' with entertainment or celebrities, help to attract the passively interested and the attention of the press; the Party Conferences draw a number of groups to hold fringe meetings, and witness the rival efforts of their respective 'Friends of Palestine' and 'Friends of Israel'. The provision of speakers, the circulation of publications to members and selected non-members, the maintenance of good relations with the national and local press, are all well-tried and regular methods. M.P.s are particular targets for published material from embassies and from British and foreign non-official organisations [22].

RESOURCES FOR INFLUENCE

Without the sanctions provided by a firm base in public opinion or by the need for their co-operation in executing policy, groups in the foreign policy field are weak in resources for the exercise of influence. On occasion a vivid crisis and a well-planned campaign, as on Biafra, may arouse enough passion to alert the Government – but these are rare. Well-maintained links among the informed élite, among M.P.s, commentators and journalists, cultivated by receptions, entertainments and foreign visits, the whole apparatus of the 'social lobby', provide a valued basis for influence [23]. In such a small body of the informed and accepted, the importance of personality and of personal connections is considerable. Many promotional groups owe their strength, some even their existence, to a single dominant personality, prepared to work long hours for little financial reward. The acknowledged expert on some aspect of foreign affairs, or the man who 'knows his way around Whitehall', is to be found bridging many groups and sitting on countless committees. Ex-diplomats are active in promotional and commercial groups, in voluntary and in paid capacities; a few M.P.s fulfil a similar connecting role.

Money is one of the scarcest resources for groups in any field – to be gathered in the foreign policy field in penny packets from individual subscribers, in larger quantities from company subscriptions and donations, and for the luckier groups in grants from the British or foreign governments. Most grants from the British Government are strictly limited to subsidising administrative costs or foreign travel; though the grant of £10,000 the United National Association received in 1968, to be repeated on a diminishing basis over the following five years, was more generally intended to assist the organisation's activities [24]. The European Movement in Britain has budgeted its expenditure during 1971 at around £200,000; most of this comes from industry, though the £7,500 which the FCO provides to assist 'in promoting a proper understanding in Europe of the British point of view on European affairs' [25] attracts the most wrath from anti-Common Market M.P.s. Money-raising ability is itself a resource for groups in some areas, as tangible evidence of public concern. The £8 million to £12 million which the aid organisations raised each year during the sixties was a useful weapon in persuading politicians that some of the public cared deeply about the level of British aid.

A base in the wider public, through a network of branches or contacts outside London, is also a valuable resource, carrying with it the ability to mount more credible national campaigns, to lobby M.P.s on a local basis, to gain wider coverage in the local and regional press; to convey, in sum, the impression of a wider grassroots appeal. The churches' ability to mobilise their local Councils of Churches, to organise local sympathisers into lobbies or new groupings at short notice, accounts for much of the considerable attention paid to their views at government level – in contrast, for instance, to the relative neglect of trade union pronouncements on foreign policy, which are rarely carried beyond resolutions at the national level. Their ability to collect a million signatures to a 'Christmas Sign-In on World Poverty' in 1969, the co-ordinated lobbying of M.P.s in their constituencies, and the establishment of World Poverty Action Groups in major centres throughout the country, were impressive evidence that church leaders were not without support on the subject among public opinion. On a very different level, the ability of Stop The Seventies Tour to mount demonstrations, and possibly to dig up pitches and paint up slogans, at cricket grounds throughout the country, considerably increased the seriousness with which both government and the MCC considered the implications of the South African Cricket Tour.

In external affairs, where secrecy is so often the rule, information is a particularly scarce commodity. One former minister gave as a reason for disregarding the advice of many outside groups the superior quality and the more solid foundation of the advice he received from officials. Reliable information, and if possible thorough research, are therefore enormously useful resources for non-official organisations. International links (which are explored further in the next chapter) provide a valued independent source of information. The churches' missionary activities, and their links with churches in Eastern Europe and elsewhere, give them access to information which the Government may well not have. Needing to assess the situation inside Biafra, for example, the FCO was anxious to meet returning missionaries to hear their reports. The close links which the Association of British Chambers of Commerce maintains with Chambers of Commerce on the continent have on occasion given it access to information on EEC developments as yet unknown to the British Government. The work of the Anti-Slavery Society is known to the Foreign Office not only from contacts in London, but from visits to British embassies abroad. Information on the machinery of foreign policy-making is itself scarce but useful; the Biafran lobby attacked the Foreign Office from the outside, but failed to make informal contact with the West African department. The value of solid and well-presented research was demonstrated in February 1970, when almost without exception the national press viewed the Government's White Paper on 'Britain and the European Communities' by comparison with the CBI report on 'Britain in Europe' – in most cases to the latter's advantage. Indeed it is possible that the strength of the influence which industrial organisations have brought to bear on successive governments over Britain's relationship with continental Europe is attributable, not simply to the financial resources at their disposal, but to the skill and competence with which their case was presented.

But possibly the greatest resource which groups in the field of external affairs have at their disposal is the relative weakness of the external ministries in the Whitehall process, which derives from their lack of a firm domestic constituency. When expenditure cuts are demanded by the Cabinet or the Treasury, the British Council, the BBC's External Services, the aid budget, information services overseas, even the Diplomatic Service and the Foreign Office itself, are forced to bear their share. When there is room for moderate budgetary expansion, there are few *political* arguments for increasing expenditure on foreign policy programmes, and few political pressures to urge the Government to do so [26]. Ministers and civil servants in the FCO and its associated departments are therefore in need of allies, of domestic support. One may suggest, for civil servants, a further psychological factor. Foreign policy officials are relatively isolated in British politics, working for much of their career at home or abroad largely unnoticed (and, some feel, unappreciated) by press, Parliament or public opinion. They therefore welcome a chance to exchange ideas, to explain (or justify) their activities and to sense that they have an interested and responsive audience.

Foreign policy makers are also aware that the strength of their negotiating position in any area of overseas policy is partly dependent on the impression their negotiating partners have of the degree of support their position commands in their own country. A divided public opinon, most of all a vocal, respected and organised opposition, weakens the Government's hand in maintaining the credibility of its military commitments or in negotiating entry into the EEC; conversely, evidence of active and united support strengthens it. The external ministries must therefore not only pay attention to, but to some extent actively cultivate, informed and uninformed public opinion.

The relationship between government departments and groups in the foreign policy field is therefore less one of confrontation than of mutual encouragement, a more subtle form of co-operation than is to be found in most areas of domestic policy. Several departments of the FCO regard it as part of their function to advise and encourage non-official organisations in their area: one department lists 'Liaison with Commonwealth Societies' as part of its official remit [27]. Examples of official assistance, in one form or another, to various groups have already been cited; one may add as further evidence the inclusion of representatives of non-official organisations in delegations to international conferences, and the provision of the Foreign Office conference centre at Wilton Park, as well as the willingness of civil servants to devote time and attention to 'their' groups. Lord Caradon when a Minister devoted a month in each year to speaking around the country for UN associations. Senior civil servants and ministers at the Ministry of Overseas Development took the initiative in encouraging aid organisations to work together, and attempted on occasion to stir the aid lobby into greater efforts to bring pressure on the Government. In an extreme case a minister or a civil servant may move over from the Whitehall process to the outside camp, as Reginald Prentice did on his 'promotion' from the Ministry of Overseas Development. The ministries and the interest groups share a common interest in raising the level of public attention given to external affairs. Ministers and officials are also aware, to a greater or lesser extent from area to area, of the need to manage their domestic opinion.

THE PATTERN OF INFLUENCE

There is then rather more interest group activity in the foreign policy field than may at first appear on the surface, and rather closer contact between government and groups. But what evidence is there of tangible influence? From the very nature of the foreign policy process this is difficult to assess. Much influence is continuous, informal and multidirectional. The businessman in regular contact with the relevant departments of the FCO and the

Department of Trade and Industry is arguably a constant influence on their interpretation of Britain's interests and of the possible alternatives for British policy. But they are also, in the nature of the relationship, a constant influence on him, infecting his attitudes with the government 'view'. The leaders of respected and accepted promotional groups are involved in a similar two-way relationship, in which official and ministerial receptiveness to their proposals depends upon their willingness to accept the reasonableness of the governmental point of view. To be certain of tracing the pattern of influence one needs to know the direction of the flow of policy, the primary source of policy initiatives inside or outside the government machinery [28]. But the uncertainty of the boundary between the official and the non-official, the overlapping memberships between groups, parties and Parliament, and the civil service itself, the whole informal élite process which characterises the discussion and formulation of external policy, stand in our way.

Some groups as we have seen are not primarily concerned with influence on day-to-day policy. The value of the activities of Anglo-Ruritanian Societies to their members and to the companies and foreign governments which support them may be compared to the value of prestige advertising and public relations for private companies. They contribute towards the creation and maintenance of a favourable public image, and thus help to alter the parameters of what is considered acceptable or desirable government policy towards them. Goodwill is a commodity much valued in international politics, as in business, even if it is in both arenas a non-quantifiable asset. No one can say to what extent the cumulative effect of generations of student exchanges, or (for instance) the knowledge of and goodwill towards Germany built up amongst key politicians and journalists during successive Königswinter Conferences, influences the attitude of policy-makers at critical points; but few would deny that they have a certain, and perhaps a considerable, long-term effect.

For those groups concerned with immediate influence on policy, there are a number of problems in assessing the success or failure of attempts at influence. On some foreign policy questions the Government is hemmed in by foreign commitments and foreign pressures, on others it is relatively unhindered; domestic influence on the latter will clearly carry more chance of success. As in domestic politics, the efforts of one coalition of groups are often counterbalanced by the effects of others. The national interests which foreign policy makers cite in defence of their resistance to group influence are often compelling; the dangers of setting precedents in dealing with one country or crisis which foreign governments will seize on in other circumstances are often real. The reluctance of the Foreign Office to bend to the efforts of the pro-Israel lobby may possibly be due, as Zionist critics have long maintained, to an established pro-Arab bias within the Diplomatic Service. But it could equally plausibly be attributed to the counter-pressure of commercial organisations, their eyes on the larger Arab market, or to the representations of the oil companies – or to a continual awareness within the Foreign Office, reinforced by other ministries, of Britain's acute dependence on oil from the Middle East, and the consequent reluctance of civil servants to recommend courses of action which would jeopardise that supply, and so threaten British industry, the balance of payments and the whole basis of Britain's prosperity. There are problems too in assessing achievements in terms of the practicality of the aims intended. The aid organisations may be seen to have succeeded in preventing any further cuts in government aid in the difficult circumstances of the period 1968–70; or they may be seen as having failed essentially to raise substantially the level of the aid budget [29]. The secrecy of the foreign policy process is a further barrier to assessing influence. Outside the business world it is often assumed that business usually gets its way on foreign policy questions; but success is often more widely publicised than failure, and the commercial organisations themselves are more aware of their numerous unsuccessful attempts to shift the Government.

The conclusion of such a short essay as this must therefore be highly tentative. It may be suggested that the cumulative effect of group pressure in foreign affairs is to exert a definite limiting influence on government policy. All governments prefer to avoid trouble. The organisation of like-minded opinion on some aspect of policy, among the wider public or among the informed élite, is noted by ministers and civil servants; though they rarely provoke a confrontation, they consider it part of their function to anticipate the likely reaction of such groups to a course of policy, and to take action to avoid or mitigate opposition.

There is likely to be more room for governmental manoeuvre, and more room therefore for the exercise of influence at lower levels of policy than at higher, on matters of commercial or on cultural relations rather than on matters close to the heart of national interest and national security. On questions of high policy the Government may plead the 'cruel necessities' of international diplomacy in its defence, may change under pressure the presentation of its policy rather than the policy itself, or may offer at most a gesture, a Commonwealth Mission to Hanoi or a Prime Ministerial visit to Nigeria, as evidence of concern. But the continuous process of consultation and discussion with outside interests and experts, which clearly affects the details of external policy, is not without influence at a higher level. The changing climate of informed opinion – itself an intangible, but none the less real, thing – may lead on central issues, as on the Common Market, to fundamental shifts in government policy. The efforts and activity of the innumerable groups and individuals who play a part in this informal foreign policy process may exert a considerable long-term influence, even if their immediate effect is rarely visible to the naked eye.

REFERENCES AND NOTES

[1] F. S. Northedge, 'The Nature of Foreign Policy' in Northedge (ed.), *The Foreign Policies of the Powers* (Faber, London, 1968), p. 28. The distinctive characteristics of the foreign policy process are more fully examined in William Wallace, *Foreign Policy and the Political Process* (Macmillan, London, 1971).

[2] J. D. Stewart in *British Pressure Groups* (Oxford University Press, 1958), Chaps. V and VI, emphasises the importance of legislation as a target for group activity, particularly in formulating and pressing for amendments at the Committee Stage. There is a substantial and confusing literature on the definition and classification of domestic 'interest groups', and on the terminology appropriate to group activity. I am following the definition proposed by Graham Wooton in *Interest Groups* (Prentice-Hall, Englewood Cliffs, New Jersey, 1970).

[3] D. C. Watt, *Personalities and Policies: Studies in the Formulation of British Foreign Policy in the Twentieth Century* (Longmans, London, 1965), p. 2 and following.

[4] The trade unions possess a potential sanction in their ability to interrupt external transport and communications. The case of the *Jolly George*, when in May 1920 during the Russo-Polish war London dockers refused to load a ship which was bound for Poland, has passed into the folklore of the movement. But the union movement's commitment to international solidarity has not proved strong enough since then to use this weapon in less revolutionary circumstances. For this incident see V. L. Allen, *Trade Unions and the Government* (Longmans, London, 1960), pp. 158–164.

[5] These were the Overseas Migration Board, 'concerned with analysing and advising on policy relating to emigration from the United Kingdom to countries in the Commonwealth', and four committees on Indian pensions. By contrast the Board of Trade sponsored 38, at least six of which were concerned with important aspects of overseas trade. P.E.P. *Advisory Committees in British Government* (P.E.P., London, 1960), pp. 24–25, 33, and appendix.

[6] Where not otherwise footnoted, information in the following paragraphs is drawn from a series of interviews with 23 non-official organisations concerned with foreign policy, carried out by the author during the academic year 1969–70 with the aid of a small grant from the Nuffield Foundation. This was supplemented by an examination of literature provided by these organisations and by a further 33 organisations which replied to a questionnaire sent out in the summer of 1970. Further information, and a useful check on the claims made by groups, was obtained by following reports on their activities in the quality press during this period, and through a number of interviews with civil servants, ex-Ministers, and M.P.s. Several interviews with civil servants and groups in the commercial area were carried out jointly with Peter Byrd.

[7] The objects of the Anglo-German Association, quoted in *Anglo-German Review*, July 1969.

[8] *Guardian*, 7th July 1969, 6th October 1970.

[9] A. R. Ilersic, *Parliament of Commerce: The Story of the*

Association of British Chambers of Commerce (A.B.C.C., London, 1960), p. 2.

[10] Wooton, *Interest Groups*, p. 93; J. W. Grove, *Government and Industry in Britain* (Longmans, London, 1962), p. 332.

[11] The League of Arab States has for instance placed a number of political advertisements in the British press, the largest consisting of a four-page advertisement in *The Times*, 25th June 1969 with articles putting the Arab case by, among others, British M.P.s from both major parties and a former British Ambassador to Egypt. The propriety of this aroused a storm of correspondence. A full-page advertisement in *The Times* on 3rd November 1969, entitled 'Korea has produced the Hero of 20th Century, Kim Il Sung', advertised the three-volume biography of 'the Great Leader of the 40 Million Korean People'.

[12] Lord Windlesham, *Communication and Political Power* (Jonathan Cape, London, 1966), p. 169.

[13] For information on the aid lobby I have relied heavily on Judith Young, *The Evolution of an Aid Lobby in Britain, 1962–1970* (M.A. Thesis, University of Manchester, 1970).

[14] In December 1970 the CBI and the ABCC announced their joint sponsorship of an independent 'Commission of Inquiry into Industrial Representation' to be headed by Lord Devlin, with the particular intention of 'eliminating duplication' (CBI Press Release, 8th December 1970).

[15] BNEC Area Councils and Committees (London, February 1970), p. 4.

[16] *The Times*, 17th October 1969.

[17] Allen Potter, *Organised Groups in British Politics* (Faber, London, 1961), p. 223.

[18] For information on interest groups and the EEC I am indebted to access to research being undertaken by Helen Wallace for a Ph.D. at Manchester University on *The Domestic Policy-Making Implications of the Labour Government's Application to Join the European Communities.*

[19] The public relations firm of Maurice Fraser and Associates used a retainer to Gordon Bagier, M.P., in 1968 to impress the Greek Government with its efforts on their behalf (*Sunday Times*, 6th October 1968, 9th March 1969). At

the trial of Will Owen, a former Labour M.P., in April–
May 1970, it was disclosed that he had received a total of
£2,300 from members of the Czech Embassy over the
previous nine years. There was however no evidence that
he had provided them with secret information, and he was
acquitted.

[20] Watt, pp. 2–15. One's impression is that the utility of
London Clubs as informal meeting places has considerably
declined.
[21] The objects of the Franco-British Society (membership
leaflet 1970) and of the Anglo-Chilean Society (communication to the author 1970).
[22] Anthony Barker and Michael Rush, *The Member of
Parliament and his Information* (Allen & Unwin, London,
1970), pp. 65–66, 108–17.
[23] Potter, p. 270.
[24] The major recipients of grants-in-aid are listed in the FCO
Estimates each year.
[25] Evan Luard, Parliamentary Under-Secretary for Foreign
and Commonwealth Affairs, in answer to a parliamentary
question from Neil Marten, M.P. (Hansard, 3rd November
1969, Vol. 790, Col. 26).
[26] It is not always remarked that the terms of reference for
the Duncan Committee laid the strongest emphasis on
saving money on the external budget.
[27] *The Diplomatic Service List, 1970* (HMSO, London), p. 7.
[28] This is, of course, a problem by no means confined to the
pattern of influence in the foreign policy field. Wooton,
pp. 96–102.
[29] *An Account of the British Aid Programme*, 1970 (the text
of the UK Memorandum to the Development Advisory
Committee of OECD), para. 29, lists public opinion among
'Factors affecting the Volume of Aid', specifically citing the
churches' Christmas Sign-In as evidence of its strength. The
reader may judge whether this is evidence of government
solicitude for public opinion, or special pleading by a civil
servant in the ODA.

BIBLIOGRAPHY

The published literature in this area is extremely sparse. Allen Potter, *Organised Groups in British Politics* (Faber, London, 1961) takes a number of its examples from the foreign policy field, and provides a useful general introduction to interest group activity in Britain. Ian Waller, 'Pressure Politics: M.P. and P.R.O.', in *Encounter*, August 1962, contains some interesting examples of foreign governmental activity.

On commercial interest groups, the best introduction is J. W. Grove, *Government and Industry in Britain* (Longmans, London, 1962). See also A. R. Ilersic, *Parliament of Commerce* (Newman, Neane and Association of British Chambers of Commerce, 1960), which is largely historical; or two recent CBI reports, *Britain in Europe* and *Britain in the World* (CBI, London, 1970), and CBI and ABCC annual reports.

There are some useful studies available on domestic debate and domestic campaigns on EEC entry. Chap. 6 in Lord Windlesham's *Communication and Political Power* (Jonathan Cape, London, 1966) covers the 1961–63 application, with particular reference to campaigning groups. Eric Nordlinger's essay in Roy C. Macridis (ed.), *Modern European Governments* (Prentice-Hall, Englewood Cliffs, New Jersey, 1968), pays rather more attention to industrial and agricultural interests. Robert J. Lieber, *British Politics and European Unity* (University of California Press, 1970) is a full-length study based on a Harvard thesis.

On the competing pro-Arab and pro-Israeli lobbies, see Andrew Roth, 'The Middle East at Westminster' in *New Statesman*, 13th March 1970; and the articles by Bryan Magee and F. R. MacKenzie in *The Listener*, 19th March 1970, and the heated correspondence in subsequent issues.

Two rather different studies of CND, Christopher Driver, *The Disarmers: a Study in Protest* (Hodder & Stoughton, London, 1964), and Frank Parkin, *Middle Class Radicalism* (Manchester University Press, 1968), cover respectively the history and the social background of the movement.

12 State Management of Private Foreign Policy

J. HARROD*

PRIVATE foreign policy may be defined as the amalgam of opinion, attitude and actions concerning a foreign event or situation held, or taken, by organisations which are not formally incorporated within the state foreign policy-making and executing machinery. This chapter is concerned only with the possibilities of state management of the actions taken by private groups abroad. It is not the intention, therefore, to discuss the activities of private groups when they act as pressure groups in the field of foreign policy as this is dealt with in the previous chapter.

The management or control of private organisations acting abroad is a contentious issue. One argument is that the freedom of action of private organisations is a basic right of democracy and that any consideration of control by the state represents a fundamental attack upon that governmental system. On the other hand, in other theories of state and society, private foreign policy does not exist, as all external activities are expressions of the policy of the ruling élite and thereby of the state which it controls.

The idea that groups or organisations from one society can be actively involved in another without operating through the state foreign policy-making machinery is certainly an international manifestation of an internal liberal democratic order. The argument for private international freedom is an extention

---

* Jeffrey Harrod is a Staff Associate and Faculty member of the International Institute for Labour Studies. The Institute does not endorse any views. The opinions expressed in this chapter are those of the author and cannot be attributed to the Institute.

of the domestic pluralist tradition whereby private organisations are permitted to challenge the government. Thus the logic requires that a similar freedom should be granted concerning the ability to dissent from government in international activities. However, the organisational freedom of action, constitutionally enshrined for the domestic arena, has never been granted with such clear legal and societal approval for actions in the international environment. But neither has there been a total interdiction or the creation of institutionalised means of control in the manner of the monist state. The latter, quite logically, decrees that every contact made abroad, either individual or organisational, is part of the external relations of the state and therefore subject to its control.

Management thus becomes, in effect, a question of the degree of autonomy private organisations can exercise in their foreign activities. If there is a high degree of state management the organisations' actions abroad are that much less an expression of private foreign policy and vice versa. The excuse for the continued use of the public/private dichotomy rests, as a result, almost entirely upon the domestic nature and structure of the organisations and in particular on the fact that the officers are not appointed by the public agencies of governments and are not formally subject to constitutional mechanisms of control.

In the case of private foreign policy, unlike other aspects of the management of external relations, it is necessary to demonstrate the importance of the phenomena to international relations and to state foreign policy. Much of this chapter will be taken up with examining and illustrating the importance of the activities of private organisations abroad.

OBJECTIVES OF PRIVATE FOREIGN POLICY

Private organisations with activities abroad can be classified according to the major objectives of their foreign involvements. Four categories can immediately be identified, those seeking financial profit, those with real or perceived vested interests abroad, those with international philanthropic objectives and those with political, religious or ideological objectives. These categories are not mutually exclusive as any one organisation may have all four objectives. Neither are they exhaustive, for incentives which precipitate international involvement may arise from a variety of domestic as well as international motives.

The corporation is the most important example in the profit seeking category. It is the most written-about private organisation in international society and one which has been given a central place both in theories of imperialism and of international conflict. The corporation has received this attention as much from its domestic position in capitalist societies as from its undoubted international power. Often it is seen as merely an instrument of the foreign policy of the governing élite, in which case there is no problem of control as independent action on its part is not possible. Historically, the question of control manifests itself as a power struggle when the corporate and governing élites do not in practice accept the same foreign policy. With the advent of Keynesian economics and the current international monetary system the governing élite has a number of instruments of control which can be used against the corporations if such a struggle occurs. Most of these are discussed in Chapters Six and Seven which deal with commercial and financial policy. For this reason, the specific problem of the corporation will be excluded in this chapter in favour of other lesser-known, but increasingly important, types of private organisation. This emphasis should not however disguise the fact that of all the private organisations acting abroad, the corporation is the most important and the one with the most far-reaching implications for state foreign policy.

The second type of organisation is characterised by international objectives which are a function of events abroad and which affect, or are perceived to affect, the organisation's domestic power and welfare. The classic example of this type of organisation is trade unions, whose leaders have, from the beginning, felt impelled to act abroad. Among the variety of reasons for this phenomenon is the continuing one that low wages abroad will be detrimental to the welfare of their members, through imports of low-wage-cost goods. Thus trade unions have attempted, often in concert with corporations, to raise wages abroad to protect jobs and income of workers at home. It matters little that economists can show that the low-wage-cost argument is fallacious, for belief in its validity has been sufficient to initiate international action. All domestic organisations trading in goods, information, expertise or personnel have similar incentives for their international activities.

The third category is composed of those organisations committed to charitable works. Originally organised for charity in the fields of education and health, these organisations have grown in power and scope and can now be generally classified as dispensers of development aid to less developed countries. The historically dominant position of the churches in charitable works has been reduced by the entry of a plethora of non-denominational groups, mainly as a response to the publicity given after 1945 to the poor countries.

The fourth and final category contains the organisations with ideological, religious or political (in the narrowest sense) objectives. Clearly such motives are included in the other objectives; corporations, for example, have often cast themselves in the role of the evangelists of free enterprise and capitalist democracy as well as that of profit seekers. There are some organisations however whose activities abroad rest solely on these objectives, such as some religious sects or political parties which conceive of themselves as part of an international movement. There are also other organisations which, for a variety of reasons, are committed to a specific international political objective, such as the maintenance of a foreign state or the independence of an ethnic group.

MEANS OF PRIVATE FOREIGN POLICY

The efficiency of state management is to a large extent dependent upon the means used to express foreign policy opinions abroad as some are more easily controlled than others.

While no detailed examination of the lobbying activities of private organisations is to be attempted here, it is necessary to mention that all private organisations' acting abroad supplement their operational activities with lobbying activities. Often these are as much concerned with the maintenance of conditions domestically, which will permit them to continue to act internationally, as they are with direct foreign policy issues.

Another form of lobbying is at the international level. Through association with other organisations in international non-governmental organisations, international pressure can be applied to national governments. Each of the above categories of organisations is thus reflected in a non-governmental international organisation such as the International Chamber of Commerce, International Confederation of Free Trade Unions, World Council of Churches, and so on. Some non-governmental organisations have also been constitutionally incorporated within inter-governmental organisations, as, for example, the consultative status granted to them by the United Nations Economic and Social Council. In one case, that of the International Labour Organisation, trade unions and business organisations are an integral part of the organisation with voting power in both the policy-making and executive bodies.

The central consideration for management, however, is the direct involvement of private organisations in another society. The means of such involvement are the transfer of funds to counterpart or associated organisations abroad or the despatch of agents as consultative advisers or organisers. Direct involvements such as these often could not be undertaken by the state as they would either compromise the main lines of foreign policy or alternatively offend the legal norm of non-interference in the domestic affairs of another state. It is these activities of private organisations which, more than any other, can be called private foreign policy and which are at the centre of the question of the relationship between them and a state foreign policy.

IMPORTANCE OF PRIVATE FOREIGN POLICY

The basic importance of private foreign policy is that, apart from its possible use as an instrument of state foreign policy, the activities of private organisations contribute to the nature of the international environment in which the state must act. While this has always been the case, the current contribution of private foreign policy to the international environment is of increasing importance. This arises from a cluster of phenomena surrounding the new efforts at international integration, especially on the regional level, and from the number of small and economically weak states which have recently been created.

Private groups have always been given a special place in both the theory and practice of international integration. This was particularly true of the functional theory of integration which placed a great deal of hope in the possibility of links forged between private organisations having similar functions in different national societies. The private group was placed in an international role of subverting the paramount position of the state, which was not considered a suitable vehicle for international integration. The origin of the theory in nineteenth century anti-state liberalism meant that any idea that private organisations should be controlled by the state, or were instruments of state foreign policy, was vigorously resisted. For this reason the role of the corporation in integration was tactfully omitted as it was not considered sufficiently divorced from the tainting hand of the state [1]. It is the residue of this philosophy which has helped to give private organisations an ideological protection against rigorous investigations into the extent of their conformity to state foreign policy.

The deliberate policies of integration, the widespread activities of corporations, the growth of inter-governmental organisations, the ease of communication and the international character of technology have likewise made private organisations more important. They have, to a large extent, been responsible for the growth of extensive international political networks and information systems below the state level. Such political networks among professional associations for example have been used to counter or support policies proposed or initiated by the states [2]. Thus state foreign policy must take cognisance of such networks when it seeks to draw support or reduce opposition from other states concerning specific policy proposals.

The second reason for the increased importance of private organisations is the potential afforded them by the presence of the less developed countries. The extreme nature of the difference in wealth between industrial countries and less developed countries has meant that private organisations in the latter often have relatively larger financial resources than governments in the former. While this may be an extreme case it remains true that the international power of private groups in industrial countries has been increased by the presence of small and relatively weak states. In a country of under a million inhabitants with a per capita annual GNP of, say £120, a small private organisation will find its funds can make a considerable impact and it becomes possible for such an organisation to find the people and finance necessary to launch its own aid programme abroad.

There are, in addition, some general effects that the activities of private groups make on the international environment. First, at the broadest and most abstract level, is the contribution that the activities of private citizens acting abroad, either as agents of private organisations or in their individual capacity, make to the image of their home state and to the prevailing national stereotypes upon which foreign decision-makers often base their policy. This may be of more importance than it sounds because one of the distinguishing factors between the activities of private organisations abroad and state activities abroad is that the former are often operational. That is, the individuals are operating what is crudely known as a 'people-to-people' programme; they are involved in the day-to-day work of foreign social organisations and, in the case of development and missionary work, are deeply involved in the life of small communities and, even more important, in the socialisation process of the children and young people. The attitudes and behaviour of such persons directly affect images upon which the political, as opposed to military power, of the state is based [3]. In an era when the notion of 'neo-colonialism' is being forged into a complex description of social, psychological as well as economic and political relations, the attitudes and behaviour of nationals abroad is of paramount importance. In the third world it is not unusual that the political élite is drawn from organisations which have been influenced and sometimes created by private groups from other countries. Second, their activities may alter the political configurations of a foreign state through support for, or opposition to, various groups in the foreign society. Finally, private organisations have been involved in specific political events abroad with serious consequences, some of which have been especially important to state foreign policy. The exact nature of the importance of private activities abroad can be more readily seen by an examination of some selected examples.

Some British Examples of Private Foreign Policy
An assessment of the magnitude of private involvement in international relations and other states is virtually impossible. In one

area, that of development aid, some rough quantification can be made. It is estimated that approximately £15 million is privately dispensed abroad every year, compared with a government aid figure of approximately £200 million. An examination of the projects supported would indicate a wider spread of influence than state aid as the money is distributed across many nations in amounts sometimes as small as £80. Another measure is the number of British citizens serving abroad in such ventures; in 1968, for example, there were nearly 2,000 British citizens on volunteer programmes in the field and over 5,000 from the Protestant missionary societies alone [4].

For other activities there is no acceptable means of quantification. While some authors have attempted to measure the dimensions of contacts through counting the numbers of letters or missions exchanged, the quantification of influence and effects of such exchanges is more difficult [5]. The importance of co-operating, advisory or lobbying missions abroad would depend upon so many social, psychological, historical and economic variables that any assessment would be bound to be value-laden. For this reason the presentation of some specific examples of British private organisations (selected mainly from the field of development aid) acting abroad is the best way to develop ideas of their influence and effects. In development aid there are three main private organisations, the Voluntary Committee on Overseas Aid and Development (VCOAD), The Conference of British Missionary Societies (CBMS) and the British Volunteer Programme (BVP).

The VCOAD was founded in 1966 and its objective was to co-ordinate the activities of the major fund-raising agencies which were already existing in the field. The founding members of VCOAD were Christian Aid, Oxford Committee for Famine Relief (Oxfam), Save the Children Fund and War on Want. All these agencies are registered charities and together dispense about £7 million overseas each year of which over half goes to African countries. Two aspects of this expenditure are important; first, with one exception, the expenditure is non-operational, that is the agencies do not have their agents in the field administering the funds supplied and, second, the nature of its distribution to both country and group [6]. The basic procedure for dispensing funds is to respond to a request originating in the requesting country which usually comes from some private group or organisation. It is clear therefore that the country which has the most intimate organisational connection with the United Kingdom, or in other words is the most permeable society, will benefit. The higher the level of integration with the donor country the greater the donation. The selection of groups to be awarded funds is also a political decision, for it is likely that if one group can produce material benefits for its adherents its power in the society is thereby enhanced. The effect is thus to promote one type of group or organisation in the society in question; it would be difficult, for example, to select a group with strong nationalist or xenophobic overtones.

The British Volunteer Programme is likewise a co-ordinating agency for voluntary service overseas, but with the difference that it is operational. At the same time, however, VCOAD will refer requesting organisations to the volunteer agencies so that it is possible that funds donated by British charitable agencies may be administered by British volunteers. The recruitment is in the hands of the agencies and assignments depend upon requesting governments as well as private groups. Like the Peace Corps and other national 'people-to-people' programmes, the volunteers are, judging by the recruitment information, conceived of as part of an image-building process as well as a charitable operation.

The Conference of Missionary Societies of Great Britain is an operational as well as aid-dispensing agency. It dispenses about £5 million per annum in funds, administers programmes involving about 6,000 missionaries and is engaged in medical, educational (both general and theological) and development projects. It works through, and in conjunction with, the host governments and existing church organisations and thus probably represents the most extensive and complex involvement in the national life of the host states.

To take a somewhat different example, the Trades Union Congress has had an extensive international programme for many years. Since the 1930s this has taken the co-operating and co-ordinating form between fraternal trade unions abroad as well as aid to trade unions in the colonies and less developed countries. The former is becoming of increasing importance with the growth of the so-called 'trans-national society' which is centred around the world-wide activities of the multi-national corporation. The ramifications of international co-operation between unions, as well as the international activities of corporations, for state foreign policy have yet to be examined with the care that they deserve. The nature of the TUC's cross-national activities however is such that it is difficult for policy-makers to avoid specific involvement in political affairs of other states. In 1961 for example the TUC, in a spirit of mutual aid to trade unions abroad, extended a £145,000 loan to striking Belgian workers; these workers were members of a union federation which was striking against the Belgian government and which had been partially responsible for two weeks of widespread anti-government riots. In the colonial and ex-colonial situations it is even more difficult to avoid political involvement as trade unions in these countries are usually closely allied with, and are sometimes indistinguishable from, political parties. Thus in 1956, in British Guiana, the TUC supported one union faction with grants and advice sometimes amounting to £200 per month on a continuing basis. That this union was striking against the incumbent government, was in competition to the government party's union and that eventually the British military intervened in support of the government, is an indication of the complexity of some situations in which both government and private groups are involved.

STATE MANAGEMENT, PRIVATE AND PUBLIC FOREIGN POLICY

The foregoing discussion and examples have shown that private foreign policy can be an important aspect of British external relations. It is now possible to examine the available means of management or control of private activities abroad. There are five basic formal means; first, the control of transfer of funds; second, control of movement of persons; third, control of communications; fourth, control of domestic legal status; and fifth, control of some aspects of international status.

Control of fund transfer has been made possible almost by accident through the foreign currency crisis after the 1939–45 war, when it became necessary to pass the Exchange Control Act. Through the regulations of this Act it is possible to block, and certainly to delay, transfer of funds out of the country. Although government use of these regulations to delay transfers for political purposes would be contravening the intention of the Act, it would nevertheless be possible. In fact, in the example of the TUC loan to Belgium mentioned above, it was seriously suggested in the British national press that such action might be taken by the Treasury [7]. The legal right of withholding or withdrawing passports has been specifically reserved as a state prerogative. This power is rarely used for any purpose except in case of war. Interference with written communications has less of a legal basis and its use as a means of control would contravene both domestic and international convention law pertaining to freedom of speech. All these means have rarely, if at all, been used but the possibility of their use could certainly be viewed as an ultimate deterrent.

The fourth formal means of control is made possible through legislation affecting the domestic status of the organisations. The leading example of such legislation is connected with charities. Considerable tax advantages are enjoyed by groups as a result of being a registered charity any many organisations with operations abroad are so registered. The Charity Commissioners and the Department of Education are the arbiters of what constitutes a charity; of particular interest here is that the charitable status of an organisation can be withdrawn if it engages in political activity. One official of such an organisation claimed that consideration of the Charity Commissioners was a constant in determining some of the actions and projects of the organisation both domestically and abroad. It is clear that such a power could be used in the case of an organisation moving into what the Government considered to be an undesirable political direction. This is even more the case since the definition of a charitable activity is extremely vague excluding, for example, activities concerning 'racial tolerance, international friendship, good understanding and sympathy' [8].

Finally, government agencies have some control over the specific international status of organisations. This arises from the incorporation of non-governmental organisations within the framework of the United Nations. Non-governmental organisations have a special status before the United Nations Economic and Social Council, the principal body concerned with the co-ordination of the specialised agencies and policy matters relating to UN economic and social affairs. The non-governmental organisations are divided into three categories in descending order of their rights before the Council and, therefore, their general international status. Organisations consider their ECOSOC listing as important for their international acceptance and prestige. As the UN committee which decides the status of these organisations and considers new applications is inter-governmental, the Foreign Office can therefore determine to some extent an application for upgrading or entry to the list.

Any use of the more extreme of these measures is never made public knowledge, and for a number of reasons it can be assumed that they are not used in any significant way. The main reason why the extreme measures of control are not used is that private foreign policy never deviates sufficiently from public foreign policy to warrant the inevitable domestic political problems that such controlling actions would create. An example of the conformity between state and private foreign policy is afforded by an extensive study of the TUC policy towards the colonies or less developed countries [9]. The TUC followed the main lines of government foreign policy for nearly thirty years. This meant changing direction as various governments accepted first self-government, then independence and, finally, the need for development aid.

Even in situations where private and state foreign policy appear to be in conflict, the conflict may be more apparent than real. Thus while the British government was supporting the Federal forces with arms in the Nigerian civil war, the Prime Minister called together a meeting of the voluntary agencies and urged them to do all they could to relieve the conditions on the Biafran side [10]. Humanitarian considerations apart, the maintenance of a British state presence on one side of a civil war and a British private presence on the other can be seen as useful, assuring that all is not lost, whichever side wins. Aid to North Vietnam would be another such instance.

In seeking the answer to why private foreign policy does not seemingly depart from public foreign policy perhaps the question which should be asked is not how the activities are controlled by government but rather to what extent they are private activities at all? Even a superficial investigation of some of the private organisations acting abroad immediately reveals two important factors, first, the close informal contact between them and the foreign policy agencies of the state and, second, the financial and personnel contacts with government.

Most of the officers of the organisations report close contact with the Ministry of Foreign and Commonwealth Affairs mainly for purposes of exchange of information. Some mention 'daily contact' and talk of exchange of 'specialist' information and of varying interpretations of events which are of 'mutual interest'. All organisations report the use of British embassies for information and general support for their operations abroad. More interesting are the government, financial and personal connections. VCOAD for example, which co-ordinates the largest fund raising bodies and helps determine which countries or groups are in receipt of aid, is 30 per cent financed by the Overseas Development Administration with which it has close contact. The largest of the voluntary agencies, the Volunteers Service Overseas, has its operational activities directly controlled by the British Council [11]. The latter organisation, set up in 1932 for 'the promotion of a wider knowledge of the United Kingdom and the English language', is 95 per cent funded by the government and nine of its thirty-member executive are nominated by government ministers. After many years of co-operating with the government in the dispensing of Colonial Development and Welfare Funds, the churches now have less formal and financial contact with government. However they still use the device of government-church-host state projects and also co-operate and co-ordinate activities with government development aid in the fields of health and education. In dealing with the colonies the British TUC set up a Colonial Advisory Committee in 1935 to advise the members of the General Council concerning TUC policy in the colonies. Members of this committee were a) members of the TUC International Committee, b) representatives of corporations with interests in the colonies, and c) government officials from the colonial office 'sitting in their private capacity'. Thus from the beginning government officials were involved in the foreign policy-making process of the TUC.

This combination of the ultimate deterrents in the means of control, the network of formal, informal and financial connections has meant that management of the private aspect of British external relations has reached a high level of efficiency. The usefulness of private foreign policy in state external relations has been well stated in a pamphlet published by the Overseas Development Institute. Listing the advantages of private organisations, the authors state '. . . an obvious one is their political

neutrality. Government aid is often influenced by political
motives, and this is recognised by receiving countries, who
naturally enough are sensitive on the point. The independent
private organisation may well find that the advice or assistance
it can give will be more acceptable as coming from an independent body' [12]. That the apparent neutrality of private organisations would be valuable to the state and should be used to its
advantage was clear to the authors, as they later advocated in
the same article that private organisations 'should enter into closer
working partnership with the Government', that many organisations could not have international activities at all unless they
get special help from 'foundations, firms and governments' and
that there should be a greater secondment of government personnel to the operations of private organisations.

These latter suggestions and the private government arrangements detailed above begin to undermine seriously the claims of
a private organisation to be independent of the state in external
relations. It becomes merely a question of degree, as was pointed
out earlier, and it may well be that, contrary to customary usage
in international relations, the designations 'private' or 'non-
governmental' cannot be applied to the actual foreign policies of
the organisations but only to their domestic status and the nature
of their staffing.

If the situation outlined here is the same for other organisations
acting abroad, and there is no evidence which indicates the
contrary, it can be said in conclusion that private foreign policy is
managed sufficiently to ensure a high probability that it will have
a useful, and sometimes important, role in furthering the interests
of the state in its relations with other states, nations and peoples.

REFERENCES

[1] For example, D. Mitrany, *A Working Peace System*
    (Carnegie Foundation for International Peace, New York,
    1943), pp. 34–36.
[2] See for example E. Miles, 'Transnational Processes and
    International Organisation : Outer Space and the Oceans',
    International Organisation, Summer, 1971.
[3] See Glyn Roberts, *Volunteers and Neo-Colonialism: an*

enquiry into the role of foreign volunteers in the Third World (privately published pamphlet, Manchester, 1969).

[4] These figures and much of the information which follows in this section were derived from interviews with officials from several aid associations and government agencies.

[5] See James R. Rosenau, 'Intervention as a Scientific Concept', *Journal of Conflict Resolution*, XIII, No. 2 (June 1969), pp. 159–160.

[6] Details of general expenditures and distribution in Africa are given in Frederick Leys, 'The Work of Voluntary Agencies in Africa', *Africa in the Seventies* (Royal African Society, April 1970), pp. 66–67.

[7] See 'TUC : Disinterested Loan?', *Economist*, Vol. 198 (January 14, 1961), p. 116.

[8] *The Observer*, April 11, 1971, p. 12.

[9] See Jeffrey Harrod, *Trade Union Foreign Policy* (Macmillan, 1972), Chapter IV.

[10] Apparently government-controlled corporations also adopted a pro-Biafran policy. See Chapter 7 of the present work.

[11] See Christopher Brown, 'Volunteerism : Naive Participation and Cheap Aid', in *Private Initiatives for Development*, special issue of *Bulletin of Institute for Development Studies*, Vol. 2, No. 3 (May 1970), p. 38.

[12] P. Williams and A. Moyes, *Not by Government Alone: The Role of Non-Governmental Organisations in the Development Decade* (Overseas Development Institute, London, 1964), p. 10.

BIBLIOGRAPHY

Jean Meynaud, *Les Groupes de pression internationaux* (Lausanne, 1961).

J. J. Lador-Lederer, *International Non-Governmental Organisations* (A. W. Sythoff, Leyden, 1963).

Bulletin of Institute for Development Studies, Vol. 2, No. 3 (May 1970). This issue is devoted to several aspects of private organisation involvement in development aid.

Jeffrey Harrod, 'Non-Governmental Organisations and the Third

World', *The Yearbook of World Affairs 1970*, Vol. 24 (July 1970), pp. 170–185.

Jeffrey Harrod, *Trade Union Foreign Policy* (Macmillan, 1972).

Robert O. Keohane and Joseph S. Nye (eds.), *Transnational Relations and World Politics*, special issue of *International Organisation* (Summer 1971).

13 The News Media and Foreign Affairs

PHILIP ELLIOTT and PETER GOLDING

INFORMATION is a prerequisite for policy-making. In liberal democratic theory one role traditionally attributed to the news media is that of supply the information which the people and their leaders need to reach decisions. As the editor of *The Times* has put it 'without information there can be no government and no government can be better than the information system on which it depends' [1]. This chapter examines some of the channels through which information about foreign affairs reaches this country. But our argument is that there is more to news than information. News can be seen as one important cultural mechanism through which society copes with endemic conflict and change. This is not to say that 'society' has directly planned the ideological role of news but that it is a consequence of various factors in the organisation and performance of news gathering, selection and presentation. This chapter is a preliminary attempt at examining some of these factors and at analysing the 'view of the world' presented through the news media. The news media can be likened to a camera, one of the tools of the trade which is typically focused on a narrow range of people, events and places in the world and typically uses a limited range of lenses to present these subjects within a range of familiar perspectives. This has important consequences, not only for the way in which the mass public can understand and interpret the world and its events, but also for the policy and decision-making process within the political élite. In other words news is not just a resource but a currency. It is not simply a raw material in the decision-making process but is itself one of the ways in which Britain's foreign relations are managed.

Foreign news has always occupied an important place in the British press. In the early stages of the daily newspaper in Britain, foreign news was supplied for those who had a specific interest in it. It consisted predominantly of overseas financial and shipping intelligence supplied to those in the commercial middle class whose livelihood depended on it. Currently foreign news seems to be provided to the general public mainly in the hope that they will be interested in it or from a belief that they ought to be. This broad contrast between an instrumental goal and more diffuse goals of information and entertainment is a considerable oversimplification, especially of the contemporary situation. Some newspapers, pre-eminently the *Financial Times*, show more trace than others of their historical function. The belief that people ought to be interested in foreign affairs is related to other beliefs about the role of a newspaper in the democratic process. But it is a contrast which serves to underline the way in which the nature and importance of foreign news has changed alongside changes in the structure and function of the press. The more the press has become a mass medium, widening the scope of its potential audience and drawing its revenue from advertising as well as sales, the more it has had to sell foreign news in the same way as other news, for its interest and entertainment value. Simultaneously this has meant less scope for meeting specific instrumental needs and perhaps also for fulfilling some other traditional journalistic functions [2].

Prior to the development of the first daily newspapers in Britain, there were various systems for exchanging financial information between the commercial capitals of Europe. Banking houses in particular had their own representatives collecting and relaying information. Initially the newspapers, like the coffee house news-sheets which preceded them, relied mainly on translating information from their continental opposite numbers. The potential value of such information, in spite of the uncertain methods through which it was secured, is illustrated by the story of the fortune which Nathan Rothschild made on the London stock exchange after he had received a copy of a Dutch newspaper, carrying news of Napoleon's defeat at Waterloo twenty-four hours before official sources brought the British government word of their army's victory [3].

The development of war news in the 19th century provides one of the clearest examples in the foreign affairs field of the shift from brief, technical, instrumental news to a more general style of reporting [4]. W. H. Russell was by no means the first correspondent sent abroad by an English paper, but the despatches which he sent to *The Times* on the Crimean War captured his readers' imaginations and helped influence 'public opinion' on the prosecution of the war [5]. As the press gradually broadened its functions beyond serving the specific, informational needs of the political and financial élites, it found new means of bringing influence to bear on such élites. Moreover, the broader interest in wars and colonial development reflected not simply an expansion in general interest but also the growth and the widening of the political and economic interests involved.

Two other developments in the 19th century were of major importance in setting the context within which the contemporary press handles foreign affairs; the spread of telegraph connections around the globe and the growth of the international news agencies. To a large extent it was the former which made the latter possible, though it is recorded that both Reuter and Havas began their news services with the help of carrier pigeons. In 1873 the first international news cartel agreements were concluded between Reuters, Havas (the French agency) and Wolff (the German). This ratified the different shares of influence which each agency had developed through the world. The smaller, national agencies were each linked to one of the big three. The news cartel was not finally abandoned until 1934, though the first world war had exposed many of the problems involved when the agencies in neutral countries were linked to only one of the agencies among the belligerents. It was this problem that allowed the American agency, the Associated Press, to move into the international news business in spite of the cartel. AP was later joined by two other American agencies, the United Press and the International News Service (since merged to form UPI) but the distribution of agency bureaux around the world still shows some traces of the original division of the world under the cartel agreements [6].

FOREIGN NEWS AND ITS AUDIENCES

These historical developments form an important background to the main aims of this chapter. These are to investigate some of the factors which contribute to the way foreign affairs appear in the British press and broadcasting media, and to consider some of the ways in which foreign news reporting contributes to the social and political process in Britain. The first question – what factors underlie the way the world is reported in the British media? – is a special case of a more general problem of how to characterise 'news' and its relationship to the society in which it is produced. In the short run the complex international system of news gathering, news flow and news processing comprises the most important set of factors accounting for the way the world appears in foreign news. At the news gathering stage there are such factors as the opportunities open for reporting in different foreign countries and possible relationships with available sources. The international system of news flow itself has generally been conceptualised in terms of the 'gatekeeper' model, as a variety of intermediaries control access to the various channels leading in different directions [7]. Within this country it is necessary to consider the organisation of the different media themselves, their policies in the foreign affairs field and the selection and presentation routines through which foreign news is passed.

In the short run any individual news item will have to fit into this system with its established criteria and work routines. In the longer run it becomes important to consider another set of factors, expressed in the various beliefs about news and news policy held by publishers, executives and journalists. These include journalistic beliefs about the absolute importance of events in the world, beliefs about what will interest different audience groups and beliefs about the potential power and responsibility which the different media can and should exercise in the formation of opinion and the influence of policy. These beliefs, and the way they are operationalised in the news process, are themselves contingent on the social and economic situation within which the media themselves and the various occupational groups working within them are set.

In an abstract sense the same interrelated sets of factors – the news production process, occupational beliefs and the socioeconomic structure of the media organisations – underlie the way domestic news is recognised and processed [8]. In the foreign affairs field however, partly due to the historical developments discussed above, these factors are found in a different combination. One of the continuing characteristics of foreign news is that by and large foreign affairs is believed to have little interest or appeal for the mass audience. But the editorial belief that foreign news is important has tended to ensure that in spite of the lack of audience interest 'the percentage of newspaper space devoted to world affairs is far larger than the percentage of readers who read these articles' [9]. Cohen, in his study of foreign correspondents in the United States, has pointed to the paradox that while editors tend to justify a policy of printing little foreign news because of low audience interest, the foreign news which is printed tends to be prominently featured on the grounds that it is important according to the *public's* sense of news value [10]. These beliefs and practices reflect a continuing desire to address 'important' audiences, as well as the mass audience on "important" topics. It is one way in which the media can aspire to exercise influence.

But to take this question of the relationship between audience demand and journalistic values further, it is necessary to make some distinctions between different audiences and their different interests in foreign affairs. Robinson and Swinehart have estimated that among the American public the 'educated élite' accounts for 'almost all the relevant foreign affairs "activity" in this country' but makes up less than one per cent of the population. Lord Windlesham has made a similar two-fold distinction from the reciprocal point of view of public opinion [11]. 'Informed opinion' comes from 'a small group of informed people close to and interested in affairs, whose opinions could directly influence events.' It is more likely to have a 'positive role' influencing policy-makers than 'popular opinions, widely held' which, he argues, tend to be a negative factor, 'a way of estimating what the public will stand for rather than an expression of what the public wants'. This way of approaching the problem immediately raises questions about the channels through which different publics come to be informed and conversely the channels which are open for the expression of opinions. For example there is the question raised by C. Wright Mills of whether, with the development of mass media, it any longer makes sense to talk in nineteenth century terms of a community of publics, forming opinions and influencing policy [12]. Mass media in mass society, he argued, have turned such publics into 'mere media markets' available for manipulation by the élite.

One problem underlying such an analysis is how broadly to define the limits of the élite. Some studies of the press and broadcasting media have investigated their role as channels of 'horizontal' communication through political, social and economic élites, as well as channels of 'vertical' communication to the mass public [13]. Seymour-Ure has taken this distinction further, pointing out that whereas 'vertical' channels to an uninformed public are likely to involve no more than 'face value' communication, 'the more a reader is informed and involved in a subject, the more he will infer from a "message" in addition to its explicit content' [14]. He illustrated this argument by examining the different levels of meaning contained in the press reporting of the 'Profumo Affair' in 1963. The point is also extremely relevant to foreign affairs because, as we shall see below, in that case it is not simply a question of supplying inside political gossip to make a story intelligible, but the broad perspectives and historical background necessary to make sense of news events in unfamiliar countries. Research on the impact of communications suggests that because the public is less familiar with foreign affairs than domestic there should be more scope for influencing attitudes and opinions in this area [15]. At the least, media coverage will play a part in directing attention towards events, people and issues in the world within the framework of an implicit set of assumptions about their relevance and importance [16].

The news media are also likely to have a multi-dimensional impact on the political élite. First the élite is likely to use some media as sources of information which are both wider in scope and, especially in the foreign affairs field, faster tha 'official channels'. Cohen has made the point that American diplomatic channels seem to be slower routes for carrying much the same material to policy-makers as the news media [17]. A recent British illustration occurred over the crisis in East Pakistan. The British High Commission in Calcutta did not collect information itself on the refugee problem because to have obtained it 'would have been "unhelpful" to relations between Whitehall and

Pakistan'. Instead the High Commission relied on secondary sources, including journalists [18].

The Duncan Report on overseas representation found that political reporting on the policies and politics of foreign countries 'has declined in recent years and now represents only a fraction of the total work of any post' [19]. According to research carried out for the committee into the effects of withdrawing two foreign posts, 'user departments of the Foreign and Commonwealth Office made it plain that their main functions . . . had been little affected by the absence of . . . political reporting' caused by the withdrawal of the two posts investigated. The report advised that the constant flows of information from posts to Whitehall were excessive and that political reporting as a diplomatic function could well be diminished in scope and quantity. To take its place the committee considered the suggestion that 'very little political reporting of any kind is needed in modern conditions . . . given the amount of international news and comments which is already available in London through the press and other public media'. The committee concluded that this was only true 'to the extent that a well-conducted post will often be content to do no more than for example comment on a specific report by Reuters or the BBC. Regular liaison between our posts and local British press and broadcasting representatives is already well-developed and of great benefit to both sides'.

A second type of impact which the media and especially the press may have on political élites is that of a vertical channel of communication upwards. This assumes of course that the policy maker is prepared to accept the press as a guide to public opinion. Publishers, editors and journalists are also liable to put forward more or less explicit opinions of their own on particular issues. This is a third type of impact which again will depend on the weight which the policy maker is prepared to give to the opinion and its holder. Qualifying the conclusion quoted above the Duncan Committee argued 'comment is the largest element in good political reporting by diplomatic posts; and if a post is doing its job properly its comments will tend to be more useful to the British Government than any available from other sources'. The committee held that as the media had their own ends to serve, the diplomatic service should be in a better position to concentrate on British government interests.

The American correspondents studied by Cohen were divided on how much weight to give to the active aspect of their role as influencers of policy. Most conceived of the press as a 'neutral transmission belt' from the executive branch of government, in which foreign policy was decided, to the legislative branch, the Congress and the public at large [20]. This view rests on the assumption that it is possible, by using some supposedly neutral criteria such as news value, to operate the belt and direct the focus of publicity, without at the same time taking active part in the process of opinion formation and policy-making [21]. In practice most reporters recognised that their work inevitably took them beyond the passive role suggested by this simple model. In all Cohen distinguished eight separate role conceptions among the reporters, culminating in 'the press as policy-maker' in which the reporters saw themselves as actors in the political process, 'trying to influence the opinions of both the public and the government official' [22].

Cohen's study goes on to investigate the closely woven web of inter-action and inter-dependence which links the press, the policy makers and their external environment. A study of this type is long overdue in this country, though it must be admitted that there are sharp differences in constitutional practice and government style between the two countries. British journalists seem much more like outsiders to the political process looking in, than their American counterparts. Nevertheless it seems likely that in general terms British politicians and civil servants make similar use of the news media to their American opposite numbers. What is certain is that there is room for much more research in this country on the part which media personnel and media products play in the political process [23]. This paper is a *prolegomenon* both to research of that type and to research into the production and decision processes of the media themselves, to investigate what lies behind the picture of the world presented in press, radio and television. Such a policy has been continuously advocated by the Television Research Committee and recently there have been several signs of research moving in that direction [24], but in the foreign affairs field little empirical research is available, apart from content analyses and general surveys of the international news system mostly carried out in the United States.

In later sections of this chapter we have attempted to supply some information and more speculation on the British situation itself. But later sections follow the argument already established that news is part of an ideological system, supported by the different interests which the various parties have in it. Audience interest, in the sense of audience curiosity, is the most dependent part of the system. Lack of audience interest, in the sense of low audience curiosity, reflects the audience's lack of involvement in the political process. For the most part they remain unaware that they have any interests at stake. Political and economic élites on the other hand have an interest in the maintenance of political and economic power, while the media themselves are also concerned with their own power, prestige and financial security.

SOME CHARACTERISTICS OF THE FOREIGN NEWS SYSTEM

Research into the international system of news flow has generally been directed towards one or both of two problems; the directions in which news flows around the globe and the 'factors which impair the "free flow of news" . . . those (negative factors) which cause the "picture of the world" as it is presented through the news media to differ from "what really happened" ' [25]. On the first topic little has changed since the International Press Institute published its survey of *The Flow of the News* in 1953 [26]. Of the five main international news agencies, two are American, one Russian, one British and one French. It is hardly coincidental that international news agencies developed outside Europe at the same time as the political centre of gravity of the world shifted away from Western Europe. Nevertheless Western Europe is still an important focus of world attention. Schramm's study of one month's news in three newspapers in each of thirteen countries showed that in most countries Britain and France separately received about as much attention as Russia [27]. In all cases (except Poland, the only East European country included in the study) each country took most of its foreign news from the United States. The national ownership of the agencies seems to be one factor behind this. Schramm found that of the five agencies only Agence France Presse did not show a marked concentration on news from its own country of origin, although Reuters did carry about as much American news as British.

Even a well-staffed news organisation is likely to rely heavily on agency services for breadth of coverage and for the initial clue that something newsworthy is happening in distant parts of the world. The various agencies have correspondents covering the globe, but agency bureaux are not evenly distributed over its surface. For example AP has 111 bureaux in the USA, 25 in Europe, 16 in Asia, 13 in Central/Southern America, 5 in Africa and 1 in Australia. Reuters has 7 bureaux in the USA, 15 in Western Europe, 5 in Russia and Eastern Europe, 13 in Asia, 11 in Central/Southern America, 11 in Africa and 9 in the Middle East. The agencies are in business to meet the needs of their customers, the national news organisations. But the familiar question in discussions of media content and customer taste, that of the relative primacy of supply and demand is also relevant to the services provided by the agencies. Working criteria on news value have to be developed and disseminated throughout the international news system to ensure that the different organisations articulate together. In the short run however the criteria and assumptions used by the agencies may get out of step with the needs and policies of particular national media. To meet their own needs and also to help them compete with their rivals, news organisations can deploy their own news-gathering resources.

Apart from the agencies, British news organisations cover foreign affairs in four main ways, through stationing their own staff correspondents around the world, by taking material from 'stringers' (often native journalists in the country concerned), by sending out reporters to cover specific stories, and through the diplomatic correspondents who work closely with the British foreign office.

Table 1 shows the distribution around the world of the staff correspondents of the British news media. The figures in the table should be interpreted with some caution. Only full-time staff correspondents are included. Even so it seems that some of these work for more than one paper under different bye-lines and so may be counted twice. These staff correspondents are backed up in every news organisation by a more or less extensive network of 'stringers' overseas. Nevertheless, in view of the costs involved, the distribution of staff correspondents is probably a good indication of priorities. Recently there has been a tendency for some organisations, in particular ITN and the *Financial Times*, to rely

TABLE 1. LOCATION OF FOREIGN CORRESPONDENTS TO THE BRITISH DAILY NEWS MEDIA (MAY 1971)

	USA	W. Europe	Russia & E. Europe	Middle East	Asia & India	C. & S. America	Africa	Australasia
Newspapers								
The Times	5	5	2	1	3	1	2	1
The Guardian	3	2	—	2	—	—	—	—
Daily Telegraph	8	10	1	1	3	1	2	1
Financial Times	4	6	—	—	—	—	—	—
Daily Express	8	8	—	1	1	1	1	—
Daily Mail*	2	1	—	—	—	—	—	—
Daily Mirror	5	8	—	—	1	—	—	—
The Sun	No Information							
Broadcasting**								
BBC	4	4	1	3	3	1	1	—
ITN	1	—	—	—	—	—	—	—

* After absorbing Daily Sketch (May 11th 1971).
** Bureaux rather than individuals.

on teams working from London, a system which can be more economical than maintaining correspondents in the traditional way, permanently located abroad. The *Financial Times* has established a team of regional staff specialists who are based on London, but who travel their areas regularly, not necessarily following the stimulus of a particular news event. A somewhat similar arrangement seems to be in use on the *Sunday Times*, though in that case more use is made of the 'fire-brigade' principle, waiting for an event before arranging coverage.

Such different ways of organising foreign coverage may have important consequences for the type of content produced. For example it seems likely that a reporter despatched from London will be forced to apply British perspectives to any story, unless he is already a specialist in the area with a fund of knowledge and experience to enable him to see a country's problems in its own terms. On the other hand, ethnocentrism tends to be a general feature of foreign reporting, not especially characteristic of the British press. Desmond quotes the instructions issued before the Second World War to the foreign representatives of the Chicago *Daily News*. These laid down the importance of recognising and emphasising the American interest in foreign developments and then made the point that American interests were all-pervasive [28]. To emphasise the domestic reference of a foreign story is one way of trying to overcome audience indifference and it also enables the news media to deal with those aspects in which they may be able to exercise most influence on their own government. On the other hand looking for the national interest or the national angle may give a quite misleading picture of events. Gould for example in a study of the press reporting of the Eighteen Nation Disarmament Committee Meeting in Geneva, July 1968, found that of all the sixteen newspaper studied, *The Times* was the most narcissist, devoting most of its attention to the interventions of the UK representative [29]. He concluded that the 'day-to-day reporting of the ENDC meetings (in *The Times*) would have given the reader a highly selective picture of the proceedings'. Other papers and other news media seem equally open to the charge of parochialism [30]. Table 2 shows the percentage of news-space devoted to foreign news by the British news media in one week in April 1971. The figures for the press show relatively little

TABLE 2. PERCENTAGE OF NEWS-SPACE (TIME
OR COLUMN-INCHES) DEVOTED TO FOREIGN
NEWS BY BRITISH NEWS MEDIA BASED ON ONE
WEEK IN APRIL, 1971

Medium	%
BBC-TV (9 o'clock News)	37
ITN (News at Ten)	37
Radio (World Tonight)	34
'Quality' Papers	22
'Popular' Papers	10

change in those presented by Seymour-Ure based on a sample of
24 issues in 1965 [31]. Seymour-Ure was also able to show that
compared to domestic news, foreign news is predominantly
political.

An exception to this generalisation are the 'popular' papers.
Other types of foreign news taken up about as much space in the
'populars' as political stories. Foreign stories in 'popular' papers
seem to be mainly of two types, first the major crises and catas-
trophies which warrant front page treatment, secondly human
interest stories or items on celebrities, stories whose foreign location
is quite incidental. Stories such as 'Frozen Baby' (in Alaska) or
'Boys Crucify Baby' (in America) represent the ultimate point in
the shift from instrumental to general interest foreign news [32].
But at least so far as the allocation of permanent correspondents
is concerned table 1 shows that some of the 'populars' are as well
or better staffed than some 'qualities'. The *Daily Express* and
the *Daily Mirror* stand out as two papers on which (rather
different) editorial policies have had the similar effect of upgrading the priority of foreign news. It seems likely that on a
purely economic basis the figures for the *Daily Mail*, following
the amalgamation with the *Daily Sketch* and the rationalisation
of editorial staff, are an accurate reflection of the worth of foreign
news to the reader of such a paper. But on the *Daily Express*,
an interest in foreign affairs and especially the affairs of the
Empire, has been necessary to support the newspaper's policies
as pursued by Lord Beaverbrook and continued by Sir Max
Aitken. The *Daily Mirror* on the other hand, at least until the
advent of the new *Sun*, has been trying gradually to introduce its
readers to more 'important' political news, among which was
foreign affairs.

The geographical distribution of staff correspondents, shown in Table 1, also underlines the way the British media as a whole concentrate attention on the USA and Western Europe. In most cases correspondents are based in the same cities even within these areas – New York and Washington in the United States, Bonn and Paris in Europe – though there are some notable exceptions. The *Daily Express* has a correspondent in Hollywood, the *Daily Mirror* one in Cannes. The location of correspondents in other areas also emphasises the importance of such factors as stage of development, trade and historical connections. Four of the six correspondents located in Africa are stationed in South Africa, one (for the *Daily Telegraph*) is in Salisbury, Rhodesia, and one (for *The Times*) has a roving brief. News tends to be more readily available in developed, western countries, but for a variety of reasons the flow is restricted between the communist world and the west, and the developing world and the west. Table 3 illustrates the preoccupation of the British news media with a few areas of the world by showing the geographical distribution of stories published in one week in April 1971.

TABLE 3. GEOGRAPHICAL DISTRIBUTION OF NEWS STORIES IN ONE WEEK'S COVERAGE IN APRIL 1971*

	Broadcasting	'Quality'	'Popular'	Total
Britain	83	123	148	354
W. Europe	19	20	12	51
USA	19	15	13	47
'Old' Commonwealth	8	0	0	8
'New' Commonwealth	14	0	0	14
Other Third World	14	17	5	36
Russia, China, E. Europe	12	5	14	31

* These figures reflect the influence of one or two unusually big stories in Russia, and the inclusion of Israel in the 'third world' category.

Looked at in international perspective the news flow seems to be greater from the west to the developing world than vice versa [33]. At present the various technical and physical means of international communication tend to lead towards a few news centres. Technical factors are backed up by problems of cost and differential pricing which appear to make the outward flow from such centres cheaper than the inward flow, particularly from remote parts of the world [34]. The flow which is maintained between the developing world and the developed seems to follow contemporary trading and investment relationships and the historical links surviving from the old empires [35]. A simple illustration of one reason why this should be so, is that in Africa physical communications are often easier between an Anglophone country and London than between that country and its Francophone neighbour. In a sense this is the problem of metropolitan concentration within a developed country such as Britain, translated into world proportions. Latin America is probably the area of the world which receives least attention from the world's news media. It has long been accepted that this is a situation which should be remedied but the attempts which various British media have made to do so, have run into sufficient difficulties to show that the present system is founded on a complex of powerful factors which cannot easily be altered.

The fourth way in which the British news media cover foreign affairs, through diplomatic correspondents accredited to the Foreign Office, is a method clearly designed to report the British point of view and the development of British policy. In the course of this century the Foreign Office has gradually taken steps to handle rather than simply ignore the press [36]. Whereas the 19th century correspondent could expect little more than a chilly 'No Comment' from any formal approach, his contemporary is able to attend a series of daily news meetings organised by the News Department of the Foreign Office for 'on the record' and 'off the record' briefings. The News Department has been staffed by senior officials within the Foreign Office, which suggests that importance is attached to it. Seymour-Ure has pointed out that although the press in general may occasionally be useful to officials, by supplying missing information faster than the Foreign Office's own sources, the balance in the exchange relationship between an individual correspondent and the Foreign Office is weighted heavily on the side of the latter. He has to rely on a single, unitary source.

Journalists often recognise that they are open to techniques of manipulation and news management but find it difficult to know how to circumvent them. This introduces the second problem in considering the international news system; the various distortions introduced in the course of the news-gathering and distribution process. The word 'distortion' is not intended to imply that there is an objective ideal which can possibly be reached. Nor is it intended as a pejorative term though the reporting of some recent events seems to warrant critical appraisal as well as an attempt to understand the factors behind it, such as we are engaged in here. As Ostgaard has pointed out, direct censorship and official interference are relatively easy to recognise [37]. Such problems have formed the basis for a series of investigations into the 'freedom of the press' around the world [38]. More debatable however is the assumption, occasionally made explicit in such studies, that where there is a free press, there is no interference with the news [39]. Government, politicians and 'official sources' can manage news in the world press in much the same way as they manage it in their own. The publication of the Pentagon Documents brought to light some particularly graphic examples of such management, for example the 36 day 'scenario' prepared to lead up to the Gulf of Tonkin resolution [40]. The Pentagon Documents also illustrate how easily a media image such as 'the Domino Theory' can become established, and underlines the point made above that the relationship between journalists and policy makers is liable to be so close that each supports the other in giving credence to the same version of reality.

Many of the problems of foreign reporting which contribute to the view of the world which emerges through that reporting, are not within the control of a single journalist. There is no obvious way in which they can be changed within the existing social and economic structure of the news organisations. Journalists are likely to be skilled in interpreting stories and writing them up as 'news' for their particular outlets. To a varying extent, depending on the outlet, this is likely to involve simplification, personalisation and dramatisation to reduce the complexity of events to the presumed attention-level of the outlet's audience [41]. Moreover the same news criteria which result in such processes of simplification are also likely to lie behind the decision to cover an event in the first place. At one extreme these various factors can lead to a system of 'crisis reporting', in which neither the journalist nor his readers have any opportunity to grasp the meaning of the events reported except by using a perspective such as 'political conflict is based on the clash of personalities', which is presumed to have universal human validity and interest. 'Quality' papers, with a more specialised staff and a more informed audience, are better able to avoid this problem. Nevertheless various commentators have emphasised that the irregular coverage given to most parts of the world necessarily results in chaos, crisis and catastrophe dominating the picture of world events in the news media. Cohen for example claimed that 'for those people who depend substantially on the mass media for their basic and continuing picture of the international environment of foreign policy, even a careful reading of foreign policy news may convey an image of an endless succession of problems having little systematic relationship to each other or to some corpus of American values and American political choices' [42].

But Cohen's second claim seems more dubious than the first. World events may appear as a succession of problems but in various ways and for various reasons the reporting of these problems tends to follow predictable patterns and to be related to a few underlying perspectives which, in the last analysis, serve the ideological interests of Western political and economic élites. One continuing feature of foreign reporting touched upon above, is its ethnocentrism. In general foreign news may be divided into three types: 'home news abroad', for example war news about a country's troops abroad which, as we saw above, was one of the first general interest types of foreign news to develop; 'foreign news at home', for example the actions of home politicians in relation to overseas crises and 'foreign news *per se*', though even in this case the factors behind the flow of news discussed above are likely to ensure that media attention is rarely directed towards events overseas unless they have some implications for the home country. The proportion of foreign stories falling into the first two categories in one week in April 1971 is shown in Table 4.

Reporting foreign news in this way tends to exaggerate the power and influence of Britain and her politicians. For example reporting the constitutional crisis in East Pakistan in 1971, British parliamentary reaction was followed by politicians' visits to the area. But the full potential of British power was not revealed until a later stage when the refugee problem had been compounded by an outbreak of cholera. On June 1st *The Times* led on the cholera epidemic; nine days later it had become a British parliamentary story – 'Labour Clash on Bengal Aid forces

TABLE 4. 'DISGUISED' FOREIGN STORIES AS PERCENTAGE
OF ALL FOREIGN STORIES IN 'TOP TEN STORIES' PER ISSUE/
BULLETIN IN ONE WEEK, APRIL 1971

Medium	Foreign News at Home	Home News abroad
BBC-TV	9	30
ITN	14	21
Radio	4	33
'Quality' papers	16	48
'Popular' papers	9	36

Commons Debate Today'; by the following day British influence
had taken effect – 'Britain's Response to Cholera Crisis Astounds
India as Deaths Fall' [43]. Preoccupation with British influence
may be a hangover from the days of empire, but it is important
to examine this point in the wider world perspective. The news
media and the international news system tend to maintain a view
of the world in which the crucial decisions about the problems
of the developing world are taken not by their leaders but by
American and to a lesser extent Russian and Western European
politicians. This may be an accurate reflection of the condition
of neo-imperialism, though few journalists would entertain such
a concept. Even so it reopens the point raised above that news
tends to concentrate on the political forms rather than the underlying social and economic structure and process.

One reason why this should be so, a reason which introduces
a second of the fundamental regularities in foreign affairs
coverage, is the 'event orientation' of news media working to
daily publication schedules [44]. The point is well illustrated by
the coverage of the cholera outbreak among the East Pakistani
refugees, outlined above. By and large medical epidemics do not
appear and disappear as suggested within the space of a few days.
Prior to the outbreak in India which attracted world attention,
the disease had been moving through the Middle East and Africa,
too slowly to clear the threshold of news attention. But this 'event
orientation' has important consequences not only in selecting the
picture of the world to be presented but also in giving credence
to a limited range of ways of dealing with world problems. Pre-
eminent among this limited range are the actions of political

leaders which can both be reported as events and emanate from 'newsworthy' sources.

Another way of dealing with such problems fostered both by the 'event orientation' and the 'human interest' style of reporting – a third of the fundamental regularities – is to attract public sympathy to immediate human problems. The reporting of the civil war in Nigeria provides a clear illustration of this phenomenon, as well as others [45]. In this war the Biafran leaders devoted considerable attention to news management, using for example Mark Press, a public relations firm based in Geneva, to release human interest material about the suffering caused by the war. The result was widespread humanitarian concern for the suffering of the common people, a concern which tended to be expressed in acceptance of and support for Biafra. In Britain this support was also related to domestic political issues since the Wilson government was supplying arms to Federal Nigeria. Himmelstrand has pointed out that although the possibility of direct propagandist intent on the part of journalists and news organisations cannot be ruled out, factors in the news gathering and production processes provide an explanation for the way the Biafran conflict was reported which is largely self-sufficient. Comprehensive research on the media coverage of the Nigerian war has yet to be carried out. Nevertheless it seems clear that the two sides differed widely in their ability to handle the world's news media and, with a few exceptions, the staff of those media were content to propagate a simplistic view of the conflict in which humanitarian concern obscured rather than clarified understanding of the political and social issues in an African country. Galtung and Ruge quote some comments of Tom Mboya on the world press in which he makes the same point in a general context. 'Mr Mboya complained of the Press (Foreign-owned) in Africa behaving and writing as though it were operating in London, Paris or New York where the problems and anxieties are entirely different from those current in Africa. . . The world's verdict on Africa . . . was often produced from subjective dispatches of foreign journalists paying short visits to the various parts of Africa. The result was that news coming out of Africa was often related to the already biased and prejudiced mind that keeps asking such questions as : "is this pro-East or pro-West?" but nobody asked : "is this pro-African?" ' [46].

A fourth fundamental regularity in foreign reporting can also be illustrated from another insight of Himmelstrand on the reporting of the Nigerian Civil War. Himmelstrand has pointed to the existence of recurring cycles in the reporting of foreign news stories. These cycles are based on the factors discussed above which contribute to the lack of continuous visibility in the news media for most countries in the world.

When a crisis story breaks little detailed information is available on what has happened. News staff have to make sense of events according to past knowledge and pre-existing perspectives. It is possible that as more information comes in it will be used to give additional perspectives and to tighten information. On the other hand if the pre-existing perspectives are strongly established only information which is consonant with them may be collected and disseminated. These views are then further elaborated in the editorial and feature pages of a newspaper or the current affairs and documentary programmes of radio and television. This process sets in motion what Himmelstrand has called a 'self-infatuation cycle'. By a process of mutual confirmation within each news organisation and across the news media as a whole, a consistent view of the crisis emerges from which alternative views and information are systematically excluded.

Such reporting cycles underly a fifth fundamental regularity in the handling of foreign affairs, the use of a limited range of perspectives and stereotypes to explain foreign stories. Such perspectives are heavily dependent on past experience or apparently similar events around the world, but in a more fundamental sense they tend to reflect the policies and interests of Britain in particular and the West as a whole. It seems likely for example that in the reporting of the Dominican crisis of 1965, stories of a 'communist takeover' in the Dominican Republic were acceptable because everyone, diplomats, reporters and public, was ready for another Cuba [47]. Felix Greene has made the same point in his account of American reporting on Communist China, a case in which lack of opportunity for first-hand observation compounds this tendency to fit the information which is available into one of the previously elaborated stereotypes about developments in that country [48]. Galtung, discussing the reporting of the 1968 Czechoslovakian crisis, has commented on the way journalists tended to see those events in terms of the previous Hungarian crisis, not so much in the sense that direct analogies and comparisons were drawn, though on occasions they were, but that Hungary was part of the 'underlying frame of mind' with which journalists approached their new assignment [49]. Any journalist faces the dual problem of making sense of events himself and then of interpreting them in terms his audience will understand. It seems a sound hypothesis that the less familiar a correspondent is with a country, the more he is likely to rely on re-applying past perspectives or on using standard human-interest news perspectives as outlined above.

CONCLUSION

But although such perspectives can be justified as an aid to understanding, they play a crucial part in creating the image of the world presented through the news media. In the course of this paper we have argued that news cannot simply be characterised as a more or less imperfect reflection of events in the world. It is possible to point to a variety of factors in the journalist's role and in the way news production is organised which produce distortions and imperfections. But the important problem is to tease out the fundamental regularities in the treatment of world events and to show how these are related to the interests of those working in news organisations, of those who control them and of those who set the conditions in which they operate. One question considered in this paper has been which countries and what type of people and events receive attention from the news media. Five fundamental regularities have also been suggested in the treatment of foreign stories – ethnocentrism, event orientation, human interest, story cycles and story perspectives. Some of these perspectives obviously reflect direct British or Western interests : others seem to be a consequence of the discontinuous flow of information, the need to simplify and the superficial fragmentation of reality which these entail. But all these perspectives have ideological consequences, in the same way as the other general regularities in news reporting outlined above. For example attention is concentrated on political leaders and political crises, limiting the range of explanations of social conflict and change which can be offered. In the same way the range of possible means considered for resolving conflict in any society are limited. There is a tendency to define those outside established governments, including illegal established governments such as that in Rhodesia, as deviant, ephemeral and inconsequential. Although in quantitative terms most media concentrate on political news when dealing with foreign affairs, there is a sense in which their handling of it is apolitical : there is more to political conflict and political process than the leaders and the forms of government.

Study of the ideological role of news is crucial to an examination of culture in contemporary capitalist society. Problems of overt bias and proprietor policy seem to be less relevant to such a study than an occupational and structural analysis of the type foreshadowed by this chapter. The apparent autonomy of the broadcasting media suggests that the connection between the interests of élite groups in society and news output is not simple and complete. To elucidate these connections and their implications considerable research will be necessary into the process and organisation of news production and into audience reaction and usage among different sectors of the population. Many audience studies have been based on a simple persuasive or information-flow model, looking at problems of comprehension and understanding. A different basic model implies investigation of a rather different range of problems.

News then is a cultural mechanism of control and influence covering not simply the mass public, but also élites, creating the imagery and rhetoric within which they too are constrained to act. The image of the world contained in news reporting is itself one of the ways in which foreign affairs are managed. This is not to say that such management is necessarily purposive and planned, but that culture articulates with the institutions of a given social system.

REFERENCES

[1] W. Rees-Mogg, 'The Role of Palinurus', in *Only Connect, Four Studies in Communication* (London, Panther, 1968).
[2] On the general development of the press in England see F. Williams, *Dangerous Estate* (London, Longmans, 1957); R. Williams, *The Long Revolution* (Harmondsworth, Penguin, 1965).

[3] R. W. Desmond quotes three versions of this story, including this, the authentic one, in *The Press and World Affairs* (London, Appleton-Century, 1937), pp. 11–12.

[4] See J. J. Mathews, *Reporting the Wars* (Minneapolis, University of Minneapolis Press, 1957).

[5] Desmond (p. 20) for example quotes their influence on Florence Nightingale.

[6] Most books on the news agencies are institutional histories such as G. Storey, *Reuters: The Story of a Century of Newsgathering* (New York, Crown, 1951); J. A. Morris, *Deadline every Minute: The Story of the United Press* (New York, Doubleday, 1957); but in addition to R. W. Desmond, see also International Press Institute, *The Flow of the News* (Zurich, I.P.I., 1953); T. Kruglack, *The Foreign Correspondents* (Geneva, Librairie E. Droz, 1955) and *The Two Faces of Tass* (Minneapolis, University of Minnesota Press, 1962); UNESCO, *News Agencies: Their Structure and Operation* (Paris, UNESCO, 1956).

[7] See for example J. T. McNelly, 'Intermediary Communicators in the International Flow of News', *Journalism Quarterly*, Vol. 36 (1960), pp. 23–26.

[8] For a case study investigating news production, content and audience reaction which develops this view see J. D. Halloran, P. Elliott and G. Murdock, *Demonstrations and Communication* (Harmondsworth, Penguin, 1970).

[9] J. P. Robinson and J. W. Swinehart, 'World Affairs and the TV Audience', *Television Quarterly*, Vol. 7 (1968), pp. 40–59.

[10] B. C. Cohen, *The Press and Foreign Policy* (Princeton University Press, 1963).

[11] Lord Windlesham, *Communication and Political Power* (London, Jonathan Cape, 1966), subsequent quotation from p. 155.

[12] C. Wright Mills, 'Mass Media and Public Opinion', pp. 577–598, in I. L. Horowitz (ed.), *Power, Politics and People, The Collected Essays of C. Wright Mills* (London, Oxford University Press, 1967). See also C. Wright Mills, *The Power Elite* (New York, Oxford University Press, 1959).

[13] These terms are used by Richard Rose in *Politics in England* (London, Faber, 1965).

[14] C. Seymour-Ure, *The Press, Politics and the Public* (London, Methuen, 1968), p. 265.

[15] J. T. Klapper, *The Effects of Mass Communication* (Glencoe, Ill., Free Press, 1960); for a more recent approach see J. D. Halloran (ed.), *The Effects of Television* (London, Panther, 1970).

[16] A point continually emphasised in the recent work of George Gerbner. See for example, 'The Institutional Approach to Mass Communications' in Thayer, L. (ed.), *Communication: Theory and Research* (Springfield, Ill., C. C. Thomas, 1967), and 'Toward Cultural Indicators' in G. Gerbner et al. (eds), *The Analysis of Communications Content* (New York, Wiley and Sons, 1969).

[17] Cohen.

[18] *The Guardian*, 17th June 1971.

[19] *The Report of the Review Committee on Overseas Representation 1968–69*, HMSO 1969, Cmnd. 4107.

[20] Cohen.

[21] A point discussed at length in Halloran.

[22] Cohen, p. 39.

[23] See, however, J. Tunstall, *The Westminster Lobby Correspondents* (London, Routledge and Kegan Paul, 1970). For another study which indirectly considers one aspect of this problem, see A. Barker and M. Rush, *The Member of Parliament and his Information* (London, George Allen and Unwin Ltd., 1970).

[24] See for example, *The Second Progress Report of the Television Research Committee* (Leicester University Press, 1969), and some of the contributions in J. Tunstall (ed.), *Media Sociology* (London, Constable, 1970), and The Sociological Review Monograph No. 13, *The Sociology of Mass Media Communicators* (Keele, 1969).

[25] See E. Ostgaard, 'Factors Influencing the Flow of News,', *Journal of Peace Research*, Vol. 1 (1965), pp. 39–56.

[26] International Press Institute, *The Flow of News* (Zurich, 1953).

[27] See W. Schramm, *Mass Media and National Development* (UNESCO, Paris, 1964, Ch. 2).

[28] See Desmond, p. 48. See also F. T. C. Yu and J. Luter, 'The Foreign Correspondent and His Work', *Columbia*

Journalism Review (Spring 1964). Smart gives voice to a similar viewpoint: 'Having hundreds of well-trained, linguistically competent professional journalists available to cover news everywhere, in peaceful as well as in troubled times, would give America a protection it has never enjoyed and would provide facts about the world on which it would be safe to make decisions.' See M. N. Smart, 'A Proposal for "Scholars" in Foreign News Reporting', *Journalism Quarterly* (Summer, 1961), p. 371.

[29] L. N. Gould, *The ENDC and the Press* (Almquist and Wiksell, Stockholm, 1969), p. 75.

[30] For a trenchant example see E. J. Hobsbawm, 'Little Englanders', *New Society* (10th April 1969), p. 566.

[31] Seymour-Ure, p. 63.

[32] These headlines occurred in the same week in April 1971 for which some results of a preliminary content analysis are reported in this chapter.

[33] See Ostgaard.

[34] On the problems of cost see *The Problems of Transmitting Press Messages* (Paris, UNESCO, 1956).

[35] On this point see O. Andreson, *Hovedstadsavisers Indhold*, Sociologiske Meddelelser 9 (1964), p. 125.

[36] See Seymour-Ure and the study by The Royal Institute of Public Administration, *The Government Explains* (Allen and Unwin, 1965).

[37] Ostgaard.

[38] See for example R. L. Lowenstein, *World Press Freedom* (Columbia, University of Missouri Freedom of Information Center Publication), or for an attempt to measure control, R. B. Nixon, 'Factors Related to Press Freedom', *Journalism Quarterly* (1960).

[39] For example Nixon says of his work that 'The present study assumes that a country with a free press normally will not interfere with the free flow of news to other countries.'

[40] See *The Sunday Times*, 20th June 1971.

[41] On these processes see J. Galtung and M. H. Ruge, 'The Structure of Foreign News', *Journal of Peace Research*, No. 1 (1965), pp. 64–90.

[42] Cohen, p. 100.

[43] See the lead stories in *The Times* on the 1st, 9th and 10th June 1971.

[44] See Galtung and Ruge.

[45] For opposing views on the coverage of the Nigerian civil war by the world's news media see F. Forsyth, *The Biafra Story* (Harmondsworth, Penguin, 1969), and U. Himmelstrand, *Världen, Nigeria och Biafra: Sanningen som kom bort* (Stockholm, Aldus/Bonniers, 1969). We are grateful to Professor Himmelstrand for allowing us to see an English translation of this book. See also U. Himmelstrand, 'The Problem of Cultural Translation and of Reporting Different Social Realities', forthcoming in report of the seminar, *Reporting Africa*, by the Scandinavian Institute of African Studies. In this paper Himmelstrand notes that some correspondents to the British newspapers stand out as exceptions to the general rule.

[46] Quoted in Galtung and Ruge.

[47] Theodore Draper, 'The Dominican Crisis', *Commentary* (December 1965); partially reprinted in *Mass Media and Mass Man*, A. Casty (ed.) (Holt, Rinehart and Winston, 1968).

[48] F. Greene, *A Curtain of Ignorance* (Cape, 1965).

[49] J. Galtung, 'The Role of Television in the Time of International Crisis'. Paper given at seminar in Hangö, September 1968, on *Television as a Political Power Factor*.

BIBLIOGRAPHY

B. C. Cohen : *The Press and Foreign Policy* (Princeton University Press, 1963).

E. Ostgaard : 'Factors Influencing the Flow of News', *Journal of Peace Research*, No. 1 (1965).

J. Galtung and M. H. Ruge : 'The Structure of Foreign News', *Journal of Peace Research*, No. 1 (1965).

J. D. Halloran, P. Elliott and G. Murdock : *Demonstrations and Communication* (Harmondsworth, Penguin, 1970).

C. Seymour-Ure : *The Press, Politics and The Public* (London, Methuen, 1968).

Postscript

14 Managing External Relations: A Comparative Perspective

ROBERT BOARDMAN
and A. J. R. GROOM

OUR DISCUSSION of Britain's external relations opened with a general survey – a traditional *tour d'horizon* – of the changes affecting Britain's position in international society in the years since 1945. It is by no means certain that the dilemmas and questions thrown up in the course of Britain's post-imperial readjustment will be resolved as we move into the 1970s and 1980s. The later decades of the century seem just as likely to be filled with anxious preoccupations on the part of the Government and the attentive public about Britain's role in a changing world. Though it is by now a commonplace, it perhaps bears reiteration that the one certainty we can be sure of in contemporary international society is the fact of change itself.

This being so, Acheson's judgement of 1962 [1] might well be an apt summation of the foreign policy problems facing any Western European State today. Change makes 'losing' and 'failing to find' roles part and parcel of international life. France, having to deal successively in the 1950s with the Indochina crisis of 1954, the Suez intervention two years later, and then the mushrooming Algerian situation, faced difficulties of adaptation comparable at least in magnitude to those of Britain. Indeed the British experience could profitably be studied in the context of the colonial and post-colonial histories not only of France but also of states such as Belgium, the Netherlands, Spain, Portugal and, further back in time, Germany and Italy.

To emphasise comparability is not merely to seek for analogies. Assuming a comparative perspective however would permit a greater degree of confidence in defining what has been unique in post-1945 British foreign policy, and what aspects Britain has shared in common with other Western, and more specifically Western European, countries. In many substantive issue-areas, Britain's problems have been held in common with those of other States. This applies perhaps most obviously at the level of 'high politics'. Gaullist France and the United Kingdom responded in differing ways to the shared predicaments of handling relations with the Soviet Union and the United States. Britain moreover is one of several developed countries which have in recent years experienced varying types and degrees of communal conflict or civil strife. One could mention also the crises that have affected Canada, Italy, Belgium or France since the late 1960s. And in Britain, as elsewhere, the formal foreign policy machinery often gives the appearance of being a vestige of an older social order, one in many ways having its roots in pre-industrial revolution society.

The fact that change has impinged on the implementation of roles at times thought vital and enduring is probably also fair comment on the foreign policy problems of the Soviet, Chinese and Third Worlds; but this takes us outside the arena of the present discussion. All that is being suggested is that the changing conditions of international society in the 1970s are serving to create a situation in which the comparative analysis of foreign policy – and clearly in this context we are thinking especially of Western Europe – becomes an indispensable teaching and research need.

Developments in comparative politics in the 1960s flowed from a dissatisfaction with more traditional approaches, or 'country-by-country' discussions. The aim, as Verba has put it, was to look beyond description to more theoretically relevant problems, beyond the single case to the comparison of many cases, and beyond the formal institutions of Government to political processes and functions [2]. Unfortunately, the intellectual mainsprings of the movement placed little emphasis on foreign policy outcomes. And International Relations scholars, for their part, displayed for a long time a reluctance to examine the domestic or transnational sources of foreign policy [3]. Recently Morse summarised the sorts of changes that are forcing a re-examination of this neglect. Processes of modernisation in the Atlantic region, he suggests, have radically transformed foreign policy. The distinction between foreign and domestic affairs has broken down; the distinction between 'high' or security, and 'low' or welfare, policies has become less important as the latter have assumed an increasingly large role; and the actual ability of Governments to control events, internal or external, has decreased with the growth of interdependence [4].

This is not the place to argue the pros and cons of the comparative perspective. Other writers have tackled the question at greater length than is possible here [5]. But a most valuable start in this direction has been made in recent studies of British in comparison with United States [6], Norwegian [7], and West German [8] foreign policy decision-making. Earlier chapters in the present volume have themselves raised many questions which could usefully be pursued on a comparative basis: the recruitment and selection of diplomatic personnel for example, the interaction of defence and foreign policies, the significance of non-governmental organisations and multinational corporations, the role of domestic interest groups and public opinion, flows of information within the foreign policy departments, economic and financial constraints on policies, the changing role of the diplomat, the nature of the foreign policy planning machinery, relationships between the 'political' and the 'permanent' sectors of the policy-making process, or the importance of the legislature in the foreign policy field. These and many other themes have been elaborated already in the context of United Kingdom policies, and there is no need to go over this ground again here.

There are however other important and interesting areas connected with the management of Britain's external relations that have been covered only marginally in the volume. First, it will be recalled that the activities discussed in previous chapters take place in a much wider operational environment [9]. Decisions and policies emanating from the Cabinet or from the Foreign and Commonwealth Office often bear the stamp of a multiplicity of influences and pressures from other governments. From the official and accepted viewpoint, this is nothing new. It has long been presumed that HMG's role is to 'take note' of the advice and proffered recommendations of other governments, inter-governmental bodies, or non-governmental organisations : but that 'in the last resort' it alone is 'responsible for taking the final decision'. In some cases this construction may be not far from the truth, and indeed it forms an important element in the mythology of sovereignty [10]. Even so, it would seem to be more realistic to assume that the operating environment of policy-making is very much broader than the more restricted frame-work, limited to the acts of 'sovereign States', would have us believe. We need to know more, for example, of such phenomena as the detailed workings of relations between officials of Govern-ments, including Britain, within the Western alliance structure, or within the Commonwealth or Western European systems.

Secondly, there are the policies implemented as the outcome of such processes. Surprisingly enough, relatively little systematic attention has been given to actual policies or courses of action : their effects on their targets in international society, and the interpretation of these effects by officials responsible for the initial formulation of policy. Comparisons of actual effects with desired or intended consequences are notably lacking. Galtung's analysis of the impact of the institution of economic sanctions against the Rhodesian authorities in 1965 suggested that the out-come may possibly have been just the opposite of that aimed at; but this study is, regrettably, an isolated example of what could be done [11]. Another writer has argued that foreign policies have a degree of immunity to changing circumstances, a self-protective barrier which ensures continuity even in the light of intense criticism [12]. If this is so, and there is *prima facie* evidence enough to make it a working hypothesis, then further investigation of this question could prove valuable.

It is apparent then – almost painfully so – that a rich field exists to be tapped for insights into the comparative structures and processes of foreign policy. This volume has we hope made a contribution, however modest, to this end. Knowledge in these areas has significant practical implications. Foreign policy goals can be achieved in other than a random fashion only if the workings of international society and the nature of foreign policy processes are well understood. If the present volume has enriched this body of knowledge, it will have more than fulfilled its purpose.

REFERENCES AND NOTES

[1] Speech at the United States Military Academy, West Point, 5 December 1962.
[2] Sidney Verba, 'Some dilemmas in comparative research', *World Politics*, XX, 1 (October 1967), p. 111.
[3] Charles F. Hermann, 'The comparative study of foreign policy', *World Politics*, XX, 3 (April 1968), p. 521.
[4] Edward L. Morse, 'The transformation of foreign policies : modernisation, interdependence, and externalisation', *World Politics*, XXII, 3 (April 1970), pp. 371–92.
[5] See in particular, James N. Rosenau, 'Comparative Foreign Policy : Fad, Fantasy, or Field?', in *International Studies Quarterly*, XII, 3 (September 1968), pp. 296–329; and reprinted as Ch. iv of his *The Scientific Study of Foreign Policy* (New York : Free Press, 1971), pp. 67–94. The difficulties of pursuing such research are spelt out at length in James N. Rosenau, Philip M. Burgess, and Charles F. Hermann, *The Adaptation of Foreign Policy Research: A Case Study of an Anti-Case Study Project*, Ohio State University : Mershon Program for Comparative Studies of Foreign Policy and Societal Adaptation, publication No. 30 (*mimeo*).
[6] Kenneth N. Waltz, *Foreign Policy and Democratic Politics: The American and British Experience* (Boston : Little, Brown, 1967).
[7] Joseph Frankel, 'Comparing Foreign Policies : The Case of Norway', *International Affairs*, 44 (1968).
[8] Karl Kaiser and Roger Morgan (ed.), *Strukturwandlungen der Aussenpolitik in Grossbritannien und der Bundesrepublik* (Munich : Oldenbourg, 1970, for Deutsche Gesellschaft für Auswärtige Politik).
[9] Michael Brecher, Blema Steinberge, and Janice Stein, 'A framework for research on foreign policy behavior', *Journal of Conflict Resolution*, XIII, 1 (March 1969), pp. 75–101.
[10] See Morse, op. cit.

[11] Johan Galtung, 'On the effects of international economic sanctions, with examples from the case of Rhodesia', *World Politics*, XIX, 3 (April 1967), pp. 378–416.

[12] Denis Stairs, 'Publics and Policy-makers: The Domestic Environment of Canada's Foreign Policy Community', *International Journal*, XXVI, 1 (Winter 1970–71), pp. 221–48.

Notes on the Contributors

Donald G. Bishop is Professor of Political Science at the Maxwell Graduate School of Citizenship and Public Affairs, Syracuse University, where at various times he has been Chairman of the Political Science Department and Chairman of the International Relations programme. He has also been a consultant to the United States Government. His principal publications include *The Administration of United States Foreign Policy through the United Nations* (1967), *The Roosevelt-Litvinov Agreements: an American View* (1965), *The Administration of British Foreign Relations* (1961), *The Future of the New Political System in France* (1959), and *Soviet Foreign Relations* (1952). He received his Ph.D. from Ohio State University.

Robert Boardman is Assistant Professor of Political Science and a member of the Centre for Foreign Policy Studies at Dalhousie University. He previously taught International Relations at the Universities of Surrey and Leicester. He has published articles in a variety of journals, including the *Yearbook of World Affairs*, *British Journal of Political Science*, and *Educational Research*, and contributed to the volume *Educational Aspects of Simulation*. He was awarded his Ph.D. at University College, London, for a thesis on British attitudes and policies towards China in recent years.

Peter Byrd is Lecturer in Politics at the University of Glasgow, where he was previously a Research Assistant working on the administration of British external relations. He has published in the *Journal of Contemporary History* and has completed work on his Ph.D. topic, 'Britain and the Anschluss 1931–1938: Aspects of Appeasement' for the University of Wales, University College, Aberystwyth.

Philip Elliott is Research Fellow at the Centre for Mass Communication Research, University of Leicester, where he has undertaken studies of organisation and production in the mass media. He has published *Demonstrations and Communication: A Case Study* (with J. D. Halloran and G. Murdoch) and *The Sociology of the Professions* and a monograph is forthcoming entitled *The Making of a Television Series.*

Sir Frank Figgures joined the Treasury in 1946 after war service in the Army. He retired in 1971. During that twenty-five years he was almost continually involved in the Treasury's external affairs. He was Alternate UK Director to the International Bank in 1948 and the UK member on the Group of Ten and at Working Party Three from 1968 to 1971. He had two periods as an international civil servant, as Director of Trade and Finance at OEEC in 1948 to 1951, and as Secretary General of EFTA from 1960 to 1965. He is now Director General of the National Economic Development Office.

Peter Golding is a member of the Centre for Mass Communication Research, University of Leicester, where he has been developing his interests in the sociology of culture with research into the role of news in different societies, and the effect of audience opinions on television programming.

A. J. R. Groom is Lecturer in International Relations at University College, London. He was previously an Assistant at Lehigh University and the University of Geneva. He has also been a consultant to GATT and SIPRI. His *British Thinking about Nuclear Weapons* and *Functionalism: Theory and Practice in International Relations* (edited with Paul Taylor) will be published shortly. He has contributed to learned journals in Britain, the United States, Canada, Switzerland, Austria and Yugoslavia. His academic interests centre on the more theoretical aspects of Conflict Research, Strategic Studies and International Organisation.

Jeffrey Harrod is currently lecturing at the International Institute for Labour Studies in Geneva. He was previously a Lecturer at the University of Colorado and the University of the West Indies,

Jamaica. He recently published *Trade Union Foreign Policy*, a study of foreign trade union activities in the Caribbean. He received his doctorate from the University of Geneva.

Andrzej Krassowski is currently on the staff of the Overseas Development Institute, London. He was previously Research Assistant in Public Finance at Columbia University. His main field of interest is the economic and institutional aspects of resource transfers from developed to developing countries. At present he is working on problems of aid management in the field. His publications include *British Aid 2 – Government Finance, the Aid Relationship* and *The Economic Policies of Nkrumah.*

Christina Larner is currently Lecturer in Sociology at the University of Glasgow. She was formerly a Research Fellow in Politics there, and worked on the history of the Foreign Office since 1918. Her other research interests include sixteenth- and seventeenth-century demonology. She was awarded a Ph.D. by the University of Edinburgh.

Peter Nailor is Professor of Politics at the University of Lancaster. His special and research interests lie in the field of Strategic Studies. Recent publications include 'Problems of Security in Europe' in *International Security* (ed. K. J. Twitchett) and 'The Military Bureaucracy: a civilian contribution' in *Horizons of War in the 1970s* (ed. Roger A. Beaumont and Martin Edmonds).

Michael O'Leary is currently Associate Professor of Political Science at Syracuse University. He has also taught at Dartmouth College. His recent publications include *The Politics of American Foreign Aid* (1967) and 'American Politics and the Third World', in Robert Gregg and Charles Kegley (eds.), *After Vietnam* (1971). He completed his University education at the University of Southern California and Princeton University.

A. N. Oppenheim is a Reader in Social Psychology at the London School of Economics, a Council Member of the International Peace Research Association and of the British Conflict Research Society, and past consultant to UNESCO, to the World

Health Organisation and other international bodies. He has a special interest in international relations, conflict studies and peace research. He has done work in the areas of simulation, small-group decision making, industrial conflict and crisis behaviour; at present he is engaged in a comparative study of foreign affairs ministries in a number of different countries. He is the author of *International Social Behaviour* (in the press), of *Questionnaire Design and Attitude Measurement*, and co-author of a number of other books and articles.

Peter G. Richards is Professor of British Government and Head of the Department of Politics at the University of Southampton. He is also Chairman of the Study of Parliament Group. His publications include : *Parliament and Conscience* (1970), *The New Local Government System* (1968), *Parliament and Foreign Affairs* (1967), *Patronage in British Government* (1963), *Honourable Members* (1959), *Delegation in Local Government* (1956).

Ian Smart is Assistant Director of the International Institute for Strategic Studies, where he has taken a particular interest in problems of using and controlling nuclear weapon systems and in the theoretical analysis of international security. He was a member of the British Diplomatic Service from 1958 to 1969, serving in Tel Aviv, London and Washington. During 1972 he is Visiting Professor of Strategic Studies at Carleton University, Ottawa.

William Wallace is a Lecturer in the Department of Government at Manchester University. He is the author of *Foreign Policy and the Political Process* (1971) and is now engaged in a study of the foreign policy process in Britain under the auspices of the Royal Institute of International Affairs. He was a contributor to *The British General Election of 1966* and to *The Age of Affluence 1951–64* (edited by Vernon Bogdanor and Robert Skidelsky). He received his Ph.D. from Cornell University.

General Bibliography

I THEORY

Bauer, Raymond A., and Gergen, Kenneth J. (eds), *The Study of Policy Formation* (New York: Free Press, 1968).

Blondel, Jean, *An Introduction to Comparative Government* (London: Weidenfeld and Nicolson, 1969).

Braybrooke, D., and Lindblom, C., *A Strategy of Decision* (New York: Collier-Macmillan, 1963).

Brecher, Michael, Steinberg, B., and Stern, J., 'A Framework for Research on Foreign Policy Behavior', in *Journal of Conflict Resolution*, XIII (1969), 75–101.

Burton, John W., *Systems, States, Diplomacy and Rules* (Cambridge University Press, 1968).

Cimbala, Stephen J., 'Foreign Policy as an Issue-Area: A Roll-Call Analysis', in *American Political Science Review*, LXIII (1969), 148–56.

Deutsch, Karl W., *The Nerves of Government* (New York: Free Press, 1963).

Deutsch, Karl W., 'External Influences on the Internal Behavior of States', in *Approaches to Comparative and International Politics*, ed. R. Barry Farrell (Evanston: Northwestern University Press, 1966), 5–26.

Easton, David, *A Framework for Political Analysis* (New York: Prentice-Hall, 1965).

Easton, David, *A Systems Analysis of Political Life* (New York: Wiley, 1965).

Edwards, David V., *International Political Analysis* (New York: Holt, Rinehart and Winston, 1969).

Edwards, W., and Tversky, A. (eds), *Decision-Making* (London: Penguin, 1967).

Etzioni, Amitai (ed.), *A Sociological Reader on Complex Organisations* (New York: Holt, Rinehart and Winston, 1969).

Farrell, R. Barry (ed.), *Approaches to Comparative and International Politics* (Evanston : Northwestern University Press, 1966).

Farrell, R. Barry, 'Foreign Policies of Open and Closed Societies', ibid., 167–208.

Frankel, Joseph, 'Towards a Decision-Making Model in Foreign Policy', in *Political Studies*, VII (1959), 1–11.

Frankel, Joseph, 'Rational Decision-Making in Foreign Policy', in *Yearbook of World Affairs*, 14 (1960), 40–65.

Frankel, Joseph, *The Making of Foreign Policy* (Oxford University Press, 1963).

Greenstein, Fred I., 'The Impact of Personality on Politics : An Attempt to Clear Away Underbrush', in *American Political Science Review*, LXI (1967), 629–41.

Gross, F., *Foreign Policy Analysis* (New York : Philosophical Library, 1954).

Hanrieder, Wolfram F., 'Compatibility and Consensus : A Proposal for the Conceptual Linkage of External and Internal Dimensions of Foreign Policy', in *American Political Science Review*, LXI (1967), 971–82.

Holsti, K. J., *International Politics: A Framework for Analysis* (New York : Prentice-Hall, 1967).

Iklé, F. C., *How Nations Negotiate* (New York : Harper and Row, 1964).

Jacobson, Harold K., and Zimmerman, William (eds), *The Shaping of Foreign Policy* (New York : Atherton Press, 1969).

Jones, Roy E., *Analysing Foreign Policy: An Introduction to some Conceptual Problems* (London : Routledge and Kegan Paul, 1970).

Kaufman, Herbert, 'Organisation Theory and Political Theory', in *American Political Science Review*, LXVIII (1964), 5–14.

Lindblom, C., *The Policy-Making Process* (New York : Prentice-Hall, 1968).

Millar, T. B., 'On Writing about Foreign Policy', in *Australian Outlook*, XXI (1967), 71–84.

Misra, K. P., 'Writing about Foreign Policy : A Note on Approaches and Sources', in *South Asian Studies*, 2 (1968), 81–90.

Mitchell, C. R., 'Foreign Policy Problems and Polarised Political

Communities: Some Implications of a Simple Model', in *British Journal of Political Science*, I (1971), 223–51.

Modelski, G., *A Theory of Foreign Policy* (New York: Praeger, 1962).

Northedge, F. S., 'The Nature of Foreign Policy', in *The Foreign Policies of the Powers*, ed. F. S. Northedge (London: Faber, 1968), 9–39.

Rivera, Joseph H. de, *The Psychological Dimensions of Foreign Policy* (Columbus: Merill, 1968).

Robinson, James A., and Majak, R. Roger, 'The Theory of Decision-Making', in *Contemporary Political Analysis*, ed. James C. Charlesworth (New York: Free Press, 1967), 175–88.

Robinson, James A., and Snyder, Richard C., 'Decision-Making in International Politics', in *International Behavior*, ed. H. C. Kelman (New York: Holt, Rinehart and Winston, 1965), 433–63.

Rosenau, James N., 'Pre-theories and Theories of Foreign Policy', in *Approaches to Comparative and International Politics*, ed. R. Barry Farrell (Evanston: Northwestern University Press, 1966), 27–92.

Rosenau, James N., 'The Premises and Promises of Decision-Making Analysis', in *Contemporary Political Analysis*, ed. James C. Charlesworth (New York: Free Press, 1967) 189–211.

Rosenau, James N. (ed.), *Domestic Sources of Foreign Policy* (New York: Free Press, 1967).

Rosenau, James N., 'Foreign Policy as an Issue-Area', ibid., 11–50.

Rosenau, James N., 'Moral Fervor, Systematic Analysis and Scientific Consciousness in Foreign Policy Research', in *Political Science and Public Policy*, ed. Austin Ranney (Chicago: Markham, 1968), Ch. 9.

Rosenau, James N. (ed.), *Linkage Politics: Essays on the Convergence of National and International Systems* (New York: Free Press, 1969).

Rosenau, James N. (ed.), *International Politics and Foreign Policy: A Reader in Research and Theory* (New York: Free Press, 1969).

Rosenau, James N., *The Scientific Study of Foreign Policy* (New York: Free Press, 1971).

Simon, Herbert A., *Administrative Behavior: a Study of Decision-*

Making Processes in Administrative Organisation (New York : Macmillan, 1957).

Singer, J. David (ed.), *Human Behaviour and International Politics* (Chicago : Rand-McNally, 1965).

Singer, J. David (ed.), *Quantitative International Politics: Insights and Evidence* (New York : Free Press, 1967).

Snyder, Richard C., Bruck, H. W., and Sapin, Burton (eds), *Foreign Policy Decision-Making* (New York: Free Press, 1962).

Snyder, Richard C., Bruck, H. W., and Sapin, Burton, 'Decision-Making as an Approach to the Study of International Politics', ibid., 14–185.

Wallace, William, *Foreign Policy and the Political Process* (London : Macmillan, 1971).

II   THE MANAGEMENT OF BRITAIN'S EXTERNAL RELATIONS : OFFICIAL MACHINERY

Ashton-Gwatkin, F. T. A., *The British Foreign Service* (Syracuse University Press, 1960).

Banks, Michael, 'Professionalism in the Conduct of Foreign Policy', in *International Affairs*, 44 (1968), 720–34.

Barnett, Correlli, *Britain and her Army* (London : Penguin, 1970).

Beloff, Max, *New Dimensions in Foreign Policy: A Study in British Administrative Experience, 1947–59* (London : Allen and Unwin, 1961).

Beloff, Max, 'Another Plowden Report : I. The Foreign and Commonwealth Services', in *Public Administration*, 42 (1964), 415–19.

Beloff, Max, 'The Projection of Britain Abroad', in *International Affairs*, 41 (1965), 478–89.

Bishop, Donald G., *The Administration of British Foreign Relations* (Syracuse University Press, 1961).

Brown, George, *In My Way* (London : Gollancz, 1971).

Busk, Douglas, *The Craft of Diplomacy: Mechanics and Development of National Representation Overseas* (London : Pall Mall, 1967).

Cecil, Algernon, 'The Foreign Office', in *The Cambridge History of British Foreign Policy, 1783–1919*, ed. A. W. Ward and G. P. Gooch (Cambridge University Press, 1923), III, 539–60.

Chapman, Brian, 'The Fulton Report : A Summary', in *Public Administration*, 46 (1968), 443–51.

Connell, John, *The 'Office': A Study of British Foreign Policy and its Makers, 1919–51* (London : Wingate, 1958).

Cross, J. A., 'The Colonial Office and the Dominions before 1914', in *Journal of Commonwealth Political Studies*, 4 (1966), 138–48.

Cross, J. A., *Whitehall and the Commonwealth: British Departmental Organisation for Commonwealth Relations, 1900–66* (London : Routledge and Kegan Paul, 1967).

Cross, J. A., 'The Beginning and End of the Commonwealth Office', in *Public Administration*, 47 (1969), 113–19.

Report of the Review Committee on Overseas Representation, 1968–69, Chairman Sir Val Duncan (London : HMSO, 1969) Cmnd. 4107.

Eden, Robert Anthony, First Earl of Avon, *The Eden Memoirs: Full Circle* (London : Cassell, 1960).

Eden, Robert Anthony, First Earl of Avon, *The Eden Memoirs: Facing the Dictators* (London : Cassell, 1962).

Eden, Robert Anthony, First Earl of Avon, *The Eden Memoirs: The Reckoning* (London, Cassell, 1965).

Eubank, Keith, 'Great Britain', in *Guide to the Diplomatic Archives of Western Europe*, ed. D. H. Thomas and Lynn M. Case (Pennsylvania University Press, 1959), 98–124.

The Civil Service, Vol. I: Report of the Committee, 1966–68, Chairman Lord Fulton (London : HMSO, 1968) Cmnd. 3638.

Goold-Adams, Richard (ed.), *The British Army in the Nuclear Age* (London : Army League, 1959).

Gosses, Frans, *The Management of British Foreign Policy before the First World War*, trans. E. C. van der Gaaf (Leiden : Sijthoff, 1948).

Guttsman, W. L., *The British Political Elite* (London: MacGibbon and Kee, 1963).

Guttsman, W. L. (ed.), *The English Ruling Class* (London : Weidenfeld and Nicolson, 1969).

Heath, Edward, 'Realism in British Foreign Policy', in *Foreign Affairs*, 48 (1969), 39–50.

Heath, Edward, *Old World, New Horizons: Britain, the Common*

Market and the Atlantic Alliance (Oxford University Press, 1970).

Henderson, Sir Nevile, *Water under the Bridges* (London : Hodder and Stoughton, 1945).

Heussler, R., *Yesterday's Rulers: The Making of the British Colonial Service* (Syracuse University Press, 1963).

Higgins, Rosalyn, *The Administration of United Kingdom Foreign Policy through the United Nations* (Syracuse University Press, 1966).

Horn, D. B., *The British Diplomatic Service, 1689–1789* (Oxford : Clarendon Press, 1961).

Howard, Michael, 'Civil-Military Relations in Great Britain and the United States, 1945–58', in *Political Science Quarterly,* LXXV (1960), 35–46.

Howard, Michael, *The Central Organisation of Defence* (London : Royal United Service Institution, April 1970).

Hüsler, Angelo, *Contribution à l'Étude de l'Élaboration de la Politique Étrangère Britannique, 1945–56* (Geneva : Droz, 1961).

Johnson, Franklyn A., *Defence by Committee: The British Committee of Imperial Defence, 1885–1959* (London : Oxford University Press, 1960).

Jones, Ray, *The Nineteenth-Century Foreign Office: An Administrative History* (London : Weidenfeld and Nicolson, 1971).

Kelly, Sir David, 'British Diplomacy', in *Diplomacy in a Changing World*, ed. S. D. Kertesz and M. A. Fitzsimons (Indiana : Notre Dame University Press, 1959), 172–203.

Kirkpatrick, Sir Ivone, *The Inner Circle* (London : Macmillan, 1959).

Langford, R. Victor, *British Foreign Policy: Its Formulation in Recent Years* (Washington, D.C. : American Council on Public Affairs, 1942).

Lyon, Peter, *The Foreign Policies of the Powers* (London : Macmillan, 1972).

Macmillan, Harold, *Winds of Change, 1914–39* (London : Macmillan, 1966).

Macmillan, Harold, *Tides of Fortune, 1945–55* (London : Macmillan, 1969).

Macmillan, Harold, *Riding the Storm, 1956–59* (London : Macmillan, 1971).

Marett, Sir Robert, *Through the Back Door: An Inside View*

of Britain's Overseas Information Services (Oxford: Pergamon Press, 1968).

Mayhew, Christopher, 'The British Diplomat', in *Diplomatie unserer Zeit (International Seminar for Diplomats, Klessheim, 1958)*, ed. Karl Braunias and Gerald Stourzh (Graz: Verlag Styria, 1959).

Nicolson, Harold, *Diplomacy* (Oxord University Press, 1942).

Nicolson, Harold, *The Evolution of Diplomatic Method* (London: Constable, 1954).

Parkinson, Sir Cosmo, *The Colonial Office from Within, 1909–45* (London: Faber, 1947).

Parrott, Cecil, 'The Foreign Office Library', in *Library World*, LXI (1960).

Parry, Clive, 'The Foreign Office Archives', in *International Relations*, 2 (1961), 211–19.

Payne, Peter F., *British Commercial Institutions* (London: Harrap, 1969).

Platt, D. C. M., *The Cinderella Service: British Consuls since 1825* (London: Longman, 1971).

Report of the Committee on Representational Service Overseas, under the Chairmanship of Lord Plowden, 1962–63 (London: HMSO, 1964) Cmd. 2276.

Robinson, K. E., 'Another Plowden Report: II. A Single Ministry?', in *Public Administration*, 42 (1964), 420–22.

Robson, W. A., 'The Fulton Report on the Civil Service', in *Political Quarterly*, 39 (1968), 397–414.

Royal Institute of Public Administration, *The Organisation of British Central Government* (London: Allen and Unwin, 1970).

Sallett, Richard, 'Wie das Foreign Office arbeitet', in *Aussenpolitik*, 4 (1953), 171–79.

Sallett, Richard, *Das Diplomatische Dienst: Seine Geschichte und Organisation in Frankreich, Grossbritannien und den Vereinigten Staaten* (Stuttgart: Deutsche Verlags–Anstalt, 1953).

Shonfield, Andrew, 'The Duncan Report and its Critics', in *International Affairs*, 46 (1970), 247–68.

Smith, Brian C., 'Reform and Change in British Central Administration', in *Political Studies*, XIX (1971), 213–26.

Steiner, Zara S., *The Foreign Office and Foreign Policy, 1898–1914* (Cambridge University Press, 1969).

350   *The Management of Britain's External Relations*

Strang, Lord, *The Foreign Office* (London: Allen and Unwin, 1955).

Strang, Lord, *Home and Abroad* (London: Deutsch, 1956).

Strang, Lord, 'The Formulation and Control of Foreign Policy', in *Durham University Journal*, XLIX (1957).

Strang, Lord, 'Inside the Foreign Office', in *International Relations*, 2 (1960), 3–21.

Strang, Lord, *Britain in World Affairs* (London: Faber, 1961).

Strang, Lord, *The Diplomatic Career* (London: Deutsch, 1962).

Tilley, Sir John, and Gaselee, Stephen, *The Foreign Office* (London: Putnam, 1933).

Verrier, Anthony, *An Army for the Sixties* (London: Secker and Warburg, 1966).

Vital, David, *The Making of British Foreign Policy* (London: Allen and Unwin, 1968).

Vital, David, 'The Making of British Foreign Policy', in *Political Quarterly*, 39 (1968), 255–68.

Walker, P. Gordon, *The Cabinet* (London: Cape, 1970).

Wallace, W. J. L., *Foreign Policy and the Political Process* (London: Macmillan, 1972).

Waltz, Kenneth N., *Foreign Policy and Democratic Politics: The American and British Experience* (Boston: Little, Brown, 1967).

Watt, D. C., 'Foreign Affairs, the Public Interest and the Right to Know', in *Political Quarterly*, XXXIV (1963), 121–36.

Watt, D. C., *Personalities and Policies: Studies in the Formulation of British Foreign Policy in the Twentieth Century* (London: Longmans, 1965).

Watt, D. C., 'Restrictions on Research: The Fifty-Year Rule and British Foreign Policy', in *International Affairs*, 41 (1965), 89–95.

Watt, D. C., 'The Home Civil Service and the New Diplomacy', in *Political Quarterly*, XXXVIII (1967).

Watt, D. C., 'Britain's Representation Overseas', in *The World Today*, 25 (1969), 328–30.

Watt, D. C., 'Overseas Representation', in *Political Quarterly*, 40 (1969), 485–90.

Watt, D. C., 'The Reform of the German Foreign Service: The Herwarth and Duncan Reports Compared', in *The World Today*, 26 (1970), 352–58.

Williams, R., 'Administrative Modernisation in British Government', in *International Social Science Journal*, 21 (1969), 100–15.

Wilson, Harold, *The Labour Government 1964–70* (London: Weidenfeld and Nicolson and Michael Joseph, 1971).

Young, Kenneth, *Sir Alec Douglas-Home* (London: Dent, 1970).

Ziebura, G., 'Zur Empirie des Aussenpolitischen Entscheidungsprozesser in Grossbritannien und Frankreich', in *Europa-Archiv*, 19 (1964), 65–70.

III THE MANAGEMENT OF BRITAIN'S EXTERNAL RELATIONS: THE SOCIAL AND POLITICAL ENVIRONMENT

Abrams, M., 'British Elite Attitudes and the European Common Market', in *Public Opinion Quarterly*, 29 (1965), 236–46.

Christoph, James B., 'The Press and Politics in Britain and America', in *Political Quarterly*, XXXIV (1963), 137–50.

Christoph, James B., 'Consensus and Cleavage in British Political Ideology', in *American Political Science Review*, LIX (1965), 629–42.

Davies, D. I., 'The Politics of the TUC's Colonial Policy', in *Political Quarterly*, 35 (1964), 23–34.

Davies, M., and Verba, S., 'Party Affiliation and International Opinions in Britain and France, 1947–56', in *Public Opinion Quarterly*, 24 (1960), 590–604.

Durant, H., 'Public Opinion, Polls and Foreign Policy', *British Journal of Sociology*, VI, 2 (1955), 149–58.

Epstein, Leon D., 'Partisan Foreign Policy: Britain in the Suez crisis', in *World Politics*, XII (1960), 201–24.

Epstein, Leon D., 'British M.P.s and their Local Parties: The Suez Case', in *American Political Science Review*, LIV (1960), 374–90.

Epstein, Leon D., *British Politics in the Suez Crisis* (London: Pall Mall, 1964).

Goldsworthy, D. J., *Colonial Issues in British Politics, 1945–61* (Oxford University Press, 1971).

Gordon, Michael R., *Conflict and Consensus in Labour's Foreign Policy, 1914–65* (Stanford University Press, 1969).

Groom, A. J. R., *British Thinking about Nuclear Weapons* (London, 1973).

Janosik, E. G., 'The Nuclear Deterrent as an Issue in British Politics, 1964–66', in *Orbis*, 10 (1966), 558–604.

Lieber, R. J., *British Politics and European Unity: Parties, Elites and Pressure Groups* (Berkeley : University of California Press, 1970).

Meehan, Eugene J., *The British Left Wing and Foreign Policy* (Rutgers University Press, 1960).

Naylor, John F., *Labour's International Policy: The Labour Party in the 1930s* (London : Weidenfeld and Nicolson, 1969).

Northedge, F. S., 'British Foreign Policy and the Party System', in *American Political Science Review*, LIV (1960), 635–46.

Northedge, F. S., 'Parties and Foreign Policy in Britain', in *Yearbook of World Affairs*, 14 (1960), 67–91.

Pelly, H. M., *A Short History of the Labour Party* (London : Macmillan, 4th ed. 1972).

Richards, Peter G., *Parliament and Foreign Affairs* (London : Allen and Unwin, 1967).

Rose, R., 'Labour's Pax Britannica', in *Political Quarterly*, 36 (1965), 131–41.

Snyder, William P., *The Politics of British Defence Policy, 1945–62* (Columbus : Ohio State University Press, 1964).

Tunstall, Jeremy, *The Westminster Lobby Correspondents* (London : Routledge and Kegan Paul, 1970).

Younger, Kenneth, 'Public Opinion and Foreign Policy', in *British Journal of Sociology*, 6 (1955), 169–75.

Younger, Kenneth, 'Public Opinion and British Foreign Policy', in *International Affairs*, 40 (1964), 22–33.

IV THE COURSE OF BRITISH FOREIGN POLICY

Allen, H. C., *Great Britain and the United States: A History of Anglo-American Relations, 1783–1952* (London : Odhams, 1954).

Austin, Dennis, *Britain and South Africa* (Oxford University Press, 1966).

Bartlett, C. J., *The Long Retreat: A Short History of British Defence Policy, 1945–70* (London : Macmillan, 1971).

Beloff, Max, *The Future of British Foreign Policy* (London: Secker and Warburg, 1969).

Buchan, A., 'Britain in the Indian Ocean', in *International Affairs*, 42 (1966), 184–93.

Caccia, Lord, *The Roots of British Foreign Policy* (Ditchley Foundation, 1965).

Calleo, David P., *Britain's Future* (London: Hodder and Stoughton, 1968).

Carlton, David, *MacDonald versus Henderson: The Foreign Policy of the Second Labour Government* (London: Macmillan, 1970).

Carr, E. H., *Britain: A Study of Foreign Policy from the Versailles Treaty to the Outbreak of War* (London: Longmans, Green, 1939).

Cunningham, George (ed.), *Britain and the World in the 70s: A Collection of Fabian Essays* (London: Weidenfeld and Nicolson, 1970).

Darby, P., 'Beyond East of Suez', in *International Affairs*, 46 (1970), 655–69.

Darby, P., *British Defence Policy East of Suez, 1947–68* (London: 1972).

Dawson, R., and Rosecrance, R., 'Theory and Reality in the Anglo-American Alliance', in *World Politics*, 19 (1966), 21–51.

Donelan, Michael, 'The Trade of Diplomacy', in *International Affairs*, 45 (1969), 605–16.

Epstein, Leon D., *Britain: Uneasy Ally* (Chicago, 1954).

Epstein, Leon D., 'British Foreign Policy', in *Foreign Policy in World Politics*, ed. Roy C. Macridis (Englewood Cliffs, N.J.: Prentice-Hall, 1967), 29–61.

Foot, M. R. D., *British Foreign Policy since 1898* (London: Hutchinson's University Library, 1956).

Frankel, Joseph, *Britain's Foreign Policy since 1945* (London: 1972).

Gelber, Lionel, *America in Britain's Place* (London: Allen and Unwin, 1961).

Goldberg, A., 'The Atomic Origins of the British Nuclear Deterrent', in *International Affairs*, 40 (1964), 409–29.

Goldberg, A., 'The Military Origins of the British Nuclear Deterrent', in *International Affairs*, 40 (1964), 600–18.

354   *The Management of Britain's External Relations*

Goodwin, Geoffrey L., *Britain and the United Nations* (Oxford University Press, 1957).

Griffiths, Sir Percival, *Empire into Commonwealth* (London: Benn, 1969).

Groom, A. J. R., 'The United States and the British Deterrent', in *Yearbook of World Affairs*, 18 (1964), 73–95.

Groom, A. J. R., *British Thinking about Nuclear Weapons* (London, 1973).

Hannah, Ian C., *A History of British Foreign Policy* (London: Nicholson and Watson, 1938).

Hanning, H., 'Britain East of Suez: Facts and Figures', in *International Affairs*, 42 (1966), 253–60.

Howard, C., *Splendid Isolation: A Study of Ideas concerning Britain's International Position and Foreign Policy during the Later Years of the Third Marquis of Salisbury* (London: Macmillan, 1967).

Howard, Michael, 'Britain's Defenses: Commitments and Capabilities', in *Foreign Affairs*, 39 (1960), 81–91.

Howard, Michael, 'Britain's Strategic Problem East of Suez', in *International Affairs*, 42 (1966), 179–83.

Hugo, Grant, *Britain in Tomorrow's World: Principles of Policy* (London: Chatto and Windus, 1969).

Ivens, M., and Bradley, C. (eds), *Which Way? Thirteen Dialogues on Choices facing Britain* (London: Joseph, 1970).

Kadt, E. J. de, *British Defence Policy and Nuclear War* (London: Cass, 1964).

Kaiser, K., and Morgan, R. (eds), *Britain and West Germany: Changing Societies and the Future of Foreign Policy* (London: Oxford University Press, 1971).

Kirkman, W. P., *Unscrambling an Empire: A Critique of British Colonial Policy, 1956–66* (London: Chatto and Windus, 1966).

Kirkwood, K., *Britain and Africa* (London: Chatto and Windus, 1965).

Leifer, Michael (ed.), *British Foreign Policy: Constraints and Adjustments* (London: Allen and Unwin, 1972).

Lowe, C. J., *The Reluctant Imperialists: British Foreign Policy, 1878–1902* (London: Routledge and Kegan Paul, 1967).

Luard, Evan, *Britain and China* (London: Chatto and Windus, 1962).

Maclean, Donald, *British Foreign Policy since Suez, 1956–68* (London : Hodder and Stoughton, 1970).

McDermott, Geoffrey, *The Eden Legacy and the Decline of British Diplomacy* (London : Frewin, 1969).

Mander, John, *Great Britain or Little England?* (London : Secker and Warburg, 1963).

Martin, Laurence W., 'The Market for Strategic Ideas in Britain : The "Sandys era" ', in *American Political Science Review*, LVI (1962), 23–41.

Martin, Laurence W., *British Defence Policy: The Long Recessional* (London : Institute for Strategic Studies, 1969).

Medlicott, W. N., *British Foreign Policy since Versailles, 1919–63* (London : Methuen, 1968).

Miller, J. D. B., *Britain and the Old Dominions* (London: Chatto and Windus, 1966).

Monroe, Elizabeth, *Britain's Moment in the Middle East, 1914–56* (London : Chatto and Windus, 1963).

Moulton, J. L., *British Maritime Strategy in the 70s* (London : Royal United Service Institution, 1969).

Mowat, C. L., *Britain between the Wars, 1918–40* (London : Methuen, 1955).

Nicholas, H. G., *Britain and the United States* (London : Chatto and Windus, 1963).

Northedge, F. S., *British Foreign Policy: The Process of Readjustment, 1945–61* (London : Allen and Unwin, 1962).

Northedge, F. S., *The Troubled Giant: Britain among the Great Powers, 1916–39* (London : Bell, 1966).

Northedge, F. S., 'British Foreign Policy', in *The Foreign Policies of the Powers*, ed. F. S. Northedge (London : Faber, 1968), 150–86.

Northedge, F. S., 'Britain's Future in World Affairs', in *International Journal*, 23 (1968), 600–10.

Northedge, F. S., 'Britain as a Second-rank Power', in *International Affairs*, 46 (1970), 37–47.

Northedge, F. S., 'Britain and the United Nations', in *The Evolving United Nations*, ed. K. J. Twitchett (London, Europa, 1971), 141–156.

Penrose, E. F., 'Britain's Place in the Changing Structure of International Relations', in *New Orientations: Essays on Inter-*

national Relations, ed. E. F. Penrose, Peter Lyon, and Edith Penrose (London : Cass, 1970), 28–79.

Pick, Otto, and Critchley, Julian, *British Foreign Policy* (London: Atlantic Education Trust, 1970).

Porter, Brian, *Britain and the Rise of Communist China: A Study of British Attitudes, 1945–54* (Oxford University Press, 1967).

Reynolds, P. A., *British Foreign Policy in the Inter-War Years* (London, Longmans, Green, 1954).

Reynolds, P. A., 'The Future of British Foreign Policy', in *International Studies*, 7 (1966), 401–18.

Rose, S., *Britain and South-east Asia* (London : Chatto and Windus, 1962).

Rose, S., 'The Foreign Policy of Britain', in *Foreign Policies in a World of Change*, ed. Joseph E. Black and Kenneth W. Thompson (New York : Harper and Row, 1963), 25–56.

Rosecrance, R. N., *Defense of the Realm: British Strategy in the Nuclear Epoch* (New York : Columbia University Press, 1968).

Rothstein, Andrew, *British Foreign Policy and its Critics, 1830– 1950* (London : Lawrence and Wishart, 1969).

Royal Institute of International Affairs, *Political and Strategic Interests of the United Kingdom: An Outline* (1939).

Royal Institute of International Affairs, *British Interests in the Mediterranean and Middle East: A Report by a Chatham House Study Group* (1958).

Russett, B. M., *Community and Contention: Britain and America in the Twentieth Century* (Cambridge, Mass. : MIT Press, 1963).

Stewart, M., 'British Foreign Policy Today', in *Australian Outlook*, 20 (1966), 109–24.

Strange, Susan, *Sterling and British Policy: A Political Study of an International Currency in Decline* (Oxford University Press, 1971).

Taylor, A. J. P., *The Trouble-Makers: Dissent over Foreign Policy, 1792–1939* (London : Hamish Hamilton, 1957).

Temperley, Harold, and Penson, Lillian M., *Foundations of British Foreign Policy from Pitt (1792) to Salisbury (1902)* (Cambridge University Press, 1938).

Thomas, Hugh, *The Suez Affair* (London : Weidenfeld and Nicolson, 1967).

Toynbee, Arnold J., *The Conduct of British Empire Foreign Relations since the Peace Settlement* (Oxford University Press, 1928).

Walker, P. Gordon, 'The Labour Party's Defence and Foreign Policy', in *Foreign Affairs*, 42 (1964), 391–98.

Ward, A. W., and Gooch, G. P., *The Cambridge History of British Foreign Policy, 1783–1919* (Cambridge University Press, 1923).

Watt, D. C., *Britain Looks to Germany: British Opinion and Policy towards Germany since 1945* (London : Wolff, 1965).

Williams, Ann, *Britain and France in the Middle East and North Africa, 1914–67* (London : Macmillan, 1968).

Williamson, James A., *A Short History of British Expansion: The British Empire and Commonwealth* (London : Macmillan, 1967).

Wiseman, H. Victor, *Britain and the Commonwealth* (London : Allen and Unwin, 1965).

Woodhouse, C. M., *British Foreign Policy since the Second World War* (London : Hutchinson, 1961).

Woodward, Sir Llewellyn, *British Foreign Policy in the Second World War* (London : HMSO, 1962).

Woodward, Sir Llewellyn, 'British Foreign Policy in Retrospect', in *International Journal*, 23 (1968), 507–19.

Younger, Kenneth, *Changing Perspectives in British Foreign Policy* (Oxford University Press, 1964).

Younger, Kenneth, 'British Interests and British Foreign Policy', in *Political Quarterly*, 38 (1967), 339–50.

Younger, Kenneth, 'Britain's Point of No Return', in *Yearbook of World Affairs*, 22 (1968), 1–14.

Zinkin, M., 'The Commonwealth and Britain East of Suez', in *International Affairs*, 42 (1966), 207–18.

Zinkin, M. and T., *Britain and India* (London : Chatto and Windus, 1964).

Index

362INDEX